"As Long as They Don't Bury Me Here"

Basel Namibia Studies Series

1   Zedekia Ngavirue POLITICAL PARTIES AND INTEREST GROUPS IN SOUTH WEST AFRICA (NAMIBIA) A STUDY OF A PLURAL SOCIETY (1972) (1997)

2   Wolfgang Werner 'NO ONE WILL BECOME RICH'. ECONOMY AND SOCIETY IN THE HERERO RESERVES IN NAMIBIA, 1915–1946 (1998)

3   Lauren Dobell SWAPO'S STRUGGLE FOR NAMIBIA, 1960–1991: WAR BY OTHER MEANS. (1998) (2ND EDITION 2000)

4   Tony Emmett POPULAR RESISTANCE AND THE ROOTS OF NATIONALISM IN NAMIBIA, 1915–1966 (1999)

5   James Suzman 'THINGS FROM THE BUSH'. A CONTEMPORARY HISTORY OF THE OMAHEKE BUSHMEN (2000)

6   William Heuva MEDIA AND RESISTANCE POLITICS. THE ALTERNATIVE PRESS IN NAMIBIA, 1960–1990 (2001)

7   Marion Wallace HEALTH, POWER AND POLITICS IN WINDHOEK, NAMIBIA, 1915–1945 (2002)

8/9 Lovisa T. Nampala; Vilho Shigwedha AAWAMBO KINGDOMS, HISTORY AND CULTURAL CHANGE. PERSPECTIVES FROM NORTHERN NAMIBIA (2006)

10 Bennett Kangumu CONTESTING CAPRIVI. A HISTORY OF COLONIAL ISOLATION AND REGIONAL NATIONALISM IN NAMIBIA (2011)

11 Inge Tvedten "AS LONG AS THEY DON'T BURY ME HERE". SOCIAL RELATIONS OF POVERTY IN A NAMIBIAN SHANTYTOWN (2011)

INGE TVEDTEN
Introduction by Michael Bollig

"As Long as They Don't Bury Me Here"
Social Relations of Poverty in a Namibian Shantytown

Basel Namibia Studies Series 11

Basler Afrika Bibliographien 2011

©2011 The authors
©2011 The photographers
©2011 Basler Afrika Bibliographien

Basler Afrika Bibliographien
Namibia Resource Centre & Southern Africa Library
Klosterberg 23
PO Box 2037
CH-4051 Basel
Switzerland
www.baslerafrika.ch

CARL SCHLETTWEIN STIFTUNG

The Basler Afrika Bibliographien is part of the Carl Schlettwein Foundation

All rights reserved.

Efforts were made to trace the copyright holders of illustrations and maps used in this publication. We apologise for any incomplete or incorrect acknowledgements.

Cover photograph:
"Woman cooking in front of her home". Shanty town dwelling in Oshakati, Namibia, September 2001.
Photographer: Jacob Holdt

Basic Cover Design: VischerVettiger Basel
Adapted Cover Design and Layout: Petra Kerckhoff

Printed by John Meinert Printing (PTY) Ltd., Windhoek, Namibia
Printed on 'triple green' paper: sixty percent sugar cane fibre, chlorine-free, sustainable afforestation.

ISBN 978-3-905758-24-5
ISSN 2234-9561

Contents

Basel Namibia Studies Series	VII
Telling their story over many years	IX
An Introduction by *Michael Bollig*	IX
Acknowledgements	XIII
Glossary	XIV
1 Introduction	1
The Setting	5
Poverty in Anthropology	11
Analytical Framework	14
Chapter Outline	17
2 The Making of Oshakati and its Shantytowns	20
Colonial Encounters	21
War and Atrocities	27
Oshakati – 'A Place Where People Meet'	31
Moving to Town	33
Urban Complexity	35
Shanty Relationships	38
Shanty Poverty at Independence	40
3 Global Space and Urban Place	43
Flows of the State	45
Flows of the Market	51
Flows of the Media	57
Democracy Comes to Town	61
4 The Shanty Population and Inequalities	65
Population and Household Characteristics	66
Material Conditions	72
Conclusion	78
5 Social Relations of Poverty	80

6 Rural Links	92
Urban-Rural Links	94
The Better-Off	96
The Poor	98
Age and Gender	101
Rural-Urban Links	103
Dealing with Uncertainty	107
7 Urban Connections	114
The Cosmopolitans	116
The Straddlers	121
Men Straddlers	122
Women Straddlers	124
The Shanty Localists	127
Localised Men	128
Localised Women	131
Social Isolation	133
8 Intra-Household Relationships	136
Forms of Domesticity	137
Cohabitation	138
Single-Headed Households	141
Conjugal Unions	145
Manhood and Womanhood	150
Intergenerational Relations	152
Violence and Abuse	154
9 Overwhelmed by Poverty	159
10 Conclusions	168
Abbreviations	173
List of Figures	174
List of Maps	175
List of Tables	175
Bibliography	176
Index	192

Basel Namibia Studies Series

In 1997, *P. Schlettwein Publishing* (PSP) launched the *Basel Namibia Studies Series*. Its primary aim was to lend support to a new generation of research, scholars and readers emerging with the independence of Namibia in 1990.

Initially, the book series published crucially important doctoral theses on Namibian history. It soon expanded to include more recent political, anthropological, media and cultural history studies by Namibian scholars.

P. Schlettwein Publishing, as an independent publishing house, maintained the series in collaboration with the *Basler Afrika Bibliographien* (BAB), Namibia Resource Centre and Southern Africa Library in Switzerland. All share a commitment to encourage research on Africa in general and southern Africa in particular. Through the incorporation of PSP into the *Carl Schlettwein Stiftung,* the series, by then a consolidated platform for Namibian Studies and beyond, was integrated into the publishing activities of the BAB.

Academic publishing, whether from or about Namibia, remains limited. The *Basel Namibia Studies Series* continues to provide a forum for exciting scholarly work in the human and social sciences.

The editors welcome contributions. For further information, or submission of manuscripts, please contact the *Basler Afrika Bibliographien* at www.baslerafrika.ch.

Telling their story over many years
An introduction

Social science studies on urban settings in southern Africa remain rare. This holds especially true for social anthropology as a discipline and for Namibia as a region. Much of the ethnography published over the past two decades – there has been a lot of ethnographic production on Namibia in the recent past – has focused *inter alia* on rural communities, identity politics, the politics of remembrance and on state-local community interactions. Despite an often publicised concern about growing poverty, both in rural and urban areas and rapidly growing cities (33 per cent of all Namibians live in an urban setting, the growth rate of urban centres is 5.6 per cent and urban poverty increasingly shapes urban landscapes), there is only a very limited number of anthropological and sociological studies on impoverished urban communities.

There are various reasons for this omission. On the one hand, social science research on urban squatter communities is exceedingly difficult both from a methodological and a humanitarian point of view and, on the other, many anthropological theories favoured over the last decade do not seem to offer a convincing perspective for an understanding of the situation of urban shanty town dwellers: neither do they play the harp of identity politics, nor are they (usually) portrayed as strategy-conscious actors optimising certain resources.

Inge Tvedten's book deals with urban poverty in a northern Namibian shanty town: its causes, its national as well as its global ramifications and the strategies employed by the poor to cope with their situation. Unlike other southern African cities that evolved along trade routes, Oshakati was founded mainly for military purposes by the colonial South African government. The town's importance grew during South Africa's war with SWAPO in Angola becoming a major basis for army operations. Soldiers – many of them of Angolan descent – moved their families and relatives to the town. After 1990, Oshakati became an important hub in the trading network between Namibia and Angola.

Since the early 1990s, Tvedten has worked in the shanties of Oshakati, which continue to grow rapidly. Repeated visits over the years brought him into regular contact with a number of his informants, thus enabling him to tell their story over many years. Initially submitted in 2008 as a PhD to the University of Cape Town, one of the book's great strengths is that it links the structural aspects of oppression and marginalisation to local agency. Tvedten's long exposure to the social dynamics of households and the fate of individuals helps him to overcome a problem that social anthropological fieldwork frequently confronts: based as it is on field studies of a year or so, it becomes difficult to predict the direction in which a certain situation is developing. Tvedten's intimate description of live histories brings the actors to life and, in this way, demonstrates the impressive scope of their agency.

Shanty town dwellers and their households form highly heterogeneous units. Household structures differ at any given moment both in and over time. The rapid increase of female-headed households is of great importance, as is the isolation of very poor males. Using extensive documentation, the author details how poverty has, unsurprisingly, become feminised during the past decades. His excellent ethnographic work paves the way for a differentiated understanding of the different types of shanty town households and the various ways in which they organise their social environment. Tvedten provides intricate accounts of self-representation by shanty town dwellers, partly relying on a number of impressive photographs taken by his informants to portray their lives.

Rural and urban links, as well as intra-household relations of shanty town dwellers, provide another critical field of analysis. In Oshakati, rural links are essential to the inhabitants' well-being. The wealthier segment of society maintains strong links to rural households of close relatives. Sometimes a rural dependence for the purpose of livestock herding and the production of millet can be identified. Wealthier households invest a considerable amount of their surplus in rural areas. In stark contrast to that, very poor households clearly lack these links to the rural hinterland. Tvedten's ethnography is at its best when describing how poor households gradually lost these rural links, having nothing to feed back into sharing networks. For a time the morality of reciprocity of kinship networks continue to provide recourse to the resources rural relatives command but, after a longer period of non-reciprocation, they become shut off from such networks.

Very poor households are encapsulated within shanty-based social relationships. While better-off households maintain strong links to the formal urban economy, poor households manage their lives solely within the confines of the shanty town. Interestingly, male-headed poor households appear more vulnerable to such isolation than poor female-headed households. While female-headed households can rely on extended networks of sharing among females, such networks of solidarity do not exist for very poor male households. For males, the step from poverty to destitution seems to be much closer. Consequently, intra-household relations are crucial. While much rapid appraisal literature takes households as the basic unit of exploration, Tvedten demonstrates the importance of intra-household relations for an understanding of the vulnerability, poverty and destitution that exist. Again, poor males are shown to be the most vulnerable segment of shanty town populations. The majority of households in shanty towns are female-headed, whilst a small number are headed by married couples, which usually belong to the wealthier segment of the shanty town population. In female-headed households, males regularly occur as temporary spouses but always stand the risk of being expelled (males as domestic nomads). For many women, it is a deliberate choice to stay single; males entering such households are always a hazard to female autonomy (given the predominant patriarchal ideology), without opening up reliable routes to resources.

Inge Tvedten concludes his analysis with a discussion of the shanty dwellers' perceptions of their situation and their options for social mobility. While recognising the limitations of Oscar Lewis' concept of "culture of poverty", Tvedten makes use of some of the ideas embedded in the concept. He explores in detail how specific epistemic and organisational structures, predominant in the shanties, contribute to the perpetuation of poverty both at the community and at the individual level. Confined and encapsulated social relations tend to reproduce a social formation that tends to result in marginality.

This book not only offers a detailed and well-grounded account of the origins and contemporary faces of urban African poverty and marginality. It provides a theoretical and meaningful framework through which to view the actors, their fates, their ideas and their activities in great detail. As such, the book succeeds in restoring some of their dignity.

Prof Dr Michael Bollig
University of Cologne
March 2011

To
Ida, Gøril, Kaja, Hanna and Ellen

Acknowledgements

This book has been long in the making. After applied development work in four slum-areas in the town of Oshakati in northern Namibia over a period of ten years, I decided to embark on a PhD-project to try to better understand the lives and coping strategies of the poorest and most destitute parts of the population in these areas. The idea was supported by my employer Chr. Michelsen Institute (CMI), and by the Norwegian Research Council that gave me a three year research grant. Presenting the project at the Department of Anthropology of the University of Cape Town (UCT) in 2003, I was invited to submit the thesis there. This seemed to me like a good idea, making it possible to relate to a department close to my geographical area and topics of interest in Africa's most reputable university. UCT also accepted a two year leave of absence when I was working in Mozambique in 2004 and 2005 on issues of poverty. Returning to CMI in 2006, I was given sufficient leeway in-between consultancies to finish the thesis and rework the manuscript into a book for a broader audience.

A number of people have given me invaluable support in the process. I would first of all like to thank my supervisors at UCT Associate Professor Andrew "Mugsy" Spiegel and Associate Professor Fiona Ross for their friendliness, constructive comments and patience. The late Professor Aud Talle from the University of Oslo gave me encouragements and valuable suggestions in the initial phase of the project. Former CMI Director Gunnar Sørbø has given me sufficient space to work on the thesis, despite its economic implications for the institute. Akiser Pomuti and Selma Nangulah of the University of Namibia (UNAM) have been my two main friends and collaborators in the field and spent hours discussing the issues at hand. Christa Schier, also of UNAM, has done the data processing. Lazarus Hangula, Sakki Nkembua, Daniel Kashupi, Herta Pomuti, Mono Mupotola, Martha Naanda, Frieda Iigonda and Gabriel Daniel have also supported my work at various stages and in various ways. Last but not least, I would like to thank the people in Oshoopala, Uupindi, Oneshila and Evululuku for their time and patience during my many stays in Oshakati.

Glossary

Local terms

Botstsoso	Petty thief
Cuca Shop	Shebeen
Efundula	Female initiation ceremony
Egumbo	Rural homestead
Ekaka	Dried spinach
Epya	Agricultural field
Kuku	Traditional dress
Okapana	Cooked food for sale
Olupale	Traditional family meeting place
Omahangu	Traditional porridge
Oshifima	Traditional Owambo porridge
Tombo	Traditional Owambo beer

1 Introduction

> These restless broken streets where definitions fail – the houses, the outhouses of white suburbs, two-windows-one-door, multiplied in institutional roads; the hovels with tin lean-tos sheltering huge old American cars blowsy with gadgets; the fancy suburban burglar bars of mean windows of tiny cabins; the roaming children, wolverine dogs, hobbled donkeys, fat naked babies, vagabond chickens and drunks weaving, old men staring, authoritative women shouting, boys in rags, tarts in finery, the smell of offal cooking, the neat patches of mealies between shebeen yards stinking of beer and urine, the litter of twice-discarded possessions, first thrown out by the white man and then picked over by the black – is this conglomerate urban or rural? No electricity in the houses, a telephone an almost impossible luxury, is this a suburb or a strange kind of junk-yard? The enormous back yard of the whole white city, where categories and functions lose their ordination and logic (Gordimer 2000 [1979]:148).

The urban manifestation of poverty reflects one of the most dramatic developments on the African continent, yielding contrasting images of affluent residential and business districts and utter misery in sprawling shantytowns or slums. More than 50 percent of Africa's population will soon live in towns and cities (United Nations 2008), and 50 percent of Africa's poor are expected to live in urban slums by 2040 (UN-Habitat 2003). Southern Africa is the most urbanised region on the continent, with Angola currently having an urban population of more than 60 percent, South Africa 55 percent and Namibia 33 percent – albeit with one of Africa's highest urban growth rates at 5,6 percent (United Nations 2008; GoN 2003). Urban migration does not seem to slow down, taking hundreds of thousands of women, men and children to towns, ostensibly in search of a better life. The large majority of these end up in poverty-stricken shantytowns, vividly described by Nadine Gordimer in her novel *Burger's Daughter* quoted above.

In the course of my 25 years of development work with urban shantytowns in Southern Africa, I have repeatedly been struck by the apparent marginalisation and seclusion of sections of each shantytown's population that are poorer and more apparently vulnerable than the rest of that population. This contradicts many of the popular conceptions and much of the development literature on urban poverty that tend to contrast such areas with the formal town and treat them as generally poor, generally deprived and generally vulnerable (UN-Habitat 2003; Kessides 2006). The people to whom I refer have comprised parts of the populations of particular shantytowns and neighbourhoods, as well as households and individual women, men and children that I have met in poor urban slum areas in places as different as Luanda, Windhoek and Oshakati.

Working with women fish-traders in Cazenga, one of the poorest shantytowns in Luanda, I met a former fish trader (*peixeira*) living in a shack in a dense and tense neighbourhood with three children from two to nine years of age. Her dwelling and her family were in a dismal condition compared even with those of others in that neighbourhood. She had a sad and introverted look, and her children bore evidence of severe malnutrition with discoloured hair, large bellies, "burnt" skin, swollen legs and lifeless eyes. She did not have the money necessary to start trading fish again, and depended on support given to her by men who stayed with her for longer or shorter periods of time. The support was hardly enough to provide for food, and tended to disappear together with the men every time she got pregnant. All other sources of support had dried up: She had not had contact with her family in the rural province of Kwanza Sul for years, and neighbours tended to shy away from her because, as she put it, "I don't think they like my life-style". When inquiring whether she wanted to take part in a small credit project she said with a sad face "No, it is no use. I will never make it".

In Windhoek, I conducted an interview with a group of six young men between 18 and 20 years of age in the shanty Okuriangawa. They all looked poorer than what was common even in these areas, and they were all unemployed. Despite it being early in the day, they had started to drink the local *tombo* brew and became quite vocal as the conversation went along. Their poverty and desperation were evident in their bodily appearances and behaviour, and in their worn-out second-hand clothes and shoes that did not even come close to their own urban ideals. They blamed their difficult situation on the government and town life. "You need money for everything: School, housing, food, clothes and drinks. Without education and the right contacts, you will not get employment. At the same time people back in the village expect us to send them something. If we don't, they will not support us either. The only things we can do is what everybody does in our situation [i.e. being petty criminals or *botsotsos*], which is not going to take us anywhere".

Coming into Oshakati for the first time, I met local authorities to prepare work for a slum upgrading project. I was told that all four major shantytowns were safe, except for Amunkambya which was reportedly very poor, full of problems and dangerous. Every night, I heard, people were beaten, raped and even killed there, and domestic violence was widespread. "The rest of us here in Oshakati do not deal with them". Two years later, I was back in Oshakati and went on my first of many visits to Amunkambya. Meeting with a community leader, she argued that the situation in the shantytown was very difficult. "People have no jobs, and the informal sector has no customers. Nothing is as it used to be. We are also getting on each others' nerves, and there is a lot of trouble here. But this is the only place we can stay. We have no life any longer in the rural areas where we come from. So we shouldn't complain, even though living in town is not really a life for an Owambo. As long as they don't bury me here".

The phrase "As Long as They Don't Bury Me Here", selected as the title of this book, epitomises the ultimate signifier of poverty and exclusion in Oshakati as well as in many other poor urban areas in Southern Africa. Not being put to rest on ancestral land in rural areas usually implies that the deceased has been too poor to leave behind the means for a proper funeral, and too socially isolated to have relatives or friends organise one and show the last signs of respect in accordance with prevailing tradition. Instead of being buried in rural Owambo in a homestead surrounded by family, relatives and friends in traditional ceremonies, the poorest are put in graves behind a second-hand car dealer in Oshakati in a graveyard littered with garbage, frequented by stray animals, and disregarded by everyone.

It is the lives and coping strategies of the poorest people in the Oshakati shantytowns[1] that are the focus of this book, and their experiences of marginalisation and social exclusion. Throughout my more than ten years of visiting shantytowns in Oshakati – carrying out surveys, taking part in discussions, sharing meals, drinking in local bars, watching kids play, visiting hospitals and schools, accompanying people to town and rural areas or just being there – it is the fate of the poorest men, women and children in these areas that has puzzled me the most. What is it, I have asked, that enables some people living in oppressed and poor urban shantytowns to strive to go on with their lives or improve their situation while others, living in the same setting and apparently under the same conditions, seem to be trapped in abject poverty and to give up making more out of their lives?

In the development literature, urban poverty is first and foremost related to levels of income, consumption and material assets (Rakodi and Lloyd-Jones 2002; Bryceson and Potts 2006). I am concerned with processes of impoverishment and marginalisation that make people become what is variously denoted the "very poor", the "ultra poor", the "poorest of the poor", or the "chronically poor" – often defined as people experiencing severe poverty over an extended period of time (CPRC 2005). Provisionally defining the poor in the Oshakati shantytowns as the 70 percent[2] of the population with a monthly household income of less than the defined national poverty line of N$ 662 (NPC 1999; see also NPC 2006), the very poor part of that group will be defined as the 37 percent of the total number of households with a monthly income of less than 40 percent (or N$ 250) of that poverty line (Hulme and

---

[1] Poor urban areas in Southern Africa are known by different names and connotations. The term "squatter area" usually connotes illegality of settlement; the terms "shantytown" highlights the poor conditions of settlements and residential dwellings; and the term "informal settlement" comprises both. "Slum" is normally not used due to the word's strong derogatory connotations, but is, as we shall see, closest to the local terms often used for such areas. In this book, the terms shantytown, informal settlement and slum will be used interchangeably.

[2] If not otherwise stated all figures in this study are taken from a household income survey carried out in 1994 of the four main shantytowns Uupindi, Oshoopala, Evululuku and Oneshila (Tvedten and Pomuti 1994) – to be compared with the most recent national (NPC 1999 and 2006) and local (OTC 2002) income surveys (see also NPC 2008 and Schmidt 2009).

Shepard 2003). The remaining 30 percent of the shanty population have an income above the poverty line of N$ 662, which makes them part of the 'better-off' (or 'less poor') section of the shanty population. While male-headed and female headed households are represented in all categories, the former have a higher average income than the latter.

Having said this, households do not function as autonomous social units, and poverty is increasingly acknowledged as multi-dimensional involving lack of material resources as well as powerlessness in relation to institutions of society and the state and vulnerability to adverse shocks (Chambers 1989; Kedir 2005; Kanbur and Schaffer 2007). My point of departure in this book is that it is the combination of political and economic oppression, low levels of income and material assets, and marginalisation through social relations and cultural perception that trap people in abject poverty. The approach makes it necessary to balance an analysis of structural oppression with a meaningful representation of social practices and relationships. The very poorest represent an underclass that I will define with reference to their position on a scale of material poverty, vulnerability and powerlessness – or 'economic position' (Bourdieu 1990, Ortner 1991). While we shall see that there is room for social change through the agency of social actors (Bourdieu 1990; Johnsen-Hanks 2002), a central theme in this book is the extent to which the poorest parts of the Oshakati shanty population remain trapped in poverty and destitution with few if any options for improving their situation.

My working hypothesis has been that social continuity and change among the Oshakati shanty-dwellers depend on the way people internalise structural oppression, their economic position, and their ability to establish and maintain social relations with urban areas (through employment, income and command of urban cultural styles) and with rural areas (through embeddedness in the land, exchange of goods and command of rural cultural styles). The importance of economic position for social relations of well-being and poverty is qualified by the socio-cultural construction of gender, with unemployed poor men unable to maintain their 'manhood' and positions as household heads leaving new space and responsibilities for women and female-headed households who pursue their coping strategies by entering close matrifocal relationships.

People avoiding becoming very poor or with upward social mobility are those who manage to relate constructively to the urban and rural social formations outside the oppressed and poor shantytown. The poorest shanty dwellers are marginalised and excluded from rural and urban relations as they cannot fill them with money or material means in an increasingly commoditised social context demanding reciprocity. Being unable to establish and maintain external relationships, they depend on shanty-based social relations and networks which further limits their access to economic resources and enhances their sense of powerlessness and vulnerability. For the most destitute part of the population having experienced long-term impoverishment and marginalisation, the discrepancy between hegemonic perceptions of urban and rural life and their own desperate situation of poverty and social exclusion makes them act in compliance with the oppressive forces in ways that further undermine their socio-economic position. In other words, material poverty has consequences of its own in the sense that it narrows the room for constructive social relationships outside the shantytowns and channels people's perceptions and actions inwards towards the shantytown in ways that tend to further impoverish and marginalise them.

The Setting

Before I start my anthropological analysis, let me here briefly introduce Namibia, Oshakati and its shantytowns from an aggregate quantitative perspective in the vernacular of economic development. With a population of 2.1 million people, Namibia is one of Africa's most sparsely populated countries. 62 percent of the population live in the former homelands in the northern one third of the national territory and 33 percent live in urban areas – all according to the most recent census and updates (GoN 2003, EIU 2008).
While being one of the world's driest countries in terms of rainfall, Namibia is richly endowed with natural resources such as minerals and marine fish, with commercial livestock production and tourism being other important sources of income. With a GDP per capita of USD 7,120, Namibia is defined as a "lower middle-income" country (EIU 2007).

Having said this, the most salient and striking feature of the Namibian economy and society is its inequality: No other country in the world reveals such a large discrepancy between the rich and poor – as measured by its Gini coefficient of 70.7 (World Bank 2007).[3] The inequality is also evident from other national aggregate data, such as the discrepancy between GDP per capita, where Namibia ranks 65 out of 175 countries, and the Human Development Index (HDI) which measures longevity, educational attainment and income and where Namibia ranks 124 out of 175 countries. A HIV/AIDS prevalence rate of 21.3 percent among the adult population contributes to the low HDI (UNDP 2007).

Moreover, these aggregate figures conceal national disparities at several levels: There are large differences in income and social development between regions, language groups (a local euphemism for ethnicity and race), and gender. Looking specifically at the urban-rural divide, urban areas are consistently portrayed as being better off than rural areas. Mean annual household income in urban areas is N$ 33,117, with the mean income in

---

[3] The Gini coefficient measures the share of income between different quintiles of the population in relation to the average per capita income. A value of 0 implies perfect equality, and a value of 100 implies perfect inequality. A country like Norway has a Gini coefficient of 25.8, and South Africa has a Gini coefficient of 59.0 (World Bank 2007).

rural areas being less than one third of that at N$ 10,531. The Human Development Index shows a similar discrepancy of 0.628 and 0.512 respectively (GoN 2003; see also NPC 2006 and 2008). However, as already argued, aggregates of this type conceal important internal differences in urban areas between the modern city and urban slums – which brings us to Oshakati.

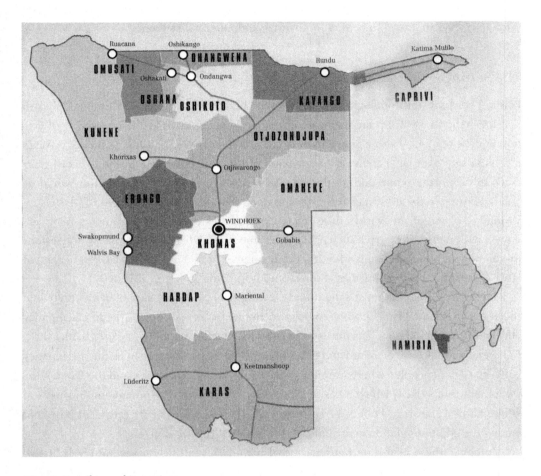

Map 1: Namibia and its regions

Oshakati is the main urban centre for 780,000 Owambo people living in northern Namibia (GoN 2003), and has an estimated population of 42,000 (OTC 2002) – which makes it Namibia's third largest town after Windhoek and Walvis Bay. Oshakati was established in 1966 as an administrative and later a military town, being the centre for South Africa's apartheid administration in the north until Namibia's independence in 1990. Oshakati is currently considered the main boom-town in Namibia, largely based on economic investments from

South African capital establishing shopping centres and manufacturing industries, and on the increasing formal and informal trade with Angola following the 2001 peace settlement there. The enhanced commercial importance of Oshakati has also led to stronger government involvement – culminating in its acquired status as a municipality, implying higher political and financial autonomy than before its municipal status (CLGF 2004).

The formal parts of town, with their tarred roads, private bungalows, gardens, shopping malls, hotels, government offices, schools, churches and a hospital, stand in sharp contrast to the informal shantytowns in which 73 percent of the Oshakati population live (OTC 2002). The focus of the current study is the four major shanty areas in Oshakati – Oshoopala, Evululuku, Uupindi and Oneshila – containing approximately 60 percent of the town's total population (Map 2).[4] The areas give an immediate impression of poverty and deprivation from their physical appearance of run-down houses and shacks, narrow alleyways and garbage as well as from the way people dress, look and move. The shantytowns are considered poor, violent and vulnerable by people from the outside as well as by its own population, as indicated by the term *obumbashi* (implying "shit" or "dirt") commonly used for these areas.

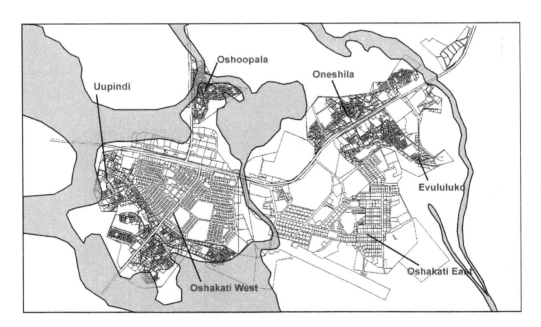

Map 2: Oshakati and its Shantytowns

---

[4] There are also five smaller and more recently established shantytowns (Kanjengedi, Sky, Eemwandi. Oshimbangu and Ompumbu), presently providing homes to an additional 13 percent of the population (OTC 2002).

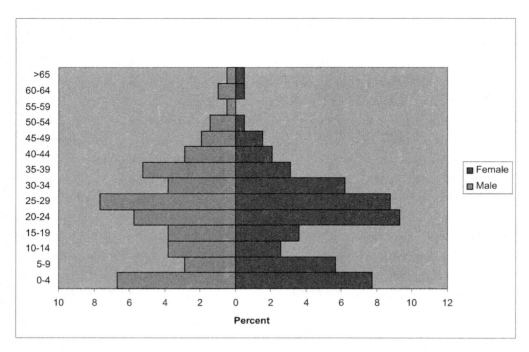

Figure 1: Population Pyramid 1994 (Age Cohorts)

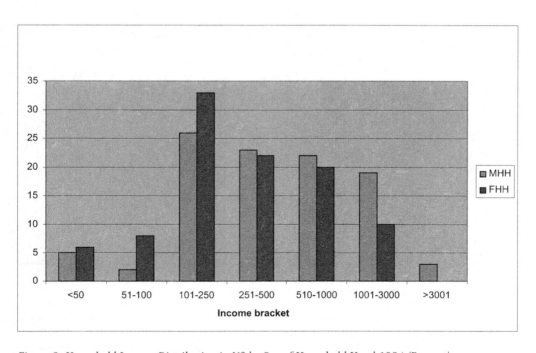

Figure 2: Household Income Distribution in N$ by Sex of Household Head 1994 (Percent)

The population in the four shanty-areas has increased by approximately eight percent per year since independence, standing at an estimated 24,000 in 2002. This means that about half the population has lived there since the time of the apartheid state, with the other half having been born there or moved in after independence. Of the 2002 population, Uupindi accommodated 9,474 people, Oneshila 6,066, Evululuku 5,378 and Oshoopala 3,167 (OTC 2002). As shown in Figure 1, the population is young with 77 percent being 34 years or younger and only five percent being 50 years or older.[5] 52 percent of the population are female and 48 percent are male, and 72 percent of the households are male-headed and 28 percent are female-headed. More recent figures show a sharp increase in the proportion of female headed households to more than 50 percent, reflecting gendered processes of impoverishment that will be a central focus in this book (GoN 2003, see also NPC 2006).

Looking at conditions of material poverty in the four shanty areas, my own applied research (Tvedten and Pomuti 1994; see also Tvedten and Nangula 1999; Tvedten 2004) has revealed a situation of general deprivation but also of important internal differentiation in terms of access to income and material resources. Let me here give a brief introductory account of these material realities as they have emerged from my applied studies, calling to mind that, for people living "on the edge", even small differences may be vital for the ability to cope in poor urban shantytowns.

Differentiation is first and foremost documented by income – being considerably lower than the averages for urban areas in Namibia referred to above. As seen from Figure 2, approximately 70 percent of households have an income of less than N$ 662 per month – putting them below the poverty line defined by the NPC (see above).[6] And 37 percent of the households are very poor by having an income of less than N$ 250 per month or 40 percent of the poverty line – effectively making them non-viable as socio-economic units and dependent on social relationships outside the household to survive. Household income is also gendered: female-headed households have a considerably lower income than male-headed households. 47 percent of the female headed households earn N$ 250 or less per month and only 10 percent earn N$ 1000 or more, as against 33 percent and 22 percent respectively for male headed households. Comparative data from 2002 (OTC 2002) show that the proportion of very poor households is relatively stable over time (with 37 percent

---

[5] All subsequent data are taken from my own survey, if not otherwise stated. The survey was done in 1994. and is based on a seven percent sample of the total shanty population. This is large enough to draw generalised conclusions (Devereux and Hoddinott 1992, and personal communication).

[6] There is, surprisingly, no official state-defined poverty-line defined for Namibia. While the issue of poverty-lines is much debated, they are commonly used to guide pro-poor policies in developing countries. An unofficial poverty line based on an income of N$ 662 was defined in a Levels of Living Survey (NPC 1999), and has represented the point of departure for all subsequent analyses (see e.g. NPC 2006 and 2008).

in 1994 and 35 percent in 2002), although that finding does not mean that over time there are no households that cross over the dividing line.

My data also reveal a close correspondence between income and other expressions of material poverty. The better-off generally have access to better housing in the form of brick houses, larger plots and superior physical infrastructure in the form of clean water, sanitation and electricity. They are more likely to own or have access to agricultural land and cattle. They own a larger number of capital items such as cars, bicycles, radios and telephones. And they are more likely to save money for future investments or use than poorer households. The materially poorest, on the other hand, tend to live in inferior iron shacks, rural reed-huts, or tents; they have limited access to water, proper sanitation and fuel; they own few if any of the capital items listed above; they have limited or no access to land, cattle or other rural resources; and they generally do not save. There is also a close correspondence between level of material poverty and education and health. 16 percent of the population 15 years or above have no formal education at all and 24 percent of those who have gone to school have grade 4 or less, implying a functional illiteracy rate of 40 percent. And health indicators (MHSS 2001; see also MHSS 2008) reveal a child mortality rate of more than ten percent, under-nutrition of 35 percent, and 31 percent being infected by HIV/AIDS.

Finally, my quantitative data show that female headed households – in addition to having low incomes – also tend to be more dependent on informal employment, have poorer housing and inferior physical infrastructure, lower rate of ownership of capital items and more limited access to rural resources in the form of cattle and land than male-headed households. And there are differences in employment, income and access to material resources between the different shantytowns. Oshoopala is by far the poorest of the four major shantytowns in Oshakati, with people in Oneshila being better off as judged by all socio-economic indicators.

My data thus reveal a situation of general material poverty, but with important internal differentiation along lines of class, gender and geographical space. As I have come to know communities and individuals better, however, quantitative analyses have seemed inadequate to understand the complexity of contexts, social relations and individual identities. Questions about why particular groups and individuals seem to remain poor and marginalized; their own perceptions about their position in the world at large and in their community; and their strategies for getting by in a harsh urban slum environment have largely remained unanswered. The objective of this book, then, is to analyse processes of impoverishment, marginalisation and social exclusion in the Oshakati shantytowns, and thereby to explain why some households and individuals seem apparently to be trapped so that they barely get by and appear to have acceded to their condition as poor people in a poor urban setting.

Poverty in Anthropology

Turning to "academic" anthropology to seek answers to my more fundamental questions about urban poverty, I was initially struck by the apparently limited attention devoted recently to issues of poverty and development, at least in leading anthropological journals and textbooks as well as among academically oriented colleagues.[7] I was of course familiar with the important critique in anthropology of the notion of "development" as a Western modernisation project (see e.g. Ferguson 1994), and of the multi-dimensional and contested realities of "modernity" and "social change" (Arce and Long 2000). However, my sense was also that mainstream anthropology had become introverted and had lost the ambition of contributing to an understanding of development issues (Gardner and Lewis 1996; see also Edelman and Haugerud 2005) – in contrast to other social sciences where applying social theories to real-world problems is essential also for academic careers. In the words of one of the most ardent critics of development anthropology, to do development anthropology is to "facilitate development, and such facilitation violates the anthropologist's credo of self-determination of local populations" (Escobar 1991:69).

With its anti-theory and anti-positivist stand (Moore 1999:5), post-modernism has made it particularly difficult to work on issues of poverty. In the words of Philippe Bourgois:

> The post-modernist anthropologists have, in their eagerness to break down hegemonic definitions and meta-narratives, made it impossible to categorize and prioritize experiences of injustice and oppression. This subtly denies the very real personal experience of pain and suffering that is imposed socially and structurally across race, class, gender, sexuality and other power-ridden categories (Bourgois 1995:14).

In a similar vein, Nancy Scheper-Hughes argues that anthropology has turned away from the plain facts of hunger as lived experiences for millions of Third World people:

> Perhaps hunger as hunger – a frightening human affliction – is simply `not good to think´ for anthropologists who, if they think of hunger and famine at all, prefer to think of them as symbols and metaphors or as positive contribution to long-term adaptation (Scheper-Hughes 1992:132).

Neither did there seem to be much help in the urban anthropology literature. The programme for the urban anthropology of the new millennium has been defined as "spatial relations, mass-media and consumption as well as urban planning and design decision-making" (Low and McDonough 2001:5-6), with urban poverty apparently disappearing from the

---

[7] Development anthropology seems to have assumed a marginal position in most anthropology departments, compared to the situation in the 1980s and 1990s. When it is taught (such as at the Poverty Politics Programme at the University of Bergen in Norway) its de-constructive point of departure makes it un-interesting for anthropological practisioners in the field.

agenda. Moreover, the focus on towns and cities is not first and foremost to understand the city in and of itself, but "a necessary part of understanding the changing post-industrial and post-modern world in which we live" (Low 1999:2). Rather, Low argues, anthropologists have left theorising the city to sociologists, cultural geographers, urban planners and historians, and have only contributed marginally to urban policy debates, despite the fact that a number of anthropologists have shown that anthropological studies are essential for understanding urban problems (see e.g. Moser 1996; Konings and Foeken 2006; Ross 2010).

Having said this, there were also important lessons of relevance for development anthropology[8] in the post-modern critique. In general terms, post-modernists were uncomfortable with the reified "othering" typical of classical modernist anthropology (Eriksen and Nielsen 2001:146). Their critique has focused on how ideas and practices of modernity are appropriated and re-embedded in local practices, "accelerating the fragmentation and dispersal of modernity into constantly proliferating modernities" (Arce and Long 2000:1). Such multiple modernities, Comaroff and Comaroff (1993:1) have argued, generate powerful counter tendencies to what is conceived of as Western modernisation, exhibiting "distorted" or "divergent" patterns of development, and re-assembling what is often naively designated as "tradition".

More particularly, the profound questioning of the assumptions and techniques used to develop and convey cultural representations and interpretations (Marcus and Fischer 1986) has been at the very centre of my own dissatisfaction with my applied work. How do we as anthropologists represent life-worlds that are so different from our own as is life in poor urban shantytowns? How can we account for the different and often conflicting realities and notions among the poor themselves of what this life is all about? And how does my own position as a researcher with a specific professional background and agenda influence the way I perceive and represent this type of society? Questions like these should, I believe, compel us to reassess key issues of methodology, perspectives and writing that are vital also in development anthropology (see Johannsen 1992; Mosse 2005).

Moreover, as we see from the calls of some leading anthropologists there is a need for a more concerned urban anthropology. Fredrik Barth states that:

> [a] highly intellectual and internal critique has set priorities and focused interest so that we have lost much of our engagement in the real world and urgent issues... Anthropologists have had pitifully little to say on the phenomena of untranscendable poverty as it affects increasing hundreds of millions of people in major cities in the world. We have not been able to articulate

---

[8] Following Grillo (1997), a distinction is made here between development anthropology (engaged directly in application, for example by evaluating a project or offering policy advice); and anthropology of development (concerned with the social-scientific analysis of development as a cultural, economic and political process).

a position, or even a noticeable interest, in the fact that human activity seems to be destroying humanity's own global habitat. And we are only marginally addressing phenomena of increasing cultural pluralism and cultural blending in the world under present conditions of communication (Barth 1994:350).

Nancy Scheper-Hughes is even more explicit:

> In the brave new world of reflexive postmodernists, when anthropologists arrive in the field everything local is said to dissolve into merged media images, transgressed boundaries, promiscuously mobile multinational industry and workers, and transnational corporate desires and commodity fetishism ... The flight from the local in hot pursuit of a transnational, borderless anthropology implies a parallel flight from local engagements, local commitments, and local accountability ... Anthropology, it seems to me, must be there to provide the kind of deeply textured, fine-tuned narratives describing the specificity of lives lived in small and isolated places in distant homelands [or] in the `native yards´ of sprawling townships (Scheper-Hughes 1995:417).

Similarly, Bruce Knauft (1997), in a more accommodating mode, argues for a productive conversation across the divide that separates objectivity and empiricist declaration from strong forms of dislocation and subjectivity.

> As opposed to quotidian realities, many newer orientations in cultural anthropology can be ironically distant from the lives of most people, even as they creatively mime features of mass media, popular culture, hybridity and commercialism ... In theoretical as well as ethnographic terms, careful description and analysis are too easily dismissed as a totalising or master narrative. Of course, matters of textuality and displacement are integral to ethnographic field research as well as to the humanities. And it remains a crucial contribution to problematise this fact. But we still need detailed accounts of peoples' everyday lives (Knauft 1997:286-287).

Individual studies out of a concerned urban anthropology, to which I will return in more detail later, have also come to be important inspirations for my book. Scheper-Hughes's (1992) *Death Without Weeping* is a politically concerned study about the "routinisation" of human suffering in the shantytown Bom Jesus de Mata.[9] Also Philippe Bourgois' (1995) *In Search of Respect* combines political concerns with thorough scholarship. Through a critical discussion of polarized race, class and gender relations he contributes to a broad understanding of problems in the American inner city. Though sharing Sherry Ortner's (1995) scepticism regarding much so-called "resistance literature",[10] James Scott's (1985) *Weapons of the Weak*

---

[9] In fact, the Brazilian anthropology of urban poverty is rich and varied (Magnani 2003; see DaMatta 1995 for an overview in English). This is hardly known to people outside the Lusophone world - emphasising the essentialisation of anthropology around the Anglo-American nexus (Eriksen and Nielsen 2001:158).

[10] Ortner is particularly critical of the absence of analyses of forms of internal conflicts in many resistance studies, which as she puts it "gives them an air of romanticism" (Ortner 1995:177).

has been important as an early example of a concerned anthropology. Equally relevant for the issue of continuity and change among the urban poor, has been Paul E. Willis's (1977) *Learning to Labour*. The book analyzes the inner meaning, rationality and dynamic of cultural processes that contribute to working class culture and the maintenance and reproduction of the social order. Together, these studies represent important and relevant insights into issues of impoverishment, marginalisation and social exclusion – insights on which I have drawn extensively.

The strong tradition of urban anthropology in Southern Africa has also been an important motivation. As Fardon (1990:24-25) states, "[i]n its simplest form, a regional tradition influences the entry of the working ethnographer into a field imaginatively chartered by others". Whilst rather marginal in other regional anthropologies, urban studies have been central in Southern Africa since the pioneering study by Hellmann (1948) of a slum yard in Doornfontein in Johannesburg in the 1930s. Later, the Copperbelt studies in Zambia in the 1950s and 1960s (see e.g. Epstein 1958, Gluckman 1961 and Mitchell 1966) were unique not only for their inclusion of the modern but also for their innovative methodological approaches (Hannerz 1980:119-162). Zambia has continued to have a central place in urban anthropology through the reassessment of the Copperbelt towns and the Copperbelt literature by James Ferguson (1999) and the work of Karen Tranberg Hansen (1997) in Lusaka.

A series of studies that is somewhat less well known, but equally relevant for my own study, is the trilogy from urban townships in East London in South Africa (Reader 1961; Mayer 1963; Pauw 1963), and which Leslie Bank has reassessed and followed up both theoretically and empirically (Bank 1996, 2002). In Namibia, Wade Pendleton (1974) pioneered urban anthropology with his book *Katutura: A Place Where We do not Stay* (see also Pendleton 1996). I will argue that an active relationship with regional ethnography is important in its own right: It increases relevance, and decreases the danger of essentialisation of anthropological analyses (Fardon 1990).[11]

Analytical Framework

There is of course a very complex set of conditions that may explain processes of marginalisation and impoverishment in shantytowns like those in Oshakati. The shanties are the outcome of complex historical processes; the shanty-dwellers find themselves in a political and economic context which brings considerable constraints and implications; and they are

---

[11] I am, of course, also aware of the problematic relationship between anthropology and the apartheid state in South Africa and South-West Africa (Namibia), and will return to this later. The relationship is the subject of intensive debate among South African anthropologists themselves (see e.g. Gordon and Spiegel 1993; Kiernan 1997; Becker 2001).

susceptible to intersecting discourses, values and practices associated with notions of modernity (defined as "images and institutions associated with Western-style progress and development in a contemporary world" [Knauft 2002:18]), tradition (associated with rurality and customary values and relationships), and their own shanty-based practises of complex social relationships and cultural constructions.

All this raises an analytical dilemma to which I will have to relate to throughout this book, as pointed out by other anthropologists who have worked with deep urban poverty and deprivation such as Scheper-Hughes (1992:533) and Bourgois (1995:17-18): Either one attributes great explanatory power to the fact of oppression (and in doing so reduces the agency of subjects), or one tries to locate the everyday forms of compliance and resistance in the acts of the oppressed (running the risk of disregarding the effects of structural oppression). What I hope to achieve in the following pages is to balance an analysis of structural oppression (Chapter 2-4), with a meaningful representation of the poorest in Oshakati's shantytowns, and one that gives voice to them too (Chapter 5-9).

To approach the problem of poverty, marginalisation and exclusion, I have found the overarching framework of structure and agency, as this is advocated in Bourdieu's *practise theory* (Bourdieu 1977, 1990, see also Wacquant 1992[12]) and further elaborated by Ortner (1984, 2006), good to think with. It has become increasingly evident to me that historically constituted and structural conditions not only shape the political, economic and social context in which shanty populations find themselves, but that history and structural conditions are lived experiences for people in the Oshakati shantytowns. These experiences matter for people's own identities, their relations to each other, their world views and hence for their actions.

Bourdieu holds a view that social systems do have a powerful, even determining effect upon human action and the shape of events, but also emphasises human agency and ordinary lives. His approach highlights economic positions and social asymmetry as the most relevant dimension of both structure and action (Bourdieu 1990; see also Ortner 1984:147). Moreover, instead of assuming priority to structure or to agency, Bourdieu emphasises the primacy of *relations*. Society does not consist of individuals, he maintains: rather it expresses the sum of connections and relationships in which people find themselves. His notion of *habitus* is related to how historical and structural relations are "deposited" in individual bodies in the form of mental and corporeal schemata of perception and action. Among poor people in places like the Oshakati shantytowns, the notion of embodiment of structural oppression takes on a very real meaning through overt bodily and cultural signs of abject poverty, vulnerability and powerlessness.

---

[12] Waquant's article is an eloquent outline of the structure and logic of Bourdieu's sociology, and appears in a volume jointly written with Bourdieu (Bourdieu and Wacquant 1992). When considered useful, I will use this as point of reference.

I have undertaken my historical and structural analysis with reference to the combined outcome of the political economy and the cultural flows of meaning (Bourdieu 1990, see also Hannerz 1992), leading to the impoverishment, marginalisation and "othering" of the Oshakati shantytowns as socio-cultural space. Both the political economy and the hegemonic cultural forms are seen as part of a framework that reflects the related processes of modernisation and commoditisation as its driving forces, and sees culture as ideas and modes of thought that are socially distributed in locally embedded flows of meaning. With the commoditisation of social relationships and requirements for reciprocity in the social context in which the shanty-dwellers find themselves, the options for establishing and maintaining social relationships outside the poor shantytowns differ between the better-off and the poor. Differences in economic positions channel social relationships in specific directions, with the better-off in positions to establish social relationships with the urban and modern and the rural and traditional social formations and the poor becoming marginalised in the shantytowns. At the same time, shanty unemployment and poverty recast male domination and contribute to the establishment of female-focussed social networks in which men have little room. For the very poorest men and women, the discrepancy between hegemonic perceptions of urban and rural life and their own poverty and desperation make them succumb to their poverty and act in ways that contribute to their own impoverishment.

My analysis of impoverishment and marginalisation of people in the oppressed and poor Oshakati shantytown thus reconsiders several basic premises in current anthropology and poverty research: It argues for the need to combine the dominant notion of global cultural flows as the defining element of socio-cultural space (Appadurai 1996; see also Eriksen 2003) with a focus on political economy for defining the shantytowns as urban neighbourhoods. It reassesses the notion of the urban and the rural as a single social universe with hybrid cultural forms (Leeds 1994; see also Lynch 2005) by arguing for the relevance of *emic* distinctions between the slum, the urban and the rural for peoples' coping strategies. It introduces material poverty as a central determinant of social relationships, reassessing the notion of *style* as "strategies of survival under compulsory systems" (Ferguson 1999:99) by showing that the very poorest in the Oshakati shantytowns cannot escape their position nor their identity as poor. It reassesses recent notions of the feminisation of poverty by arguing that while female headed households and women may be poorer than male-headed households and men in material terms, resources flowing between women in female-focussed networks reduce their vulnerability and lead to greater social mobility (Moore 1994; see also Cornwall 2007). And it challenges the 'romantic' anthropological notion of organised and every-day forms of resistance among oppressed and poor people (Scott 1985, see also Ortner 2006) by arguing with Bourdieu (1990, see also Wacquant 1992) that the very poorest appear to contribute to their own destitution by acting in short-term and *ad hoc* ways and give up making more of their lives that together seem to trap them further in chronic poverty.

I see the broad analytical framework and related theories that will be presented and discussed in more detail as I go along as linked together in a way that will provide ways to understand the connections between structural political, economic and cultural processes; the way these relate to economic positions and identities of the shanty-dwellers; and the implications of their economic positions for social relations of poverty and marginalisation. My theoretical approach resembles what South African anthropologist Andrew Spiegel (1997) has called "a new materially grounded culturalism", which he advocates as a working paradigm for the anthropology of contemporary Southern Africa. This is when he says that "A rather eclectic mix of theories and approaches is required. It must build some of the more useful insights of recent interpretative approaches and revived pragmatist theory into materialist analyses" (Spiegel 1997:10).

Chapter Outline

Pursuing my central research question of why some people in the Oshakati shantytowns strive to go on with their lives and improve their situation while others seem trapped in abject poverty and to give up making more out of their lives, the first part of my study (Chapter 2-4) focuses on the historical and structural processes leading to the establishment and maintenance of the Oshakati shantytowns as poor, urban neighbourhoods.

In *Chapter 2*, I trace the making of the shantytowns historically, from early colonial encounters in the late 19th century to Namibian independence in 1990. I show that German and South African colonialism had a strong impact on everyday lives in the form of changing authority-structures, socio-economic differentiation and gender relations – albeit without wholly destroying traditional structures. The outbreak of the Namibian war of independence in the mid-1960s exacerbated processes of differentiation, and the poorest and most marginalised men and women migrated to Oshakati only to find themselves marginalised again, this time in an apartheid urban space in dense and tense shantytowns. With independence and the withdrawal of South African forces and administrative structures, Oshakati initially experienced a decline in socio-economic conditions – with people with a more mixed socio-economic background starting to move in as the new Swapo government asserted itself.

In *Chapter 3*, I set the stage for the Oshakati shantytowns as part of contemporary global and national space. Emphasis is given to the articulation between cultural flows associated with the state, the market, the media and social movements and their material implications; and the complexity of Oshakati and its shantytowns as urban place. I argue that poor informal settlements are at odds with the modernising project of the independent state, commercial capital and cultural images of modernity. They and their residents are therefore oppressed and marginalised politically, economically as well as in sociocultural terms – all further contributing to the constructed otherness of shantytowns. By following a selected number of shanty dwellers in their encounters with oppressive structures, I am able to show how the implications of those encounters relate to the economic position of the shanty-dwellers themselves.

I end the first part of the study in *Chapter 4* by outlining the implications of the historical processes and flows emanating from oppressive structures for population characteristics and material conditions in the shantytowns, revealing a general situation of poverty and deprivation but also with differences in levels of income between the very poor, poor and better-off shanty dwellers. I also expose the close correspondence between economic position, gender and material well-being and poverty. Existing quantitative data give some basis for assessing trends in population, household headship and income poverty and differentiation over time, but the chapter will also reveal the limitations of survey data for explaining social relations of poverty and processes of social marginalisation and exclusion.

In *Chapter 5*, I set the stage for the second part of the study on social relations of poverty (Chapter 5-9) with a theoretical introduction on the importance of economic positions for the type and nature of social relationships across shanty, urban and rural social space; the implications of the ongoing commodification of social relationships for processes of impoverishment and marginalisation; the notion of social reproduction of households being closely related to changing economic responsibilities and socio-cultural space for men and women; and the idea that oppressive forces make the poorest act in ways that effectively contribute to their own impoverishment and marginalisation. Still by way of introduction, I also present the shanty-dwellers own perceptions of the shantytowns as distinct socio-cultural space through their own photographs.

In *Chapter 6*, I show how the shantytown residents' social relations with rural areas and kin have to be filled with material content over time to be viable and to live up to rural people's expectations. While the better-off households manage to maintain a "double rootedness" by maintaining an urban base but keeping the options open for eventual rural retreat, the poorest are eventually marginalised from their rural relations, thus increasing their material poverty as well as their vulnerability and social exclusion. I also show that poor women and their children are less susceptible to rural exclusion than poor men, due to the former's more enduring social relationships in a matrilineal setting and the higher expectations vested in urban-based men as providers for rural kin.

In *Chapter 7*, I analyse urban social relationships. Employment and income in the urban and modern setting are vital for the shanty-dwellers, but they demand education and command of urban cultural codes that the poorest often do not have. Erratic and piecemeal employment and the informal economy represent alternative sources of employment and income, with the latter and most stable being dominated by female-focussed networks. Impoverished and marginalised from the rural as well as the formal urban context, the remaining option for the poorest is retreating to the shantytowns. Here options for income and viable social relations are limited, leading men to become entrapped in impoverished and frequently violent social relations and women to seek relations primarily with other women or social isolation.

In *Chapter 8*, I analyse social relations of inclusion and exclusion in the household as the basic unit of social reproduction, showing how the stress of poverty has implications for internal household relations. While the better-off tend to marry, to ground their relationships in an extended family context, and to be relatively stable, the poorest tend to establish *ad hoc*, more socially isolated and less stable relations of cohabitation. Poor women increasingly establish female headed households and matrifocal networks as alternative forms of social organisation, while poor unemployed men become redundant to the social reproduction of the household and are increasingly marginalised as 'domestic nomads'.

In *Chapter 9*, I argue that long-term experiences of impoverishment and social marginalisation of the very poorest from rural and urban areas and from shanty-based networks and households as basic units of social reproduction on the one hand, and what is perceived as an impossible discrepancy between hegemonic perceptions of a good life and those people's own situation of abject poverty on the other, represent socially constituted principles of perceptions and appreciations that have implications for coping strategies. Their salient features are a sense of giving up making more out of ones life, and acts of emergency and despair that lead to further impoverishment and marginalisation.

In *Chapter 10*, I sum up the analysis by concluding that the Oshakati shantytowns are caught up in historical and structural processes of oppression and impoverishment, with economic position and gender being central for the shanty-dwellers' ability to establish and maintain vital social relationships outside the shantytowns. The part of the shanty population trapped in deep and chronic poverty are those who are unable to maintain such relationships, with the very poorest and most marginalised succumbing to their situation as destitute.

2 The Making of Oshakati and its Shantytowns

The colonial encounter, first under the Germans from 1885 to 1915, and then under South Africa until 1990, had profound implications for the creation of Oshakati and its shantytowns as localities as well as for relations of class, gender and ethnicity. Ending two decades ago, it is also lived experiences for a large number of shantytown-dwellers. The objective of the present historical chapter is to provide a backdrop so that we will be able to make sense of Oshakati and its shantytowns as geographical space and of the identities and social relations of poverty of the shanty-dwellers as they currently unfold. Understanding relations of poverty and processes of marginalisation and social exclusion, I argue, also necessitates an understanding of how the past impinges on the everyday social and cultural practices and how it is used instrumentally in people's coping strategies (Bourdieu 1990, see also Spiegel 1997).

Anthropological literature on colonialism and its implications for people's current lives often focuses on historical discourses between the colonial state and colonial subjects, in Foucault's sense of social constructions of reality with particular emphasis on the power of classification (Pels 1997). As Stoler (1995) argues, questions of racial identity, class distinction and sexuality pervaded the colonial discourse, with far reaching consequences for the objectification of colonial subjects.

As underlined by Comaroff and Comaroff (1997), however, the primary objective of colonialism was political control and economic exploitation of colonies and their subjects. "Social worlds cannot" as they put it, "be the product of conversation alone" (Comaroff and Comaroff 1997:410). The point is to demonstrate how, in particular periods, colonialism, capitalism and modernity constituted and played off each other, manifesting themselves simultaneously *both* as political economy and as culture.

Of particular relevance for the making of colonial subjects was the process of *commodification* (Comaroff and Comaroff 1997:34). Changing patterns of production, exchange and consumption, wrought in part by the civilising mission, in part by an expanding market in labour and goods, "recast existing regimes of value and property and altered the construction and representation of personhood, status and identity" (ibid.). In many settings this process was exacerbated by an increasing urbanisation, particularly towards the end of the colonial period.

The making of colonial place, identities and social relationships as presented by these scholars resemble the making of Owambo and Oshakati. The colonial state, the missions and merchant capital had diverse interests, but essentially championed commercial production, wage-work, contractual relations and racial identity (Moorsom 1995). Having said this, Owambo also represents a special case. The system of indirect rule and the policy of apartheid had particularly strong implications due to the geographical isolation, its sparse population and the consequent ease of control for the colonial administration. As I will show the colonial encounter led to changing relationships between political authorities and subjects, old and young and men and women – with an important implication being the pauperisation, impoverishment and marginalisation of parts of the Owambo population.

An additional aspect of the colonial encounter of particular relevance for Owambo and Oshakati is the extreme atrocities committed during the liberation struggle, primarily by South Africa (Leys and Saul 1995, Hangula 2000), but also within the SWAPO movement (Groth 1995). Handling the aftermath of conflict in a post-conflict setting is, of course, nothing exceptional in a Southern African context.[1] In the case of Owambo, however, practically all inhabitants were affected by the brutality of war as members of the colonial army or the resistance movement or as civilians (Herbstein and Evenson 1989). Having said that, I will argue that the implications of war on the current identities and social relationships of the Oshakati shanty dwellers are mediated by a joint feeling of having lost the peace by being marginalised and excluded from post-war and post-independence developments.

Finally, the urbanisation process itself introduced further complexities in the formation of the Oshakati shantytowns and their subjects. Urbanisation in Owambo was late due to the distance from main trading routes and other population centres, with Oshakati being established only in 1966 (Hangula 1993b). Many of those moving to Oshakati were pauperised, poor and marginalised rural dwellers trying to make a living as soldiers for the already then detested apartheid state and in the increasing informal economy around the town. Urbanisation thus represented a critical disjuncture with rurally based class, gender and ethnic identities, with the migrants' marginalisation being exacerbated by the negative rural perception of Oshakati as an apartheid town. In Oshakati itself, the marginalisation of poor rural migrants into the town continued with the strict delineation of the town into a formal white town, a formal black township, and informal poor black shantytowns where most of them ended up. After independence a more mixed group of people started moving in, but still dominated by poor rural migrants.

Colonial Encounters

The colonial encounter came late in Owambo. Although the Portuguese had set foot on the northern coast of present day Namibia already in 1484, the vast desert lands isolating

---

[1] Similar situations exist in towns and cities in Angola, Mozambique and South Africa, and historically also in Zimbabwe. In fact, shared memories of conflict are probably the rule rather than the exception in many localities in these countries.

Owambo both to the west and to the south effectively postponed colonial settlement for 400 years (Williams 1991). The establishment of missionary societies in Owambo from the 1870s, and German colonial occupation from 1884 implied a more direct foreign impact, although white colonial presence was still very limited. The Germans saw Owambo primarily as a labour reserve and used traditional leaders for recruiting labourers to farms and mines in the southern parts of the country (Siiskonen 1990). And both Finnish and German Rhenish missionaries initially tried to "save souls" by starting at the apex of the social hierarchy, in the hope that the subjects of the kings and nobility would follow (Tönjes 1911, Silvester et al. 1998).

The direct impact of the colonial power, missions and traders increased during the first two decades of the 20th century. The German need for labour from Owambo increased after the German-Herero war of 1904-1905, when the German colonisers killed nearly 60 per cent of the Herero population on which it had primarily depended for labour (Krüger and Henrichsen 1998). Wage labour was enforced through taxation and, by World War I, as many as 10,000 Owambo men per year were sent south as migrant labourers with an additional 2,000 men working in Angola on the Moçámedes and Benguela Railway (Moorsom 1995). At the same time, particularly the Finnish missions had changed strategy to one of reaching out to the common man and woman directly by intensifying missionary activities and establishing mission schools (Siiskonen 1998). By 1909 the German and Finnish Lutherans had missionary stations in all seven Owambo kingdoms,[2] and the Owambo membership of the Finnish church increased from 2,873 in 1913-1914 to 23,000 by 1930 (Moorsom 1995:10).

Both developments put increasing pressure on the socio-economic and cultural fabric of matrilineal Owambo society, which had been characterised by hierarchical political authority through king- and clanship; subsistence production with options for accumulation of wealth through unequal access to cattle and land and tribute; and ward- and household authority vested in male members of matrilineages (Estermann 1957, Williams 1991). Labour migration and taxation, combined with several years of severe drought, had the effect of increasing the number of Owambo dependent on cash income (Silvester et al. 1998). Missions meanwhile worked against the traditional authorities and (albeit inadvertently) male dominance by opening up alternative means of social mobility through education, and by discouraging important traditional practices affecting women. Their insistence on monogamy and their attacks on the female initiation ceremony *efundula* in particular aimed at the very heart of chiefly and male authority (Hartmann 1998).

---

[2] These were Ondonga and Uukwanyama in the east, Uukwambi in the centre and Ongandjera, Ombalantu, Uukwaludhi, Uukolonkadhi in the west.

From 1915[3] South Africa as a colonial power had a stronger and more direct impact on Owambo society, through a body of new laws to regulate the flow of labour and to control the indigenous population (Banghart 1969). South African policies towards Namibia were spearheaded by three men with strong interest in the territory. These were the Rhenish missionary Heinrich Vedder; Louis Fourie, who was medical officer to the South African administration; and C.H.L. Hahn, who was Native Commissioner in Owamboland from 1929 to 1946. Together they produced the famous book *Native Tribes of South West Africa* (Hahn, Fourie and Vedder 1928). Their work had large implications for the objectification of black subjects as "natives", allocated to specific "native reserves" (Hayes et al. 1998).

South Africa's main objective with its colony was to secure cheap labour for farms, mines and the expanding fishing industry in the central and southern parts of the South West Africa Territory (Silvester et al. 1998). Increasing capitalisation and commodification of Owambo society, combined with long periods of drought and famine particularly in the 1920s, contributed to making labour migration the single most determinant aspect of the South African colonial encounter. Between 1910 and 1930 the average number of Owambo men on migrant labour contract was rarely less than 20 per cent of the adult male population and, after recovery from the great depression in the mid-1930s, not less than 25 per cent (Moorsom 1995).

Migrant labourers usually stayed away for 18 months, often with only a few weeks in Owambo before entering new contracts out of fear of losing the goodwill of their employers (Mbuende 1986). Owambo women were from the very beginning excluded from the colonial regime's recruiting mechanisms, although a small number went illegally to work as domestic servants or in the informal economy in towns in the central parts of the country (Hishongwa 1983). Conditions of work were generally harsh with long working hours and crowded living conditions in single quarters, and salaries were low (Moorsom 1995).

An important implication of the labour migration system at the level of individual households and extended families was the changing role and responsibility of women. With such a large number of able-bodied men absent for long periods, women had their workload dramatically increased to include agricultural as well as domestic work (Banghart 1969, also Frayne 2005). A result of the increased workload was often deterioration of farms and homesteads and, in combination with what women perceived to be small remittances from their husbands, this often created mutual suspicion (Hayes 1998). It also contributed to a weakening of the polygamous, as well as the nuclear, household institutions (Hishongwa 1992; Becker 2000).

---

[3] That year, the invasion of "South West Africa" was led by the famous Boer generals Smuts and Botha in the name of supporting British and Allied war efforts against Germany (Silvester et al. 1998). A mandate was awarded by the League of Nations for a trusteeship of the territory in 1920, which lasted until 1948.

With the increasing dominance of money from labour migration among people in Owambo society, the importance of new parallel forms of wealth in western goods and in knowledge became part of a wider socio-economic struggle (McKittrick 1998). Many European cultural artefacts – names, clothing, hospitals, oxcarts, ploughs, bicycles, even literacy – were increasingly adopted by the Owambo people with the necessary means. Employment and cash income had become an alternative economic base for many men – challenging the authority of traditional powerholders with their wealth in land and cattle.

With time, the influence of traditional authorities continued to decrease, the number of Christian converts continued to grow and the traditional social fabric continued to change (Mbuende 1986). Losing the battle against the "native" going "modern" (and hence the very rationale for the system of indirect rule), direct control by the South African colonial and apartheid state tightened from the early 1960s following the report of the South African state's Odendaal Commission (GSA 1963) and the introduction of apartheid-style Bantustan policies as a particularly ruthless form of colonial order. With this followed stronger direct political control – and the introduction of Bantu education with the state taking over the educational responsibility from the missions (O'Callaghan 1977). The objective of the education was, in the words of the then South African Minister of Native Affairs Dr. H. Verwoerd, "to teach natives from childhood to realise that equity with Europeans is not for them" (quoted in Hishongwa 1992:14).

Parallel with the tightening of political and cultural control, the economy of Owambo changed from being primarily subsistence oriented with injections from migrant wages, to becoming increasingly commoditised. The number of trading licences in Uukwanyama, for example, increased dramatically from the early 1960s, and an increasing number of people were trading without licences as small-scale traders, butchers and eating house proprietors, illegal liquor-dealers and lorry-owners (Moorsom 1995). Perhaps most important was the commodification of agricultural production itself, with land as well as cattle becoming objects of exchange and many men losing ownership or control of both (Tapscott 1990; Frayne 2005).

With this development, economic differentiation as well as pauperisation increased. Perhaps the clearest indication of this is that, by the 1960s, cash income was necessary for the large majority of peasants to avoid real hardships (Moorsom 1995, Devereux et al. 1996). Both the extended and nuclear family showed signs of disintegration, as indicated by an increasing number of poor, destitute households (Hishongwa 1992). Women also found that their security was no longer firmly rooted in the reciprocities associated with kin relations in a working matrilineal system, and many became increasingly dependent on own income generation through informal economic activities beyond traditional agricultural production (Hishongwa 1983).

As we shall see later in this chapter, the poorest and most marginal of Owambo's rural dwellers formed the main group of men and women who moved to Oshakati and its shantytowns from the mid-1960s – carrying with them the type of historical experience I have just described. Having said that, I have also claimed (with Bourdieu 1990) that the way in which historical conditions are deposited in people in the form of mental or corporeal schemata for perception, appreciation and action will depend on people's own personal histories and current economic positions.

Fairweather (2003:284-285) has argued that for people in Owambo nostalgia for the past is a "way in which people distance themselves from the real past and put it safely in a box, while at the same time creating an imagined past that has positive implications for the construction of contemporary identities". While this might indeed apply to some of the less poor shanty dwellers, I have only rarely encountered such positive perceptions of the past among the poorest people in Oshakati's shantytowns. For them, "the old days" (*omathimbo gonale*) are primarily associated with confusion, hardship and oppression, and embodied in their very identities and perceptions of themselves as poor. As the following three cases indicate, people's own rural history seems to be reflected in their historical imagination.

Daniel Shapi[4] is an older, relatively well-off man in Oneshila who had moved to the shantytown in the early 1980s to set up a small sewing-business. He told me he had grown up in a large family, with a father who was a sub-chief and had several wives. He was always well-dressed and elegant, and made a point of telling me that he wasn't really a shanty dweller but lived there for what he called "practical reasons" (apparently the low costs of land and buildings where he ran his business). Since he moved to Oshakati he had maintained strong links with his rural village in Ohangwena where he had land and cattle, and where his first wife (*omukukuladhi gwambanda*), and two daughters with their children continued to live. His notion of Owambo history and tradition was overall positive in conversations I had with him. He referred often to Chief Mandume's brave resistance against the South Africans (in 1917, see Hartmann 1989); to the role of the missionaries who gave the Owambo "God and education" as he put it; and to what he said was the "necessary struggle" against the apartheid regime.

Simon Namene in Uupindi was one of the poorest men in the shantytown, and bore evidence of his destitution by living alone in a run-down shack, dressing in rags and being skinny and constantly ill. He told me he had moved to the shanty in the mid-1970s; joined the South West African Defence Force (SWATF); and, after independence, experienced a dramatic downfall from being a well-paid soldier to becoming poor, unemployed and marginalised. Since he joined the colonial forces, he had had no contact with his village

---

[4] All names of local people in this book are fictive. To further assure anonymity, people are also placed in an other shanty-area than where they actually live.

of origin and his family there. From my conversations with him I understood that he had grown up in a poor family in Omusati; that he had long faced hunger there because people had stopped sharing "as we were all poor"; and that he eventually became a soldier because "there was nothing else I could do". For him, Owambo history and tradition seemed to be enmeshed in negative connotations of poverty and marginalisation as if history took place for him rather than by him – thereby increasing his sense of poverty and isolation in the shantytown.

Kornelia Uutoni was a single mother living in Uupindi when I met her in 1994. She stayed in a shack with her sister and four children, making ends meet by selling cooked food (*okapana*) in the town centre and running a small shebeen (*cuca*-shop) from an extra room in the shack – making it possible for one of the sisters to look after the children. Kornelia Uutoni told me she had grown up in a poor family with many children, and became pregnant already at the age of 16. The father of the child was an older man who refused fatherhood. She gave birth in the village, but said it was very difficult for her to stay there both because her father really didn't want anything to do with her and because she didn't think she would ever be married as a single mother. She therefore left for Oshakati in 1988, at the age of 18. Admitting that life had been hard in Oshakati, she had no nostalgia for the past: "I think the most important thing that has happened is that we [i.e. women] can make our own lives. In the old days we didn't have land and cattle, and we had to ask for everything. This meant that men could do anything [pointing at her child when saying this]. At least nobody could stop me when I wanted to leave. I even received a little help from a woman in a neighbouring homestead who worked as a cleaner at the mission".

In sum, then, the pressure on traditional Owambo society from the colonial authorities and apartheid, the church and the system of labour migration led to changing social relationships along lines of political authority, gender and age. This was exacerbated by an increasing importance of employment and income to make ends meet and leading to what, with acknowledgement to Comaroff and Comaroff (1997), I have denoted a "commodification" of relationships. Owambos losing out in the process, by limited access to employment, income and rural resources, found themselves increasingly pauperised and detached from rural society. For them, Oshakati came to represent an alternative social and economic setting from the mid-1960s. In order to get a full picture of the making of Oshakati shantytowns within an historical context, however, two significant developments after the mid-1960s have to be taken into consideration. One is the establishment and early development of Oshakati as urban space; the second is the war of liberation. Parallel in time and mutually reinforcing, I will start with the war of independence which continued until independence in 1990.

War and Atrocities

Though there are historical examples of resistance against German and South African domination in Namibia[5] and although several resistance movements were formed in the 1950s,[6] the forced removal of people from Windhoek's Old Location to Katutura in 1959 is generally considered to be the starting point of the struggle for Namibian independence (Pendleton 1974, Leys and Saul 1995). The so-called "Windhoek Shootings" on 10 December 1959, in which 11 people were killed and many more were wounded, radicalised the population – in the same way as the Sharpeville massacre did in South Africa in 1961. From then on the war of liberation was fought with the South West Africa People's Organization (SWAPO) and its armed wing, the People's Liberation Army of Namibia (PLAN), in the lead. It is estimated that around 75.000 men, women and children went into exile, of which 69.000 went to Angola (Sparks and Green 1992:31). Many of these were teachers, nurses and young students, and many received higher education while abroad (Groth 1995).

Direct military activities increased in number and frequency in the late 1960s, following the Battle of Omugulumbashe on 26 August 1966 and enhanced PLAN activities inside Owambo through a strategy of sabotage, ambush and retreat (Brown 1995). From the 1970s, the war of independence came to affect practically everybody in Owambo either directly or indirectly: Many were involved by having children flee into exile or through supporting PLAN fighters making excursions into the region. And an increasing number of people became directly involved on the South African side through employment with the South West African Territorial Force, SWATF (an offshoot of the South African Defence Force SADF made up of about 30,000 indigenous Namibian troops); or the counter-insurgency Koevoet (counting 3,000 men, most of whom were born and bred in the war-zone) (Sparks and Green 1992).

As opposed to other Namibians, people from the war zones (Owambo, Okavango and Caprivi) were not recruited to the colonial army through forced conscription, but attracted by salaries and other material compensation such as extra pay for killing SWAPO soldiers. Such conditions primarily attracted poor and marginalized young men in rural communities who had few if any alternative options for employment and income. By the early 1980s and up to 1989, Pretoria had an estimated 100,000 troops stationed in Namibia at any one time, the majority of them in Owambo, alongside its own total population then of around 360,000 people (Lush 1993:43).

---

[5] Including the expedition to remove King Mandume in 1917 and the so-called Iipumbu-affair in 1932 (Leys and Saul 1995, Hartmann 1998).
[6] These were the labour organisation Owamboland People's Organisation (OPO); the South West Africa National Union (SWANU); and the Herero Chief's Council (Dobell 1998).

The war of liberation thus dominated life in Owambo for more than two decades. People's fear for their lives and property had implications for social relations within households, neighbourhoods, villages, and – as we shall see in the next section – between the rural areas and the emerging towns. A dawn-to-dusk curfew, imposed by the SADF and lasting 11 years from 1979, was particularly hated, and had implications not only in terms of the harassment and assassination of many who broke it, but also by disrupting people's previously ordinary daily habits in the homestead, in agricultural fields and grazing areas as well as in their leisure time (Hebstein and Evenson 1989).

The war also split families and communities, often putting barriers between militant youngsters and older people concerned to maintain rural social order and peace (Leys and Saul 1995). Perhaps most seriously, families of young people who joined SWATF or Koevoet faced hostility from other members of the local population, and were viewed with suspicion because of the special treatment they sometimes received from the apartheid authorities. The war thus brought distrust between people and further affected the sense of community that was already quite fragile after years of colonial policies of oppression (Hangula 2000).

A dominant theme in any history of the Namibian war of independence and its effects in Owambo must be its physical and psychological brutality (Brown 1995). I have found it very difficult to obtain detailed histories and narratives from the many shanty-dwellers who were involved in atrocities,[7] and will use an excerpt from a literary account by Kaleni Hiyalwa (2000) to exemplify the type of violence committed by some of the shanty-dwellers and the suffering of victims from the war who also currently live in the shanty-towns (see also Groth 1995 and Erasmus 1995 for first hand accounts of atrocities committed against Swapo detainees and suspected SWAPO collaborators respectively).

> I was exactly nine years old in May 1976. After parting with my schoolmates, I went to our homestead. But as I approached the homestead, something happened to me. The hair swelled off my head and body. My heart started to pound as if I had a noisy machine in me. Something had happened. But what was it? I couldn't tell what was happening to me. Maybe that was just a vague feeling, I thought. I stood and tried to think. I tried to force myself to calm my emotions so that I could think well again. When I entered the homestead, in the right corner of the entrance, I saw something that made me go wild for a moment. I was seeing a human arm…
>
> I was staring at the hand I knew so well, the hand which [had] generously fed me every day of my life. Like a mad person, I began to run about. I headed to the kitchen, calling out for my mother. I couldn't believe what I saw near the entrance of the homestead. I stopped just in front of the kitchen, and called. I hesitated, and entered the kitchen, hoping that I would see my dear mother, but there was no one there. At that time, I gathered courage. I knew my

---

[7] This may have been related to the personal pain felt by many, but should also be seen as an expression of a "culture of silence" in the shanty-areas that I will discuss further below.

mother was somewhere. But where? The other big question was whether she was alive. Meme! Meme! I called out...

Then I thought of going to Meekulu's place to look for her. Meekulu lived just two kilometres away from our house. My mother was an idol of Meekulu ... Meekulu ran about the place, just as I had done before. She passed me as she ran round the homestead. And there she was. Meekulu stood as if the blood had drained out from her veins. I saw her falling to the ground still screaming. My heart leaped as I struggled to run towards her. What I saw was unbearable. Meekulu was kissing two dead bodies laid in a row. They were my mother and father. What struck me most, was that they were naked. When Meekulu stood up to hug me, my head whirled and darkness covered my eyes and brain (Hiyalwa 2000:1-2).

Despite the shanty-dwellers' reluctance to share stories from the war with me, people retained and shared "flashes" of what for them had been devastating experiences of death, brutality and the drama of waging war among ones own people – and some remained traumatised and were among the poorest in Oshakati's shantytowns. People have difficulties explaining how such atrocities could take place, and often refer to "indoctrination". As a Koevoet member told the journalist David Lush in 1989:

When we joined Koevoet they took us away for perhaps two to three months and showed us how to use the weapons and told us who we should use the weapons against. During the time we did not see anyone outside the camp where we were doing the training. They filled our heads with information about SWAPO, and I tell you, when I came out of that training, if you had told me my mother was a SWAPO, I would have killed her without hesitation (Lush 1993:75).

But there are also contextual issues at hand: For South Africa, issues of apartheid politics and economics merged with notions of race and sexuality (Becker 2000). For SWAPO, a fear of spies merged with an authoritarian ideology, obsession with power and anti-intellectualism (Groth 1995). And Owambo men joining the colonial army that I have talked with told me that options for employment and income in a situation of poverty and despair really gave them no choice but to do as they were told.

Malkki (1997) has argued that people who have experienced such atrocities carry something in common, something that deposits in them traces that can have a peculiar resistance to appropriation by others who were not there. What Malkki (1997:92) calls "momentary, out-of-the-ordinary moments of shared history" can produce (more or less silent) communities of memory that can powerfully shape what comes after. In the Oshakati shantytowns, it took me a long time to figure out the signs and symbols of historical belonging, with variations around statements of having worked for the "police" separating former SWAPO soldiers, SWAPO detainees, SWATF soldiers and Koevoet. Women, younger people and others who were less directly involved in the atrocities – but not necessarily less affected thereby

– talked about the suffering and described individuals' fates, but rarely in a way that might take their stories too close to the shantytowns themselves. One of the memories I heard referred to by women was when Caspirs (armoured personnel vehicles) with dead bodies attached to them had come driving through the shanties, apparently to scare people off from supporting "the terrorists". But no woman ever pointed out to me men who had taken part in such atrocities, in other ways than saying that "they are still among us".

Despite their different experiences of physical and psychological brutality as former enemies, people in the Oshakati shantytowns are in a peculiar way united by not having taken part in the developments following from peace and independence and from sharing identities as poor slum dwellers. Too much seems to be at stake in fragile communities like the Oshakati shantytowns to let revenge guide discourses and actions. It leads to a culture of silence, but not to a loss or rejection of memory. Even people who know that their neighbour committed atrocities against their family, friends or village will relate in daily life to the extent of "borrowing soap from each other" (*taa paathana oothewa*) – a common phrase idiomatically indicating trust and friendship. Shilongo Haluteni was a former Koevoet-soldier, now unemployed and living in Uupindi. He sold torches, batteries, pots, pans and other cheap commodities directly to people in the shantytowns (with the help, I later discovered, of a former colleague working for a hardware-store). Asking a woman (who, I knew, had lost her husband who had been a PLAN fighter) how they could deal with him, she explained that people in the shantytown had to relate to anybody who could help ease their problems. The "silent communities" are most clearly revealed when those involved are no longer part of the shantytown community: When former Koevoet soldiers or collaborators die, only very few people tend to show up to pay their last respects, as if those staying away signal that the people concerned have finally got what they deserved.

For former soldiers both on the South African and SWAPO sides and other people affected, then, memories of war and atrocities were largely submerged – that is except for the most traumatised shanty-dwellers who cannot get away from them. Rather than creating internal frictions and dominating social relationships between former enemies, the shared experience of not having gained from peace and independence and finding themselves in poverty and destitution seem to have increased the feeling of marginalisation and vulnerability in relation to society outside the shantytown.

But it is a fragile sense of community, as demonstrated by the strong reactions from poor shanty-dwellers when a column of 23 cars with ex-soldiers from SWATF and Koevoet approached Oshakati in August 1994 (see also *Namibian* 4 August 1994).[8] They were mainly young men from 25 to 40 years, wearing nice clothes, discmen, jewellery and other signs of

---

[8] The Namibian soldiers, who had been considered particularly susceptible to acts of revenge, had been given practical and economic support to settle in South Africa at the time of independence.

affluence. Practically everybody in the shantytowns was angry, not only because the people coming reminded them of war and atrocities but also of their own poverty and vulnerability. An old man from Amunkambya, tried to calm tension down outside a *cuca*-shop [shebeen] in Oshoopala: "It is true that they have new cars and fancy clothes, but they are *mbwiti* [a person who is considered to have lost his or her Owambo roots and identity]. They don't have an *egumbo* [rural homestead] in Owambo, and they cannot visit their people in Oshakati without creating turmoil". "That is true", responded a young man just having sent around a jug of *epwaka* [a local beer]."But I don't have an *egumbo* either, and nobody seems to care that I am here."

The arrival of the United Nations Transition Assistance Group (UNTAG) in mid-1989 was meant to secure a peaceful transition to independence, following the signing of a cease-fire between South Africa and SWAPO on 1 April that year (Sparks and Green 1992). Namibia finally became independent in 1990. One incident at the very end of the era of South African occupation symbolises the atrocious character of war from which most of the people in the Oshakati shantytowns had been affected: It was the killing of 260 PLAN combatants crossing the border into Namibia in the first five days of April 1989 in order to give themselves up to UNTAG in Oshakati to celebrate independence. Many of them were subsequently buried in a mass grave on the outskirts of one of Oshakati's shantytowns.

The final section of this chapter will focus on the development of Oshakati itself as part of apartheid's political economy, showing how the pauperised and war-affected Owambo population ending up in Oshakati and its shantytowns were further impoverished and marginalised.

Oshakati – 'A Place Where People Meet'

Oshakati was established in the mid-1960s as a direct result of the Odendaal Commission's report (GSA 1963) and South Africa's colonial homeland policy in Namibia. The South Africans wanted a new "capital" for Owambo from which they could pursue their political and commercial interests, preferably in a place that was a geographical and demographic centre for the 'homeland' (*bantustan*) that the policy went about creating. A suitable place was found in the Uukwambi tribal area near to the villages of Erundu and Otshipuku and close to the Okatana River. It was also a central place in relation to the different tribal areas in Owambo, and was given the Oshiwambo name *Oshakati* ("A place where people meet") (Hangula 1993b).

Oshakati rapidly became the administrative and commercial centre of Owambo as planned, and people from its hinterland as well as from other parts of what was then known as South West Africa started to move into the new town. They took up positions as professionals and labourers, and as small-scale businessmen and petty traders in the informal economy. Oshakati's spatial outline wore the characteristics of the apartheid policy with a clearly demarcated white area (Oshakati East) and a formal black township (Oshakati West) (see Map 2). As the houses in the black township became overcrowded, the poorest labourers and the self-employed tried to meet their accommodation needs by erecting iron shacks or traditional dwellings on the periphery of the formal settlement area – further entrenching the spatial distribution of race and class.

By 1970 Oshakati had 2,950 inhabitants (Claessen 1978:52). From then on, the war of independence had significant impacts on developments: The population grew as people joined the South African Defence Force, or moved to town to escape war and seek economic opportunities. Oshakati effectively became a fortified town, as a large number of South African police and soldiers moved to the area. Oshakati East in particular became surrounded by watch-towers, security fences and bullet-proof walls around houses, and movements in and out of the town were strictly controlled (Dobell 1998).

During the 1970s and 1980s the population increased particularly in the then expanding poor informal settlements around both Oshakati East and Oshakati West. Alongside the large number of Namibian SWATF soldiers who were placed in the shantytowns, poor rural dwellers who had moved to Oshakati to seek desperately needed employment and income also settled there. Many were women and children, depending on social and economic relations with soldiers and with people employed by resident South Africans. From 1975 and Angolan independence, an influx of refugees from southern Angola added to the population. The four main informal settlements that developed were Oneshila, Amunkambya (now Oshoopala), Omashaka (now Evululuku) and Uupindi. At the time of independence in 1990 the population in Oshakati was estimated at 37,000 people, of whom around 85 percent lived in informal settlement areas (Urban Dynamics 2001).

On the face of it, then, Oshakati is what Southall (1961:6) in the early days of urban anthropology called a "Type B" town. These were towns of rapid expansion, closely associated with European power, with employment opportunities supplied by colonial capital, and with a sharp discontinuity between them and the surrounding African society. Several towns in the southern African region were the objects of urban anthropological studies at that time, most notably through the Copperbelt studies in Zambia by people like A.L. Epstein (1958), Max Gluckman (1961) and J.C. Mitchell (1969), and the East London studies in South Africa by D.H. Reader (1961), Philip Mayer (1963), and B.A. Pauw (1963). These will be points of reference in the coming pages since all looked at characteristics of what they called *urbanisation*, defined by Eames and Goody (1977:45) as "the shifts in locus of economic activities, political power and population concentration to urban centres", and at *urbanism* which they defined as "the sociocultural consequences of urban life" (Eames and Goody 1977:45).

Common for all these studies is that none of them are explicitly concerned with issues of poverty (Hannerz 1980:161). One anthropologist who did explicitly refer to poverty in South African townships was Oscar Lewis's (1996 [1966]:396) He acknowledged that urban poverty is a special kind of sociocultural condition characterised by low income, lack of property ownership, absence of savings, absence of food-reserves, and a chronic shortage of cash. I will relate to his notions of the social implications of oppression and economic deprivation in this chapter, while leaving out his much more controversial notion of a specific 'culture of poverty' that has been criticised for blaming their poverty on poor people themselves (Eames and Goody 1996; see also Lamont and Small 2008).

Moving to Town

Let us look first at migration to Oshakati in more detail. I have argued that the ground for urbanisation into and urbanism in Oshakati had been laid in the Owambo population through a long period of male migration to other urban areas in the central part of Namibia, and a gradual commodification within Owambo society and of Owambo social relations. The commodification process found expression in labour, land, cattle and staple food all increasingly becoming items of monetary exchange; in European goods becoming increasingly available in Owambo itself particularly from the 1950s; and in the fact that, as Moorsom (1995) has demonstrated, for an increasing number of Owambo people cash income became necessary for survival.

Despite this, moving to Oshakati did not have the same connotations as moving to the larger urban areas in the central parts of Namibia. On the one hand, Oshakati was not considered what was called *ondolopa* (a "real town") and people moving there were not considered real *oombwiti* ("town-like people"). Urbanism had increasingly become associated with employment, income and an urban lifestyle: Windhoek in the 1950s and 1960s was a place of hard work, single quarters and corrugated iron shacks, but also of beer halls, dance halls and the "vibrancy and swing of leisure time" (Wallace 1998:134). Oshakati had little of this, and was primarily associated with the South African colonial administration, military occupation, limited employment opportunities and increasingly also poor and violent shantytowns. In fact, the *only* real rationale for moving to Oshakati, according to self-proclaimed local historian Jacob Stefanus to whom I will return later, was to earn money.

Professionals initially moving to Oshakati were mainly from the central parts of the country where access to education had been better than in the northern "homelands". Some local small-scale entrepreneurs moved to the town, and established small shops, tailors, butchers, drinking outlets, and lodging-places (Moorsom 1995). But the large majority were poor and uneducated people from rural Owambo seeking low-paid unskilled jobs or self-employment in the informal economy (Hangula 1993b). Moreover, when the South Africans started to recruit police and soldiers in Owambo at the end of the 1960s, they deliberately chose the poorest and least educated in order to form them as soldiers in their own image – able to wage war against their own people (Leys and Saul 1995). "Most people who joined the South African police or army", an older man in Uupindi told me, "did so secretly without asking permission, as they were always ashamed".

Urbanisation and urbanism through labour migration had always, claims Banghart (1969) and Hishongwa (1992), been associated with men and manhood. Women had been discouraged from migrating to urban areas by the traditional authorities which claimed that their going to town violated the existing rural social order, and by the colonial state because of its apartheid politics of separate development in which women were seen to belong in the Bantustans. Moreover, women were faced with few prospects for their own employment and income generation except by working in the growing but low paid informal economy or attaching themselves to employed men. The women who did leave rural Owambo to come to Oshakati were often poor women, and with a bleak future in the rural areas, many of whom were unmarried mothers. Leaving the village they were called *iikumbu* ("loose girls"), and were stigmatised for their lifestyles in Oshakati as the following song from the 1970s indicates (recited to me in 2001 by an old woman in a rural Owambo village):

Moshakati sha Nangube	You cannot get in with a traditional
Kamuiwa na Delela	Owambo woman's dress. You have to wear a
Shapo Oshikete una, ile utete	skirt, or cut it to make a miniskirt, short
Uninge obuila ile uninge	trousers or underwear. Yesterday I did not rest.
Onghela nghuhalele, hailongo	I have been looking for my sister. I found her
Mumwamene Ondemukonga fiyo ebundu	in Erundu in Oshakati
Moshakati shanangube	
Moshakati sha nangobe	It's there my sister went, she was
Onwaile mumwamene	a virgin girl. Now she is
Ailemookadona, paife	pregnant, in an advanced state.
Okuna edimo, eli medalelwa	When she gave birth the child was
Peni. Eshi odala okana	named Deliberate, "the thing that
Ondekaluka "Nashitjani" oshimina	was deliberately done". That is
Shaningilwa owina osho kashina	not a problem. Get ready, we have
Oshilonga fikama tuye keumbo	to go back home
Haimbodi ya Shomwele	Haimbodi and Shomwele,
Tuala owuna keumbo	Take the children back home.
Ounona tewaji omeya	The children are drowning.
Moshakati omuna emhuangha	In Oshakati there is a hyena
Tulili oukadona.	that eats girls.

ya shomuele tuala omona kuembo	Shomwele, take the children
Ya shomuele tuala omuna keumbo	back home
In Oshakati of Nangube	

Individuals' options and ability to maintain links with their respective rural areas of origin varied with their possession of land and cattle; their own status and income in Oshakati and their ability to support rural family; and the geographical location of their village in relation to the war zone. However, the large majority of Owambo migrants to Oshakati were poor, and continued to find themselves in deep poverty once there. Even those who had become SADF soldiers or other functionaries of the South African bureaucracy in Oshakati and earned well, found it difficult to openly display their newfound wealth. I have heard described a heated discussion between two mothers, where one was mocking the other for receiving "blood money" from her son in the South African military forces. The other is then said to have responded by referring to the other lady's son in exile for SWAPO: "And what do you get? Dirt and sand?"

The initial phase of urbanisation in Owambo thus stands in contrast to what has been reported to have occurred in central Namibia (Pendleton 1996), the Copperbelt (Gluckman 1961) and East London (Mayer 1963), where early urbanisation was associated with employment, income and modernity and where links with rurality and tradition persisted in one form or another. Most Owambos moving to Oshakati were forced to do so by circumstances of poverty, stigmatised by moving to militarised locale that affected the life of every Owambo, and had few if any options for supporting their families in the rural areas.

Urban Complexity

In looking at the making of Oshakati as urban space in more detail in the following pages, I will give special attention to the issues of density of settlement; mobility; heterogeneity; demographic disproportion; economic differentiation and administrative and political limitations – all key aspects of Southern African urbanism in a number of studies (Mitchell 1966, see also Hannerz 1980 and Bank 2002). Having shown how Oshakati became established and populated primarily by poor rural migrants from Owambo, the purpose in this section is to show how the development of Oshakati lay the ground for processes of further impoverishment, marginalisation and exclusion of the shanty-towns as urban space.

There is hardly any written evidence about the internal development of pre-independence Oshakati as a military town.[9] Much of the following empirical data are thus based on

---

[9] One of the few exceptions is Jim Cooper's (1988) book *Koevoet!*, which is essentially a glorification of war and brutality.

accounts of people living there during my various fieldwork visits. They include the already mentioned self-proclaimed Oshakati shanty-historian tate Jacobus Stefanus. His perspective can be regarded as fairly balanced, as he was one of the first black businessmen in Oshakati who depended on the occupying South Africans and who has also had a long-term (first hidden, then open) affiliation with SWAPO.

Despite its initially small population, Oshakati became more densely populated from the early 1970s and the militarisation of the town, affecting the range of contacts townspeople had with each other. The South Africans had allocated specific areas for a black location (Oshakati West) and informal settlements. And there was a curfew for all blacks in white areas. Moreover, the annual flooding of large parts of the town from the *kuvelai* drainage system forced people into confined areas in the shantytowns (see Map 2). The town's population density soon stood in stark contrast to that in rural Owambo, where there were no concentrated villages and individual homesteads were located in the middle of large fields. From a situation where people knew each other as "whole persons" (Hannerz 1992:41-42), the shanty-dwellers came to know each other from particular kinds of activities in a context of increasing socio-cultural complexity.

The population was also increasingly heterogeneous in so far as people from all seven Owambo groups were resident in the same shantytown, bringing together people who had historically had little contact. Moreover, the Angolan population of Oshakati also grew, particularly from the mid-1970s when men, women and children fled the fighting following independence in Angola in 1975 (Tvedten 1997) and Unita[10] soldiers came to join the special Koevoet forces. Many of the Angolans were ethnically linked to Owambos, but their position as refugees and soldiers soon stigmatised them and isolated them in specific shantytowns. Many Owambo people also came into direct contact with white South Africans for the first time, either as public or private employees, or in the military forces.

With the majority of people coming to Oshakati being young men, women and children, there was a demographic disproportion in the shanties that also stood in sharp contrast to the rural areas that had long been dominated by women, children and older men (with younger men being absent labour migrants). Hardly any older people moved to Oshakati, even though some visited to go to hospital or to buy foodstuffs and commodities. Some shanty-dwellers were able to send their children to rural relatives to be taken care of, but for most this was not an option due to the location of their village in the war-zone, poverty or the stigma of living in a town like Oshakati.

---

[10] The rebel movement "National Union for the Total Independence of Angola", headed by Jonas Savimbi.

With a mixture of well-paid soldiers on the one hand,[11] and a majority of people in dependency relations or relying on the low-income informal economy on the other, economic differentiation soon developed in the shantytowns. While people in formal employment were secluded in Oshakati East and Oshakati West, and had access to a large variety of special stores and commodities, the shantytowns were dominated by stores stocked with food, alcohol, cosmetics and other items for immediate consumption. Ample access to these types of goods was a deliberate strategy by the South Africans, who, in the words of an ex-Koevoet soldier repeating what he said he had heard from his South African commanders, saw a "money-hungry soldier as a good soldier".

Soldiers in particular developed a special form of conspicuous consumption, trying to prove themselves that way to other soldiers, civilians and perhaps particularly women in the shantytowns. As José António, a former soldier in the feared 32 Battalion of the South African Army, told me:

> We used to drink a lot of beer and liquor, and no *tombo* (traditional Owambo beer). We had a lot of money, and at that time any soldier drinking *tombo* was laughed at. We had meat every day, and did not eat *ekaka* (a traditional spinach) in our house.

Looking at spatial relations, the separation between Oshakati East and Oshakati West and the town's shanties (see Map 2) was strong. White South Africans living in Oshakati East were isolated behind wired fences and with their own separate schools, stores, social clubs etc. The degree of social, cultural and racial separation that existed is also indicated by people in the shantytowns not being able to recall one single case of "illegitimate"[12] children in Oshakati, despite the large presence of white officers and soldiers there. The shantytown's separation from the professionals in Oshakati West, while not underpinned by racial divisions, was maintained by the latter's access to separate stores and other facilities. Some of them have since told me how they looked upon the shantytowns as different and dangerous. For that reason, they explained, they might occasionally go to shops and bars on the periphery of shanties along the main roads, but never inside the settlements themselves.

People from the shantytowns emphasised their own sense of isolation from Oshakati East and West, which we shall see still exists. But they also described how the shanty areas differed from one another. Oneshila and Uupindi were built around existing settlements primarily by civilian migrants, and soon developed the largest clusters of informal businesses due to their proximity to the main road through Oshakati. Omashaka (now Evululuku)

---

[11] A regular soldier would earn from R 1,500 to R 2,000 per month, with up to R 3,000 being paid in bonuses after raids and involvement in combat (*iiponohela*). In the same period teachers and nurses earned around R 1,000 (pers.comm). Jacob Stefanus).

[12] Such children would also have been illegitimate in a legal sense: There was an increasingly harsh "Immorality Act" which deemed interracial sex illegal (Erichsen 2001:15).

and Amunkambya (now Oshoopala), on the other hand, were primarily established for and dominated by SWATF soldiers, which added to their separateness. These two latter areas were generally considered poorer and more violent than the other two – a distinction that we shall also see still exists.[13]

The matrix of population density, ethnic heterogeneity, demographic disproportion, economic differentiation and administrative and political limitations represented a significant contrast to life in rural areas, just as Mitchell (1966) claimed had been the case on the Copperbelt. Its impact in the Oshakati shantytowns was particularly strong, due to the limited contact people there had with both their rural hinterland and the formal urban parts of the town (Oshakati East and West). Such constraints meant that the situation in Oshakati was quite different to that which had prevailed in the Copperbelt where links with rural areas were more actively maintained and urban space less segregated, and it made the conditions in Oshakati's shantytowns exceptionally volatile.

Shanty Relationships

Those conditions seem first of all to have led to mobility and impermanence of social relations. This was perhaps most evident and dramatic at the level of households as the basic unit of social reproduction. Still according to *tate* Stefanus and other informants with a long history in the shantytowns, young girls and women who moved to town took up residence in dwellings with men, both for economic reasons and for personal security. Cohabitation soon became common, in strong violation of Owambo customary practises and without involving kin as a source of social security. For many, "serial monogamy" with girlfriends (*aaholi*) came to replace formal marriage or polygamy. An older former Koevoet soldier told me how he had lived with "at least ten different women" during the late 1970s and 1980s, emphasising that it was only one at a time as "marrying and having several wives" was difficult in the shantytowns.

The permeability of household relations was further exacerbated by the density of settlement and contiguity of houses. Most people in the shantytowns lived in small one or two roomed corrugated iron shacks, with limited space for privacy, and in violation of the elaborate cultural codes, documented by Estermann (1957) and Williams (1991), that related to homesteads and domestic space use in the rural areas including the separate dwellings related to age and gender. The traditional family meeting place (*olupale*) for family discussions, to transfer traditional family virtues, and to entertain guests was particularly central

---

[13] Asked to estimate the proportions of men who would have been soldiers versus those who would have been civilians in the four shanty areas towards the end of the colonial era, tate Stefanus estimate of 8 civilians and 2 soldiers out of every ten men in Oneshila, 6 civilians and 4 soldiers in Uupindi, 5 civilians and 5 soldiers in Omashaka and 3 civilians and 7 soldiers in Amunkambya.

in such a context. Yet in the shantytowns, an ever-growing number of bars and *cuca*-shops[14] took over this role, but without the presence of elders and the cultural and moral connotations of the *olupale*. The distinction between private, social and public space became blurred, increasing the pressure on the households and interpersonal relations within them.

With social isolation, atrocities of war, economic dependency and alcohol abuse, many marriages and cohabitation arrangements were marred by violence and brutality in a setting where this was commonplace (Lush 1993). Assaults and even murder were widespread, particularly, people in Oshakati have told me, when edgy soldiers came back from days in the bush hunting SWAPO soldiers or "terrorists" (see also Erichsen 2001). Away from, and often marginalised by, their villages, women in town could not, in situations of domestic violence, seek refuge with brothers or other matrilineal kin as they might have done in the rural areas, and I was told that the police too did not follow up cases of violence among the shanty population.[15]

While early Southern African anthropology emphasized that urban settings were characterized by a wide set of relations and networks (Wilson and Wilson 1945; also Hannerz 1980; also Moore 1994) this was not the case to the same extent in the Oshakati shantytowns. A large number of people who were unemployed remained in the shantytowns during the day, most of whom were women. Also, within Oshakati's shanty communities neighbourhoods tended to be small and closed as a result of the general insecurity and violence. Outsiders were treated with suspicion, and often only two or three of one's neighbours were close enough to really be trusted or to trust each other. Mingling between men and women was more common than in the rural areas, but as one woman in Oneshila told me: "We were not really speaking nicely as in the village, but more drinking and shouting".

Both soldiers and other employed men had their own particular networks outside the shantytowns, the former characterised by relations of strict authority and discipline. Also, men working for the South African government administrations and businesses were subject to strict control by a "*baas*" (equivalent to "boss"). They were obliged to go back to the shanties after work in terms of the elaborate "Native Urban Areas Proclamation" (Seckelman 2001:24) and various military regulations. Only a few women had formal employment outside the shanty areas, usually working as domestic workers. During most parts of the 1970s and 1980s women's contacts with the formal parts of town were thus more limited than for men, but this changed with the expansion of the informal economy into the formal

---

[14] Small informal alcohol outlets mainly selling traditional brew, equivalent to *shebeens* in South Africa and named after the Angolan beer "Cuca".

[15] Domestic violence was not equally emphasised by the early urban anthropologists, possibly because of their detached involvement with the urban population they studied as argued by Ferguson (1999) and Bank (2002), but probably also because the Copperbelt and East London were not to the same extent marred by structural oppression and poverty at that time.

areas towards the end of the 1980s as evidenced by the establishment of the Omatala open market in 1987.[16]

What the above indicate is that Oshakati's early urbanisation had wide-ranging implications for division of social space, as well as for social organisation at the level of the community, households and individuals. For marginalized and poor migrants to Oshakati, moving to town implied a weakening and at times discontinuity of links with rural areas and their extended family. In Oshakati, they came to find themselves in a kind of urban space where they were again poor and marginalized, this time by apartheid structures that manifested themselves in dense and tense urban shantytowns. The journalist David Lush described the Oshakati shantytowns in the late 1980s, that is at the end of the period treated in this chapter, in the following way:

> As we drove through rutted, muddy alleyways barely wide enough for the car to fit through, music blared out from shacks built of corrugated iron, scraps of wood, plastic sheeting and crushed beer cans. Almost every shack seemed to sell alcohol of some kind or another, and drunken men – some dressed in fashionable casual clothes, others in their uniform – lurched from one hovel to another, most still clutching their rifles.
>
> Dogs and pigs scavenged through the piles of garbage dumped at random along the alleys, while barefooted children dressed in filthy rags ran through the streets or skulked outside their squalid homes. Women, with babies on their backs or at their breasts, sat cooking crouching over open fires in front of their houses. Few women bothered looking at us as we passed, but those who did glared at us blankly before returning to their pots or conversation with the people they were sitting with.
>
> The whole camp stank of wood smoke, excrement and decay. We turned one corner and were confronted by the skull of an antelope stuck on the top of a pole, leering down at us with a manic grin and two beer cans balanced on its huge horns. I yelped and reversed the car back the way we had come. Children were the only ones to react to us as we crawled through the squatter camp. We came across a group of youngsters playing on a patch of wasteland and, as we approached, we were spotted by one small girl who shouted a warning to her friends, and they all fled into the location, screaming as they went (1993 :72).

Shanty Poverty at Independence

The characteristics of poverty in the Oshakati shantytowns right until independence find resonance in the work of Oscar Lewis (1966). In relation to the larger society there was a lack of effective participation and integration of the poor in major institutions; at the level

---

[16] The step-by-step amendment of the apartheid laws (the prohibition of credits to natives law, the 72-hours-clause, the influx control, the curfew, the prohibition of acquisition and property of urban land for blacks etc.) took place earlier in central and southern parts of the country than in the militarised north and Oshakati (see Seckelman 2001:28).

of the community there was a minimum of organisation beyond the level of nuclear and extended family; at the level of the family there was a disintegration of traditional family and household structures; and at the level of the individual there was a feeling of marginality, helplessness and inferiority. Giving a sympathetic interpretation of Lewis, these characteristics were largely generated and reproduced by political and economic forces outside the control of the poor themselves, rather than due to the personal failings and acts of the poor themselves, as Lewis's critics suggest was his argument (Eames and Goody 1996; see also Small, Harding and Lamont 2010).

Having said this, there is no basis to conclude that the processes of marginalisation and exclusion had led, by the time of independence, to chronic poverty in the sense of severe poverty and vulnerability over time. Nor is there evidence to suggest that there was a specific culture of poverty in Lewis's sense of poverty also involving more permanent behavioural and personality traits. For the first-generation migrants to Oshakati's shantytowns, identities and relations were fluid and contradictory, based on a special political and economic context and on a sense of exclusion from the rural as well as from the urban, yet still offering a glimmer of hope for the future. There was thus no prevailing perception that the values and goals of the larger society were unattainable.

For many, the rural world had effectively had to be left behind and people were cut off from it through lack of rural resources such as land and cattle, through the stigma that came from their living in a repressive apartheid town, and through their limited income which made it difficult for them to support rural relatives. And yes, the white urban and modern town was effectively out of reach because of apartheid with its class and race characteristics and the limited education among the shanty-dwellers. Both sets of circumstances created a sense of "us against the others" – or in the words of Tate Jacobus: "There was a lot of problems here before independence, but there was also a sense of community (*uukumwe*). We didn't like the South Africans, and the rural people didn't like us". Yet, with the soldiers' wages securing access to basic means of food and shelter for many within the shanty-population, people were marginalised and vulnerable rather than poor. And they continued to aspire to eventually re-establishing rural ties and achieving the goals of being modern urban citizens once the war had ended.

Immediately following independence in 1990 (i.e. from the time I myself started to follow events in Oshakati and its shantytowns), some of the Oshakati shanty dwellers who had been soldiers in the SWATF and Koevoet were given economic and practical support to settle in South Africa. Some, who had managed to maintain agricultural possessions and linkages with their rural relatives, moved back to their villages to try to re-establish themselves as rural dwellers. And some, with the necessary resources or contacts, moved to urban areas in the southern part of the country that were seen as offering better opportunities (Tvedten

2004). But the large majority of people in Oshakati's shantytowns remained there, under very difficult circumstances: Soldiers lost their wages, leading to people in the informal sector losing much of their income, and the new government initially hardly made its presence felt. As we shall see in the coming chapters, in the years following independence the majority of people moving in to the shantytowns were poor rural Owambo still pushed by a deteriorating rural economy and pulled by the hope of obtaining employment and an urban life-style. But as the town opened up and the economy grew an increasing number of people with education and employment in the private or public sector also settled there for lack of alternatives – increasing the socio-cultural complexity and internal differentiation between the very poor, the poor and the less poor.

The next chapter picks up the theme of structural political and economic oppression in which people in the Oshakati shantytowns find themselves in the contemporary world, and the related theme of the flows of meaning affecting people there. I address these issues in order to assess the combined outcome of history and structural oppression for the formation of the shantytowns as poor urban space, and its implications for social relations of poverty and processes of marginalisation and exclusion within the shanty population to which I return in the second part of this book.

3 Global Space and Urban Place

In this chapter I focus on Oshakati and its shantytowns as urban spaces and places within a global and national context of post-independence Namibia. Having demonstrated in the previous chapter that pre-independence Oshakati and its shantytowns were the outcome of an articulation between traditional Owambo society and colonialism, apartheid and war, I will now show how post-independence Oshakati has opened up to the wider world outside through the new independent state, through capital markets, the media and social movements. My objective is to show how shanty residents' lives have become incorporated into the political economy and the cultural flows that emanate from it on a scale beyond Oshakati itself, processes that both expand and confine the room for manoeuvre for the shanty population. I want, to use Bourdieu's (1990:26-29) terminology, to pursue the "objective structures" or the distribution of the resources that define the external constraints bearing on representations and interrelations of the people in the Oshakati shantytowns.

To pursue these issues in more detail, I will apply Hannerz's (1992) notion of 'cultural flows' and their political and material implications – or, simply, their 'flows'. Hannerz's framework makes it possible to demonstrate how cultural flows are filled with both meaning and materiality, having structuring effects in local contexts, such as those of the Oshakati shantytowns, as systems of classification of social agents and distributions of material resources (c.f. Bourdieu 1990). By insisting that people relate to these flows through different horizons and perspectives, Hannerz's model enables one not to lose sight of local processes and relationships at the expense of "global flows" – something many other globalisation theorists seem to do (Buraway 2000; Eriksen 2003).

In line with this Vilho Shilunga, sitting outside a *cuca*-shop called "bin Laden" in Oshakati's Uupindi shantytown in October 2001, eating a portion of (American) Kentucky Fried Chicken, listening to (the European group) Travis on the radio, drinking (South African) Castle beer and wearing an old T-shirt with a picture of (the Namibian) President Sam Nujoma may be seen to be caught up in global cultural connections. But, then again, for him it may also be just another name, just another song, just another piece of meat, just another beer, just another T-shirt and just another day struggling to survive within a life-world largely confined to the shantytown.

Hannerz (1992:48-49) argues that four organisational macro-frameworks encompass most of the cultural processes and their material implications in the world today, all fostering "deliberate and explicit flows of meaning", albeit with differing symmetries and asymmetries of input quantity and scale.[1] These are *flows of the state* ("the organisational form which involves a degree of control over a territory on the basis of concentrated, publicly acknowledged power"); *flows of the market* ("[a]s meanings and meaningful forms are produced and disseminated in exchange for material compensation, more or less centring relationships are set up of producers and consumers"); *flows of movements* ("... even when their ultimate concern is with distribution and use of power or material resources, they are often very much movements in culture, organisations for consciousness raising, attempts to transform meaning"), and *flows of the media* ("each medium ... through its symbol system, creates its own potentialities and enforces its own constraints on the management of meaning, in its way of reaching into people's minds, and possibly their hearts as well" (Hannerz 1992:27).

Still according to Hannerz (1992:101), from a macro-angle there is a range of costs and constraints relating to these flows in the sense of asymmetries of power and of material resource linkages which channel the distribution of meaning and meaningful form in society – often with alignments of distributions of meaning with power and material interests through ideology, secrecy and censorship. Seen from the micro angle, people manage meaning from where they are in a social structure (Hannerz 1992:65). At any time, Hannerz argues, an individual is surrounded by flows of externally available culturally shaped meaning which influence his or her ordering of experiences and intentions. Also here the type of ordering is closely related to economic position, gender, ethnicity and age.

The outcome of these processes for Oshakati is the town as urban *neighbourhoods*, or "situated communities characterised by their actuality, whether spatial or virtual, and their potential for social reproduction" (Appadurai 1996:178-79). After a decade of independence and hegemonic flows of the market and modernity, Oshakati in late 2001 gave a different impression than the Oshakati I found during my first visit ten years earlier as shown from my recorded notes (translated from original notes in Norwegian):

> Still coming in from the east a broad two-lane road is lit up by street lighting, and numerous shops, bars and dance-halls (including "Put More Fire", "Club Fantasy" and "Cape to Cairo") mark the outskirts of the Oneshila and Evululuku shantytowns. The streets into the shanties are still gravel but broader than before, and larger brick-houses are much more frequent; electricity lines criss-cross the areas; some houses have TV antennae, and communal as well as private toilets and water-taps are installed. Approaching Oshakati East, there is an Engen gas station, a Kentucky Fried Chicken outlet, modernised private houses (some of which boast

---

[1] Here I have taken the liberty of rephrasing Hannerz somewhat. He originally talks about four frameworks viz. the macro-flows of the state, the market and movements and the micro "flow of life". As I read him, however, he actually treats the media as a fourth macro-flow the way I do here (Hannerz 1992:26 ff). His micro "flows of life" will be treated in Chapter 5-9 on everyday practices and social relationships.

satellite TV dishes), and a large shopping centre with most of the best-known South African chain stores represented. Further on towards Oshakati West is the entrance to a new three-star hotel called Oshakati Country Lodge, an internet café, a large new pharmacy and the fast-food chain "Nandos". The Omatala open market bustles with life and one can purchase all kinds of goods and services, ranging from the latest in Western music to the staple crop *omahangu*, in apparent defiance of a second large shopping mall that houses liquor stores, the Standard Bank, small Chinese shops, supermarkets and the originally Brazilian "Universal Church" advertising salvation from sins and physical deficiencies (for a small fee of course). The biggest contrast to my earlier visits is perhaps that the town bustles with life. Cars, minibuses and huge trucks (bicycles are no more to be seen) compete for space with people all over, with *iilumbu* (whites) in suits and ties and Himba people in their traditional attire of leather clothes and red ochre epitomising the broad spectrum of town-dwellers. The shantytowns too are much more densely populated, and have expanded considerably, but have retained an overall impression of poverty and fatigue.

In the following pages, I will follow the cultural and material flows emanating from the state, the market, the media and social movements, and their implications for Oshakati and its shantytowns as urban space and place. I do so to show that a central aspect of these flows is the way they function as ideologies and material bases of a modernity in which the Oshakati shantytowns have little or no room. "The capability of neighbourhoods (such as urban slums) to produce context and to produce local subjects" Appadurai (1996:185) writes, "is profoundly affected by the locality-producing capabilities of larger-scale social formations". My goal in this chapter is to explore the extent to which such large-scale formations enable or limit the production of context and local subjects in Oshakati's shantytowns.

The implications of these flows in the practice of everyday life and for social relations of the very poor, the poor and the less poor in the Oshakati shantytowns are the subject of later chapters. In this chapter I will follow only a small number of shanty residents in their articulation with these flows – in order to ascertain how people "deal with the forces that oppress them" as Bourgois (1995:55) has put it.

Flows of the State

For the rulers of the young Namibian state, developing national identity, political cohesion and control represented severe challenges. State boundaries had been rather arbitrarily drawn by the old colonising men in Berlin in 1884-85;[2] with only 1.4 million people in a

---

[2] The Berlin Conference drew a line across the territory of the main Owambo group, the Kwanyama, leaving one-third in Namibia and two-thirds in Angola; Caprivi was incorporated into Namibia to fulfil Chancellor von Caprivi's dream of a German corridor to East Africa, separating the Mafwe and Subia from the Lozi in Zambia; while the coastal town Walvis Bay remained under South African jurisdiction until three years after independence (Hangula 1993a).

country the size of France and Spain put together, populations were spread and had limited contact; and political power and economic resources had become sharply divided along lines of race, class and gender after years of colonialism and apartheid. In addition, the Swapo leadership had come back from exile elsewhere in Africa or in Europe with their own cultural inventory to build a nation they hardly knew (Sparks and Green 1992).

Urban areas represented one of the most severe challenges to nation-building. Here the economic contrasts were most visible; expectations for development and modernity highest; and the political loyalty most fragile with concentrations of people from different parts of the country and people having fought on different sides during the liberation struggle. At the time of independence, 28 per cent of the population lived in cities and towns. And urban slums and shantytowns represented between 50 and 80 per cent of the population in urban areas (Tvedten and Mupotola 1995). Defined outside the legal parameters of the state (with illegal land occupation, with an informal economy outside the reach of the Ministry of Finance, and high rates of social unrest and crime), they were in many ways *in* but not *of* the state.

Looking at flows from the state to the level of Oshakati and local government, these were first and foremost characterised by limited transfers of economic resources and political decision-making (Tötemeyer 2000, see also CLGF 2004). Local politicians and bureaucrats were caught between the low level of resources made available by central government and the high level of expectations from the local populations following promises from the SWAPO government after independence. This put them "in the front line" of the flows of the state so to speak. As such, the flows were mediated and interpreted through face-to-face interaction and social relations, bringing "people back in" (Hannerz 1992:16) and opening up for situations of non-sharing of political ideology as culture.

The different perceptions and interpretations of the flows of the state can be exemplified by the notions of "municipality" and "town", having significant practical implications for the autonomy and accountability of local government. Graefe and Pyroux (2001) have shown how Namibia's central state structures (through the Ministry of Local Government and Housing dominated by a cadre of white town planners) defined and perceived Oshakati as a *town* throughout the 1990s with limited autonomy, while the Town Council (dominated by an influential town clerk) defined and perceived it as a *municipality* with much wider political and economic rights and obligations. Thus the population had expectations that local government was not able to fulfil; local government abrogated responsibility by referring to limited funds and room for manoeuvre from central government; and central government blamed unfulfilled promises on the incompetence of local government.

Following the flows of the state further, towards the Oshakati shantytowns, one finds that urban slums are consistently perceived by central as well as local government as being at odds with modernity and urbanisation, and therefore also as illegitimate (NPC 2001, Urban Dynamics 2001). During a visit to Oshakati in 2001, the then Minister of Local Government Nickey Iyambo complained that despite places like Oshakati having been proclaimed as towns after independence, the shantytowns were still dirty. He said people were allowed to sell meat and *tombo* without any controls, animals wandered all over, and shacks were being put up anywhere without any planning. "All this must stop" the Minister said *(The Namibian*, August 20, 2001).

Equally important is the dominant perception of the "otherness" of the shanty population, as exemplified in a statement by Oshakati's mayor in a meeting I had with him in 2001 when he said: "The biggest problem for us to become a real town is still [referring to our previous meeting two years earlier] the informal settlements". The shantytowns are thus regarded as disrupting the images of Oshakati as a modern town by their physical characteristics; and shanty dwellers are generally distrusted for their not being good law-abiding and tax-paying citizens. Both the shantytowns and their population are, as one Oshakati town council employee put it, "in the way of development". The dilemma for political powerholders in Oshakati was that the shanties were too big to be discarded, and potentially too important politically to be ignored. They were therefore tolerated in the short to medium term, and regarded as spaces that would have eventually to be brought into hegemonic perceptions of urbanity.

Perceived from the shanty dwellers' perspective, the state and local government had come to be seen as institutions that were not for them. Oshakati's shanty-dwellers were very much aware of the development that had taken place in the formal part of town with new roads, street lights, modern buildings, expensive shops, fancy cars and an increasing number of *iilumbu* (white people). And they knew equally well that hardly any such development was taking place in their own areas. Their feeling of being left out was exacerbated by an increasing number of evictions to make room for the modern development taking place in the form of government buildings, formal housing, commercial shopping centres and roads. People living on the outskirts of Oshoopala were evicted in 1996 to make room for a large new shopping centre; people living in the Sky I shantytown were evicted in 1999 to make room for the enlarged main road through Oshakati; and eviction from the informal market *Omatala* has been a long-drawn struggle between the town authorities and the informal traders working there (see e.g. *The Namibian* July 19, 2002).

From the perspective of the shanty-dwellers, other visible expressions of the flows of the state were the police and the state's tax-collectors. To safeguard income for the state in a situation where people were too poor to pay income tax and businesses were too shadowy to be reached, direct taxes on land and charges for electricity, water and sanitation remained the most accessible sources of income for local government.[3] In 1999 tariffs for water and electricity in the shanties were introduced for the first time since the establishment of the town; this despite local government having defined the shanties as illegal. The limited number of public taps, often in a poor state of repair and frequently broken, that were assigned to a defined neighbourhood were sealed off if insufficient money was collected. Besides the implications of limited access to water for well-being and health, lack of water frequently creates friction between those who have paid and those who have not. This type of collective punishment is seen as yet another proof that the state is not for the poor.

With the state's perception of the shanties as illegal urban space (making "the agents of the state less restrained in their exercise of authority" as Foucault [quoted in Merry 2001] has argued) and the fact that there is a high rate of crime in Oshakati, encounters between the shanty population and the police are frequent. Arrests are commonplace and, as the Acting Regional Chief of Investigation emphasised in a conversation I had with him in 2001, the large majority of people who are convicted and imprisoned in Oshakati come from these areas. For the shanty-dwellers, the bias of the police is verified by their inability or reluctance to make themselves available when called to deal with crimes affecting shanty-dwellers, ranging from petty theft to domestic violence and rape. People in Oshoopala were angry in early 2001, when a young man raped a young girl and the police did not come when called – and became even more angry when some older men later took the culprit to the police-station only to see him released the next day because "the police never helps us out" as they put it.

As Appadurai (1996:192) puts it, the challenge facing those who aim to produce neighbourhood in settings like urban slums derives from "... the tendency of the national state to erase internal, local dynamics through externally imposed modes of regulation, credentialisation and image production". In Oshakati, the state's project of producing neighbourhood has been only partially successful. While keeping control of slum areas that accommodate more than 70 per cent of the population, the project of penetrating everyday life and making the Oshakati shanties part of the state and its development efforts through "forms of allegiance and affiliation" (Appadurai 1995:189) has been less prominent.

This is largely related to the state's perceptions of urban modern space. Scholars drawing on Foucault's analysis of the art and rationality of governmentality (Merry 2001, see also Ferguson and Gupta 2005) have explored how urban social orders are increasingly based on governance of space. Governmentality, according to Merry (2001:18), refers to the "rationalities and mentalities of governance and the range of tactics and strategies that

---

[3] In 2000, the most important sources of income for local government in Oshakati were electricity, water and permissions to occupy municipal land (PTOs) (Urban Dynamics 2001; see also CLGF 2004).

produce social order". In addition, Merry (2001:19) adds, "spatialised forms of ordering are connected to the intensification of consumption as a mode of identity formation along with neo-liberal approaches to government". Thus spatial governmentality can be seen as a system that provides development and safety for those who can afford it, while abandoning the poor in unregulated public places.

This idea finds resonance in Oshakati. The state's perceptions about urban, modern space is perhaps best illustrated by the "Five Year Development Plan for Oshakati", prepared for the Oshakati Town Council by a private consulting company Urban Dynamics (Urban Dynamics 2001).[4] Based on an arguably biased reading of colonial development,[5] the plan outlines a town sharply delineated into industrial/business, public/institutional and residential space.

The shantytowns are variously described as "legal" and "illegal", even though none of them is formally legal in the sense of having been publicly proclaimed. The perception of some as illegal seems to be based on the extent of their residents' poverty and the extent to which violence is believed to characterise a particular area, as well as the potential of an area's presence for interfering with normative urban development. Even though the Five Year Development Plan acknowledges the existence of shantytowns and poor residents, they are consistently referred to in negative terms: "The informal residential component of Oshakati is very big and could bear considerable threat to the Council if an amicable solution to address the existing situation is not found within the foreseeable future"; and "[i]llegal occupation of land must be considered an offence and dealt with accordingly" (Urban Dynamics 2001:26-27).[6]

For the shanty-dwellers, the spatial delimitation of Oshakati into formal and legal areas and informal and illegal areas acts against their own interests where proximity of residential, business and public space is historically grounded and vital. This is why moves described earlier to relocate shanty dwellers evicted from the central parts of town to areas outside the town meet with such opposition *(The Namibian,* June 13, 2002): Such relocations mean that domestic responsibilities (such as looking after children and cooking) cannot be combined with business activities; walking to business areas in the centre of town takes a long time or eats up large parts of the profit if transportation by taxi (the only publicly accessible

---

[4] Many of the town planners working for Urban Dynamics had had a previous career in the apartheid colonial state and the Ministry of Regional and Local Government and Planning.

[5] As illustrated by their introduction to Section 3.4, where it is stated that "[u]pon independence, Namibia inherited a well-functioning physical infrastructure, strong institutional underpinnings for market development, a stable macro-economic framework, and a reasonably well organised and stable public sector" (Urban Dynamics 2001: 12) – without mentioning the unequal and racial development upon which this was based.

[6] An even more flagrant discrepancy between urban development plans and socio-economic realities is evident from a recent (2009) 'Concept Master Plan for Oshakati', made by the Belgian Buro of Architecture (www.bar.be)

means of transportation) is necessary; and distance to public institutions (such as the hospital, the police station and the Town Council offices) is seen to further weaken their own involvement and participation in the flows of the state. One time at the Omatala market, I witnessed a regular fistfight between a lady selling meat and a municipal inspector. Using words in Oshiwambo my bystander did not want to translate, she apparently threatened to bewitch and kill the town clerk if he moved the market to where "nobody will come to buy my meat".

The flows of the state involve a degree of control based on concentrated acknowledged power, but without "penetrating the nooks and crannies of everyday life" (Appadurai (1996:189). For shanty-dwellers, the impact of the flows of the state depends on where they are situated in the social structure. People with resources and the perspective to utilise what the state has to offer (in terms of security, employment, physical infrastructure and social services) will do so. For the poorest, however, the state is most noticeable for what it does not do, through its non-involvement in the shanties as urban neighbourhood and how it thereby contributes to poverty through its agents' constructions of the poor as 'other'. I will return to the implications of the flows of the state for the lives of Oshakati's shanty-dwellers in the second part of this study, but as an example of how such flows confine the room for manoeuvre of the poor in the shanties I will end this section by accompanying Nghinaunye and Imanuel Nambadja, two Evululuku residents, in their attempt to secure legal title and a business licence for their small tailor-shop.

Nghinaunye and Imanuel Ombadja are brothers who lived together in Omashaka (now Evululuku) when I first met them in 1993. They had left their village in the neighbouring region of Ohangwena at independence, to try their luck in Oshakati. Neither of them had finished secondary school, but they had a special interest in and talent for tailoring and dress-making and wanted to make a living out of that. At that time, clothes were not easily available in Oshakati. New clothes (albeit in old styles) were sold at a few local stores. Only a few travelling salesmen (normally of Asian origin) found their way to Oshakati. And the few active local tailors (normally old men) mainly did repair work. The brothers' main competition came from an NGO, Development Aid from People to People (DAPP), which sells second-hand clothes collected in Europe and the United States. Nghinaunye and Imanuel's business idea was to make clothes after the styles they saw on models they found in glossy South African magazines, which would (they told me) sell well. The brothers wanted to set up their business in the iron shack where they lived, built an additional room for that purpose, and even hired a young woman to cook and clean for them so they could concentrate on making and mending clothes.

During the following months, however, their marginality and exclusion in relation to the flows of the state became increasingly clear to them. Initial attempts to get support in the form of loans to buy an electrical sewing machine from the Small Informal Industries Division of the Ministry of Trade and Industry (into whose programme their small industry should have fit perfectly) received no response. And an application to the locally-based parastatal, National Development Corporation (NDC), was turned down because neither brother could produce a proper identity card. A small loan was finally obtained from the Private Sector Foundation, but it was large enough only to buy a second-hand machine. With an electric machine and the consequent need for electricity, they approached the Town Council to be connected to the electricity grid passing by the shanty. However, this turned out to be impossible. They were told, by an officer in the OTC Technical Department, that "Omashaka is not really part of the town". After repeated attempts at getting connected (including a failed attempt to connect illegally), the brothers gave up and decided to exchange the electric sewing machine for a hand-driven one.

With the business picking up, Nghinaunye and Imanuel and their shack soon became the target for *botsotsos* (local thugs) looking for money and other valuables. After having been repeatedly broken into, they contacted the police to ask for help. But none was forthcoming: They could not produce a business licence (obligatory by law, but in practice impossible to get for informal businesses), and were told that the police did not patrol the shanties as they were outside their areas of responsibility (a lie, according to Nghinaunye, who claimed that they were really afraid of being beaten up). The brothers ended up hiring an ex-soldier as protection – but he took off with most of the money they had at the end of his first month.

By the end of 1994, their business was in disarray. Their experiences with agents of the state had consistently reminded them of the marginality of Omashaka as an informal settlement, the insecurity and unpredictability of their own lives as slum-dwellers, and of how limited were the flows of the state into their domain. Facing problems of being able to deliver on time and keeping prices down, they finally gave up in the face of competition from DAPP, an NGO tasked by government with supplying Owambo with cheap clothing but which most likely, as Hansen (1995) has shown, ultimately benefited large international second-hand clothing syndicates.

Flows of the Market

Cultural flows emanating from the market have had a strong impact on Oshakati and its shantytowns, both in economic terms and as signs and symbols of modernity. I showed in the previous chapter how capitalism came to Owambo through labour migration, cash income and western goods, replacing subsistence agriculture and bartering as dominant modes of production and exchange. With the establishment of Oshakati as urban space, the importance of market flows for production, exchange and consumption increased – effectively commoditising many social relations and making money an agent of social transformation (Gregory 1997). This was the result not only of the flows of the market coming to Owambo and Oshakati, but also of the need to signify a distinction (Bourdieu 1990) between urban and rural areas. Those who moved to Oshakati were expected to demonstrate their successes in the urban economy by purchasing commodities that they could bring back home, even though we have seen that many of the poorest migrants were not in positions to do so.

Today the hegemony of the flows of the market is more directly apparent in the changed urban context of Oshakati. Large shopping centres are filled with Western market commodities (mainly produced in South Africa); individual traders from Angola to China supply goods of different types on a smaller scale; and large signboards spread all over Oshakati advertise everything from Volkswagens to powdered milk. Also in the shantytowns, the flows of the global market are apparent. Posters from the real "globalites", such as Coca-Cola, Carlsberg Beer and Nike, have made their way into even the darkest corners of the smallest *cuca*-shops in the most marginal parts of the shanties. And the informal markets are filled with Western goods, including cheap watches, cassettes with the latest in American music, and second-hand clothes supplied by the global "Development Aid from People to People". In one sense, then, Miller (1995:1) seems to be right in stating that there has been a shift in the consciousness of the people we study who "almost all now view themselves in direct relation to an explicit image of modern life".

Recent economic anthropology has tended to focus on consumption in order to relate to global flows of the market at the expense of focusing on production and exchange, and to view consumption primarily as processes producing identity and distinction (Narotzky 1997).[7] The structure of consumption is in turn seen to reflect and create the identities of social groups, as well as difference between groups. However, the anthropology of consumption has been criticised for not recognising that needs have a material basis (Carrier 1996:128). While the notion of consumption for identity construction presupposes an aspect of choice of what to consume, what characterises poor people in the Oshakati shantytowns is exactly that their range of choice is limited by their poverty. As we shall see in later chapters, people in the shanties find themselves caught up in a "tension zone" (Hannerz 1992:65) between hegemonic cultural forms of consumption and modernity, and their own situational experiences of poverty and despair.

Put differently, while the flows of the state stopped short of managing wholly to enter the poorest parts of Oshakati's illegal shantytowns, the flows of the market have indeed entered them, but with varying options for people to respond. When, for example, Matheus

---

[7] Gregory (1997) argues that these changes were mirrored in academia when language of "culture" and "identity" replaced that of "society" and the "individual".

Kashupulwa in Uupindi buys a worn-out second-hand pair of jeans from a local trader, this is not because he finds it 'cooler' than to buy a new pair of Levis in the Game Shopping Centre in town, but because that is all he can afford. In this way, consumption can be seen as a reflection of your socio-economic status rather than what someone wants to be or identify with. The consumption of worn-out jeans produces an identity of not being fully part of the hegemonic flow of modernity whilst remaining on its edge – which adds to the feeling of marginalisation and exclusion.[8]

At the same time, rurality and rural items have negative connotations and were even ridiculed in the Oshakati and shantytown setting. This is not because things rural are considered negative *per se*, but because it is not considered to belong in an urban setting: Traditional rural foodstuffs (including the staple *omahangu*) are hardly accessible in the markets. People coming in from rural areas are ridiculed for "spending hours" when following traditional greeting procedures. Rural *kuku* dresses are consistently associated with rural backwardness. And people insist on building brick houses or iron shacks because "they are urban", despite admitting that traditional dwellings made of sticks and grass will be cheaper, healthier and easier to move if they are forced to relocate. In line with this, as we shall see in Chapter 6, people going to rural areas strive to prove themselves as town dwellers by emphasising signs and signals of urban success.

Within a setting of hegemonic flows of the market and modernity, and a social reality dominated by unemployment and poverty in informal settlements, private capital has poured into Oshakati. The town has come to be seen as the hub of promising economic developments in northern Namibia and southern Angola, together representing a potentially huge regional market (*The Namibia Economist*, 29 August 2003). This development has taken place particularly since the proclamation of the town in 1995, and intensified with the peace in Angola from 2001. For the Oshakati population, then, life necessities are, as Narotzki (1997:40) puts it, "procured in a context where capital accumulation is the driving force organising material reproduction".

I shall look first at the flows of the market in terms of employment and income (coming back, again, to how the very poor, the poor and less poor shanty dwellers relate to them in later chapters). Formal employment has the advantage of representing a source of high and (equally importantly) consistent income, and it fulfils cultural expectations of urbanism and modernity: Formal employment is, as Hannerz (1992:52) puts it, a matter of specialised knowledge and control of particular forms of meaning and networks. This is knowledge and control that most people in the shantytowns do not have, effectively leaving professional employment (as teachers, nurses, administrators, accountants etc.) out of reach for the large

---

[8] Hansen (1995) has described how the use of second-hand clothes is turned into a positive identity of belonging in a poor settlement in Lusaka in Zambia.

majority of the shantytown population. There are some semi-skilled employment options, particularly in public sector hospitals, government institutions and construction, but these are the subject of fierce competition and are guarded vehemently by those who hold them.

The formal market for employment is dominated by the private sector that sells commodities produced elsewhere. More labour-intensive manufacturing industries have been inhibited by the large neighbouring economy of South Africa supplying the Namibian market.[9] The few existing manufacturing industries, such as Coca-Cola and Meatco, have a long history in the town and supply the local market. However, access to potential employment opportunities for those with minimal formal skills is restricted by local managers tending to recruit labourers through personal networks favouring family and friends that commonly exclude shantytown residents. All that is sometimes available is occasional, piecemeal work in warehouses, loading and unloading trucks, and as day-labourers in construction – all being badly paid, unpredictable and without any labour rights.

An influx of South African trade and service industries since the mid-1990s has created potential for new employment in department stores, fast food chains, hotels and warehouses. However, notions held by employers of urbanism, modernity and the market effectively hinder access to employment for the large majority of the shanty population. Firstly, the latter do not have proper addresses and often no identity cards, both of which are necessary for this new type of impersonal relations of employment. Secondly, most lack the required skills in terms of formal education and language (with English being mandatory and Portuguese preferred due to the importance of the Angolan market). Recruitment also tends to have a strong gender bias by favouring women. As one store manager told me in 2001: " I only recruit beautiful young girls. The customers want something nice to look at".

A final alternative formal employment option for shanty dwellers is as guards for private security companies (many owned by senior government officials, thus demonstrating the close relation between the state and certain branches of private capital). Security guards are used to protect public as well as private spaces, and there are literally dozens of them inside and outside private businesses as well as public institutions. However, the security companies recruit solely ex-soldiers, for two main reasons. One is that they have experience in handling weapons and dangerous situations. The second is that they will accept extremely low wages because, like most other shanty dwellers, they lack of alternatives. They were consequently earning wages as small as N$ 150-200 per month for working eight to ten hours working days, seven days a week.

This limited access to formal employment has led to a dependence on the informal labour market, usually yielding very low but consistent returns, for the large majority of the

---

[9] More than 90 per cent of all commodities sold in Namibia are produced in South Africa (EIU 2008).

shanty population. The informal market represents a special form of modernity, functioning, as Hansen and Vaa (2004) suggest occurs elsewhere, in the interface between global flows of the market and an embedded local context of social relations and reciprocities. Informal employment options in Oshakati include a wide range of occupations such as sale of locally made bread, rice, fatcakes, meat, fish, and other "urban" foodstuff (*okapana*), sales of cheap, imported commodities, accommodation and liquor outlets, taxi-driving and car-washing, tailoring and hairdressing, panel-beating and carpentry, running *cuca*-shops and beer-brewing, and providing services such as in sex work and traditional healing.

For the state and private commercial capital, the existence of poor shantytowns and unregulated economic activities represent a challenge to their attempts to create a modern urbanism with high capital accumulation and consumption. This is exemplified by Namibian central government policies of regulation that effectively inhibit informal economic activity – such as a proposed law to have separate toilets for men and women wherever food and drinks are served, which would effectively close 90 percent of the *cuca*-shops if implemented; and local government's repeated attempts to close and relocate the large informal market at *Omatala* (*The Namibian*, August 23, 2005).

The flows of market commodities reaching Oshakati are not designed to fit poor urban neighbourhoods on the periphery of the market economy. First of all, the price level of most of the capital goods and a large part of the imported foodstuffs is simply too high to draw in customers outside a limited class of professionals and businessmen. People earning an income around the poverty line of N$ 662 (which, as we have seen, are among the better-off in the shantytowns) would have to work four weeks to buy a radio, eight weeks to buy a bicycle, 12 weeks to buy a bed and 16 weeks to buy a sofa in one of the new department stores.

Furthermore, for the majority of the shanty-dwellers, the culture of modern consumption as an important aspect of contemporary urban style is difficult to relate to as it does not speak to them. At the end of 2001, Whoopi Goldberg posed the following question from huge sign-posts along the main road through Oshakati: "*Do You Only Have TV, or Do You Have DSTV?*" The large majority of shanty-dwellers do not have electricity; very few have TV; an even larger majority do not know what DSTV is; and (to quote a young man from one of the shantytowns) "Who the hell is Whoopi Goldberg?" If anything, the poster had the effect of giving people in the shanties the feeling of further alienation from a global flow of the market they were not really part of.

The "systematic non-sharing" (Castells 1999:3) of the flow of the market is also evident in more subtle ways. Buying in modern stores and supermarkets requires a certain cultural knowledge about neo-liberal markets that not everybody possesses. After having spent some hours observing people in a new clothing store, a new pharmacy and a new food market in Oshakati, I realised how many cultural codes one needs to master. One must dress and behave in a certain manner to get in at all (many were refused entrance while I watched); one has to be able to walk through the store and relate to the staff (many of whom are white) with a certain confidence so as not to raise suspicion; one must understand what is said and written on signboards and price-tags; one must remember to save the cash-slip to show at the exit when one leaves; and one must figure out what to do if one later regrets what was bought.

For shanty-dwellers, then, constant attempts are made to relate effectively to the flows of the market. But, for most, consumption is primarily directed towards the distorted forms found in the informal market. I was discussing this with the white manager of one of the fast food outlets who could not understand why (to paraphrase him slightly) people did not buy his fat, global chickens in his slick new and clean premises with pop-art on the walls for 16 Namibian Dollars a piece, instead of buying skinny, local half-breeds roasted by an old woman on dirty sidewalks in the hot sun for 8 dollars. It is not, I have argued, solely a question of price. Global flows of the market do reach practically every corner of the shanties with its hegemonic ideology. But the discrepancy between its messages and meanings and the realities of people's lives become too big – apparently for the agents of the global flows as well as for the local shanty-dwellers.

In this sense, then, the quasi-modernity of skinny chickens, second-hand trousers, iron shacks and fat-cakes become the alternative for many. This does not mean that the global flow of the market does not have the upper hand: As we shall see in the next chapters, people will cross over when they have the possibility of doing so, as a sign of an improved standard of living, upward mobility and ability to establish identities (albeit briefly) that are seen to be closer to the hegemonic flows of the market and modernity.

The implications of the flows of the market for employment and access to material means and commodities for the shanty dwellers will be analysed more closely when I present and analyse the social relations of poverty in the second part of this study. For now, I will exemplify how these flows constrain the room for manoeuvre for poor shanty dwellers by accompanying 12 year old Domingo Kambode from the Oshoopala shantytown into the world of football which is, I would suggest, one of the most pervasive manifestations of flows of the global market (Giulianotti and Robertson 2009).

When I met Domingo in Amunkambya (now Oshoopala) for the first time in 1994, he seemed like an unusual youngster. Normally children ran around me, yelled *oshilumbu* (white guy!), and laughed, even if they had met me many times before. But Domingo always seemed totally preoccupied with playing football with a ball made of rags tied together with a string, showing off his certain talent.

As I got to know him better, I realised that he was totally captivated by the dream of becoming a professional football player. Domingo was convinced that professional football was a way of getting rich. He knew about Manchester United and most of their players at the time (I never really found out how); and he also knew the names of South African players who had made it in Europe and Namibian players who had made it in South Africa. His only direct contact with "real football" was at local games at the Oshakati stadium, where his favourite team was (the local) Liverpool. When I asked him why he wanted to become a pro, he always emphasised the money rather than the fame.

The problem for Domingo was that he had absolutely no chance of reaching his goal. His slow realisation of this has stuck with me as one of the saddest experiences during my period of more than ten years of visiting Oshakati – even though we shall see there are more dramatic implications of the tension zone between the power of the flow of the market and shanty realities. Amunkambya was (and still is) the poorest and most violent of the shanty areas, and Domingo lived with an informally employed mother, a father originally from Angola with major alcohol problems, and four siblings who were all younger than he. There was never enough food to eat, he had to do a lot of household chores, and he had quit school (there was no money for him to go to school, his father told me early one morning as he got into his fourth beer) – all factors inhibiting a football career from the outset. Moreover, there were no organised sports activities for children in the shantytowns where he could practise and learn, and no money to buy proper shoes, pads, a football and other equipment. Had he become good enough, obstacles from race to greedy agents would have had to be tackled. At the end of 1995 Domingo had stopped playing football and given up his dream of becoming a football millionaire.

Flows of the Media

Judging from much anthropology and related science, there is nothing more global than the global flow of the media with media-messages seen to reach every corner of the world (see Askew 2002 and Rothenbuhler and Coman 2005 for overviews). A problem with many post-modern "transnational anthropologists", however, is that they often lose sight of social differentiation, poverty and differential media access within particular populations. Here I argue and demonstrate that only part of the media-messages potentially reaching the Oshakati shantytowns actually do so, and that the media messages that do reach people there tend to do so in forms that present the messages of the global world, the state and the market in ways that enhances the shanty population's sense of marginalisation and exclusion.

On the face of it, and seen from Windhoek, Namibia's capital, the country has it all in the form of a rich flora of written, audio-visual and electronic media. The truly transnational media are present in the form of satellite transmissions of CNN, BBC, ESPN and South African channels (of which the pan-African *Supersport* reaches the largest audience); there are the short-wave transmissions of Voice of America, BBC World Service and Deutsche Rundfunk; and a selective sample particularly of weekly editions of British newspapers (to maintain Commonwealth family links?). In the last few years, of course, the world has also come to Namibia through the Internet, readily available for the non-computer owners who can afford it at Internet cafés.

Nationally, the Namibian Broadcasting Corporation (NBC) transmits radio programmes 24 hours a day, including several hours of transmissions in local languages such as Oshiwambo. Its television station, albeit squeezed economically,[10] with a limited schedule of 6-7 hours a day and a dominance of imported programmes, now reaches most parts of Namibia. There is also a rich selection of newspapers, ranging from the exceedingly boring government weekly *New Era* to the exceedingly speculative *The Observer*,[11] and with the daily *The Namibian* as the most important publication, historically due to its independent voice during apartheid and currently implied by the numerous interventions from government to change its focus or stop it from coming out.[12] The government and private business also actively use flows of the media for information campaigns (such as for AIDS prevention), and advertisements to sell goods and services (to reach the would-be well-off, normally with the option of credit as a central part of the message). Windhoek, finally, boasts media-related institutions such as a large and impressive national library; two national publishing companies (Gamsberg MacMillan and Out of Africa); a number of bookshops with a broad range of international and national publications; and a modern movie theatre (too expensive for the large majority of Windhoek residents, but still there).

Seen from Oshakati, the media are less spectacular with several outlets reaching the town in interrupted streams and patches. Until the early 1990s the transnational flow of the media hardly reached directly into the town at all. It was intercepted by the South African colonial government or too distant from regional transmitters; and news from the 'big world' was siphoned through national intermediaries (the only exception was Radio Swapo transmitted from Angola and Zambia, but that was siphoned through their ideology department). Today in Oshakati international newsprint is hardly anywhere to be seen (because of the limited market), and the short-wave transmissions are, for some reason, nearly impossible to catch. With improved conditions for receiving satellite signals from global television

---

[10] This must be the explanation for why they transmitted "News from China" on prime time for several months in 2001, and transmit hours of third-rate American evangelists every Sunday.

[11] The paper seems to have one editorial principle: At least one murder must be covered in pictures and text on the front page, preferably involving cross-race rape and murder (or even better in the opposite order).

[12] Blaming the paper for being anti-government for a period in 2000-2002, the authorities stopped all government advertising in the paper with serious economic repercussions for its owners.

and the coming of the internet, however, the options for being reached directly improved towards the end of the 1990s but only for those who could afford it.

National media flows are also less than omnipresent than they are in Windhoek. Oshakati has no public library. Only a small bookstore exists. And video shops are few and far between, expensive and with "loans restricted". This leaves national newspapers and the NBC as the most accessible sources of media flow. *The Namibian* and *New Era* (both with their own correspondents in Oshakati) now reach the town the day of their publication and are sold in formal stores, while a paper like the Afrikaans-language *Die Republikein* has a special monthly edition for the country's northern regions that is also available in Oshakati. Television in Oshakati is still in its infancy, but the number of TV antennas in the formal parts of Oshakati is a sign of growing distribution. NBC radio, finally, is by far the most accessible media source. Not only do national transmissions reach the town loud and clear; NBC's regional office, located in Oshakati, transmits ten hours a day of its own locally produced programmes.

Being accessible in town, however, does not necessarily mean that the flows of the media reach their audiences in the Oshakati shantytowns. Poverty, illiteracy, language and access to necessary infrastructure determines the catchment area of the flow of the media to an extent that often seem to be overlooked by the most ardent media globalists (Askew 2002). There are very few TVs to be seen in the shanties (and even fewer that are working); electronic media reaches only a select few due to price and the cultural competence needed to enter the world of Internet cafés; trips to the movies in Ondangwa or to a video shop tend to be expensive; and it is quite rare to see people read printed media. The main exception are radios, that are owned by 56 percent of the households in the shantytowns (see Chapter 4).

The flows of the media that reach the shanties, then, tend to do so via intermediaries, in accordance with what the media analysts call a two-step theory (Askew 2002). The major papers *The Namibian* and *New Era* are written in English with only condensed summaries and selected articles in Oshiwambo and Afrikaans. *Die Republikein's* special edition for the northern regions of Namibia, Lanterna, has longer articles in Oshiwambo and is free of charge, which partly explains why this is probably is the most widely read publication – though it appears only monthly. And the flows of the radio are to a large extent channelled through the Oshiwambo Service of the NBC. About one half of the programmes are translated from national broadcasts, with the other half being produced in Oshakati itself. The most relevant arena for studying the context of the flow of the media reaching the Oshakati shantytowns, then, is not the global news agencies, where news are produced, but an editorial staff in Oshakati where it is reassessed, condensed and translated.

At this stage in its flows, however, the media has a tendency of becoming "unfree" through interceptions and acts of censorship. During and since the election in 1999, for example, comments and questions to the Open Line Inquires programme from the Oshakati office of NBC about the opposition party Congress of Democrats (CoD) were often censored (with callers being cut off the air as the most conspicuous case in point). And critical questions related to President Sam Nujoma (such as about the construction of an airfield just outside his home village in the Owambo region of Omusati) are consistently rejected or ridiculed. Incidents like these have fuelled perceptions amongst parts of the shanty population that the media and the government are two sides of the same coin, implying, as it were, "the alignments of distribution of meaning with power and material interests" (Hannerz 1992:101).

The global flows of the media reaching Oshakati, then, do so with less of a free flow than what is often theorised (Askew 2002). There is, in a sense, a "trichotomy" between the national capital city, the formal parts of Oshakati and the shantytowns in terms of access to media flows, ultimately with implications for differences in cultural capital, knowledge and world view. Whereas the power-holders of the state and private capital have access to the more subtle media flows of the complexity of the urban-dominated modern world, people in the shanties are largely left with images in the form of censored messages from the state and unattainable imagery from the market – adding, as we shall see in the second part of this study, to their sense of marginalisation and exclusion. For now, this is perhaps best exemplified by huge billboards with images representing urban and modern successes that the shanty dwellers cannot avoid seeing. Better than words can express, the "dark" and "lovely" lady staring down from one of the many hoardings along the main road in Oshakati is worlds apart from the old shanty-dweller passing in her traditional rural *kuku*-dress on the way back to her shack in one of the Oshakati shantytowns (Figure 3).

Figure 3: Worlds apart

Democracy Comes to Town

The final cultural flow in Hannerz's (1992) organisational macro-framework is that of social movements – also seen to carry with it political, economic and cultural implications. "Even when their ultimate concern is with the distribution and use of power or material resources", Hannerz (1992:49) writes, "[movements] are often very much movements in culture, organisations for consciousness raising, attempts to transform meaning". In our case, a potentially powerful movement for developing local democracy, participation and empowerment in the Oshakati shantytowns ended up in a distorted version when confronted with shantytown realities of poverty and differentiation – effectively marginalising the poorest parts of the population it was meant to reach on the way.

Democracy reached Namibia with the transition to independence around 1990, impelled by the Western powers involved in the change from South African colonialism to an independent state (Sparks and Green 1992). In tandem with national democratic development reaching down to the level of local government through elections in 1994, democracy came directly to the Oshakati shantytowns in 1993 through the "back door" with the Danish non-governmental organisation Ibis[13] and in the form of the Oshakati Human Settlement Development Project (OHSIP). Formally part of the Ministry of Regional and Local Government and Housing, with a large Danish money-bag and an expatriate staff, the project set out to improve conditions in the shantytowns through trying to instigate a democratic and participatory process.

Development in the Oshakati shantytowns through the OHSIP project included roads, electricity, water and sanitation. It was important as the first real development intervention in the shanties, potentially reaching large parts of the poor urban areas with "empowerment" as well as "development". As will be seen below, it fits well with two distinct theoretical trajectories in social movement theory (Gledhill 2000:185), one concerning social movements for resource mobilisation, and the other with issues of identity and consciousness.

Ibis's Oshakati Human Settlement Development Project came with its own vocabulary and discourse, epitomised in words like 'democracy' 'poverty alleviation', 'participation' and 'accountability' (OHSIP 1992). Inherent in the rhetoric was the language of the women's movement, the environmental movement and the human rights movement. As Ferguson (1994:18) argues, with reference to Foucault, discourse is a practice, it is structural, and it has real effects. The thoughts and actions of development organisations are shaped by a world of acceptable statements and utterances, and what they do and do not do is a product not only of various interests but also of a working out of a complex structure of knowledge.

---

[13] Funded, as are the large majority of the non-governmental (*sic!*) organisations in the world of development, by government.

The movement of democracy through the OHSIP project reached more directly into the shanties than the flows of the state, the market and the media, "being right there" so to speak and concerned with mechanisms of power and the relation of power to knowledge. Democracy in the Oshakati shantytowns was first of all to be accomplished through the establishment of Community Development Committees (CDCs) as local associations (Frayne et al. 2001). The tasks of the CDCs were to be representative bodies in the community; to represent the community in relation to the state and the OHSIP project; and to carry out their own development work through self-funding activities, mainly in the form of brick production for sale in the shantytowns. The CDCs also received some initial support from the project for constructing community centres and administering CDC election campaigns.

The CDCs were elected by people in the shantytowns themselves through an elaborate election process and under the principle of one household – one vote. Elections were undertaken on the basis of nomination processes where, in principle, anybody could stand for election but where representation of women was promoted by the project. The CDC was to have ten members, constituting themselves by selecting four office-bearers and managers of different sub-committees. As part of the process of "consciousness raising [and] attempts to transform meanings" (Hannerz 1992:49), CDC elections followed formal rules, with regulations on campaigns, secret ballots, external election observers etc.

In parallel with the flows of democracy reaching the shantytowns, the construction of infrastructure was to be based on *community participation*, yet another catchword of the democratic movement. People were to dig ditches for water pipes, carry sand and gravel for improvement of roads, transport and erect electricity poles, and dig canals for sewage – all voluntary. Additional small community projects were garbage collection and disposal, tree-planting and digging small embankments and canals to steer floodwater outside the shantytowns. Participation, as OHSIP conceptualised it, did not, however, include community-scale physical planning, which was done by an outside consulting company comprising white Namibians and South Africans who did little in the way of 'community consultation'. [14]

The political context against which the OHSIP project was set was that of a central government trying to consolidate itself; a local government in limbo with inadequate funding; and a local population in which the political culture and processes were quite different from those conventionally associated with democracy and where many people's experience was one, during the colonial presence, of being told what to do rather than to engage in processes of constructing policy and intervention activities (see Chapter 2). For central and local

---

[14] Resulting, as it were, in a number of contradictions between formal planning outcomes and local knowledge. Disregarding shanty-dwellers' warnings about the course of the *oshana* flood water, the then Minister of Local and Regional Government and Housing opened one of the main roads through Uupindi in 1994 knee-deep in water...

government, the very establishment of the CDCs in the shantytowns was seen as a threat to the formal national democracy they were in the process of installing. As noted earlier, the state saw poor informal urban settlements as the potentially most important threat to its own authority, and local government feared for its own legitimacy, if any elected shanty body was now seen to deliver development that local government agents were not themselves able to. The ensuing ambiguities soon led to strained relationships between the "top-down" democracy of central government and the Oshakati Town Council (OTC), and the "bottom-up" democracy of the CDCs under Ibis's wing. In an open letter (dated 17.06.94), the Mayor and chairman of the OTC accused Ibis of "[i]nvolving itself in the politics of our local communities for its own ends ...[while] it does not have any mandate to do so".

Even within the shantytowns, the notion of democratic participation and community development created tension and suspicion, and Ibis/OHSIP's efforts ultimately led only to very limited legitimacy for the CDCs with the population they were meant to serve. As we shall see in the second part of the study when pursuing the implications of the cultural flows of social movements for social relations of poverty, what effectively happened was that the better-off in the shantytowns (professionals, small-scale businessmen, the young and educated) had their perspective and horizon directed out of the shanties towards the formal town and its opportunities and therefore did not get involved. In contrast, the poorest and most destitute (struggling to make ends meet and with few resources in terms of social relations and education) did not capture the ideas and possibilities inherent in the process of establishing the CDCs as a democratic forum and largely withdrew. And for the in-between group of poor, the CDCs became an arena for personal ambitions and shanty politics.

My last impression of the democracy coming to the Oshakati shantytowns came from the CDC election in 2001 where the focus had by then turned to form rather than content, as indicated by a letter of complaint sent to the OHSIP project staff by a losing candidate (reprinted with permission):

> Dear Sir. We the undersigned residents and members of the Oneshila community settlement area hereby have the pleasure and strong will to seriously express our deep-seated concerns, dissension and great displeasure over the manner, atmosphere and environment under which the recently organised community based elections were prepared, supervised and held in Oneshila... Among the issues being highlighted and discussed were inter-alia: 1) The constitutionality, legitimacy, transparency, fairness and democratisation of the election; 2) The issuance of voters registration papers to the deserved and rightful plot/householder; 3) The eligibility, qualifications and disqualification of potential registered candidates; 4) The voters qualifications and the principle of voting system, in terms of the CBDO Constitution; 5) The electoral procedures followed on the polling day; 6) The allegations of the evils of corruption, irregularities, untold manipulations and evidences of election rigging or gerrymandering; and

7) The election results and the so-called newly elected committee leadership structure. The meeting also decided that the recent[ly] held elections be declared null and void pending the outcome of the investigation committee due to be established in due course. And that the so-called new elected committee be unreservedly considered unconstitutional. (Signed)

The losing battle of the flow of democracy and participation against longer established local level political processes and meanings finds resonance in Castells' (1996:3) statement that "[s]ocial movements tend to be fragmented, localistic, single-issue oriented and ephemeral, retrenched in their inner-worlds... In such a world of uncontrolled, confusing change, people tend to regroup around primary identities, religious, ethnic, territorial, national". The story of how democracy came to the Oshakati shantytowns is a useful reminder that even powerful global flows meet realities with their own logic in the form of political realities and social relations of class, gender and ethnicity – realities where unequal distributions of material means and other resources tend to take on a pivotal role.

By using Hannerz's (1992) framework of cultural flows of the state, the market, the media and social movements, I have shown how such flows move through (real or virtual) social relationships, being twisted and turned before they reach the Oshakati shantytowns. Their basic impact has been one of marginalisation and "othering" of the shantytowns and their inhabitants. For the state the shantytowns are at odds with the project of modernity and governmentality. For the market the shanty population is important, but out of reach in its structural form as most of the shanty-dwellers can only afford its informal and second-hand expressions. The media largely carry the messages of the state and the market, with its expressions deepening the discrepancy between hegemonic flows and real lives for the poorest. Finally, social movements – carrying Western ideologies of democracy, participation and gender equality – meet realities where only parts of the population are in positions to relate to their ideas.

In Bourdieu's (1990:50) terminology, the flows accounted for are constituted by the distribution of material resources and means of appropriation of socially scarce goods and values. The material implications of these forces for the Oshakati shanty dwellers depend on where they are in the social structure. They carry not only oppression, but also opportunities for those who can relate to them. This brings us to the issue of shanty poverty and inequalities, which are closely linked to both the historical processes and the structural conditions treated so far – and to the immediate lived experiences of people in the shanties and their social relationships of impoverishment and social marginalisation that are the focus of the remaining chapters of this book.

4 The Shanty Population and Inequalities

History and what, following Hannerz (1992), I have called the cultural flows of the state, the market, the media and social movements treated in the first part of this study carry with them demographic and material manifestations, as well as implications for identities and social relations of poverty in the Oshakati shantytowns. The cultural and material flows of oppression thus lead a "double life" (Bourdieu 1990, Wacquant 1992:7): They are constituted by the "distribution of material resources and means of appropriation of socially scarce goods and values", as well as by the kinds of "mental and bodily schemata that function as symbolic templates for conduct, thoughts, feelings and judgements of social agents" that will be the subject of the second part of this study (Chapter 5-9).

While the material distribution of poverty is the outcome of cultural, political and economic processes, then, material poverty is also embodied and has consequences of its own: It narrows the room for manoeuvre and directs perspectives, acts and events in specific directions. As such, poverty is structural and its presence as a concept cross-cultural. What Bourdieu (1990) argues, in his attempt to transcend theories of structural oppression and individual agency, is that social structures do not determine outcome, but they do make some outcomes more likely than others (see also Kuper 1992:6). Here I have also found Mary Douglas's (1982) distinction between poverty and destitution useful. While poverty implies, for her, a restriction of choice, she uses the word destitution to refer to a state in which the main problems are those of subsistence and survival and where there is virtually no choice at all. "Subsistence problems", she maintains, "are not only physical problems, they are emergencies" (Douglas 1982:17).

To end the first part of this study, I approach the issue of population and material poverty by outlining demographic characteristics and material conditions in the Oshakati shantytowns through their quantitative expressions. I present the outcome of a survey originally undertaken in 1994 to produce a synchronic profile of socio-economic conditions for the Ministry of Regional and Local Government and Housing and OHSIP (Tvedten and Pomuti 1994)[1], and compare this with some more recent but less systematic data to offer a sense of some trends over time (OCT 2002, GoN 2003, NPC 2006, see also NPC 2008). The 1994 sur-

---

[1] The survey interview schedule itself contained questions to gather a broad set of data on population, social organisation, housing, employment, income etc., all of which were collected with the purpose of mapping socio-economic conditions in the shantytowns in order later to be able to assess changes in these conditions following planned OHSIP project interventions (see Chapter 3). However, a follow-up study was never commissioned neither by the MRLGH nor the OHSIP project, possibly because they realised, even without a further survey, that the outcomes and impact of their project interventions were not as envisaged.

vey revealed a situation of general poverty and vulnerability. It also showed how individuals and households found themselves in diverse positions in relation to income, employment, housing, access to land and cattle, savings and other markers of poverty. The three more recent surveys are more limited in scope and not directly comparable, but give some basis for assessing trends primarily as regards population, household headship and income poverty and differentiation (see below).

Quantitative data are often needlessly shied away from by many anthropologists (Knauft 1997). Some things (like population and access to material resources) can be measured, compared and assessed without necessarily postulating causality in any scientific sense. Moreover, quantitative data and statistical analysis may, as Little (1991:174) points out, "be a preliminary way of probing a complex range of social phenomena for underlying regularities". The strength of combining quantitative data with grounded anthropology and interpretative analysis of poverty is exactly that some of the asserted underlying regularities can be critically assessed (Carrier and Miller 1999).[2]

The central theme in the next pages, then, is the severe poverty and vulnerability of Oshakati's shantytown population – poverty and vulnerability that follow from the historical developments and cultural and material flows of oppression and marginalisation to which the Oshakati shantytowns and their inhabitants have been subjected. A further related theme is the differences in access to income and basic means of livelihood that separate the very poor, the poor and the better-off in the shantytowns. The distribution of material poverty has strong bearings on social relationships and the kinds of processes of marginalisation and social exclusion that will be the subject of the second part of this book.

Population and Household Characteristics

There is still controversy over the exact size of the Oshakati population, and data differ. The population peaked in the late 1980s with an estimated population of 37,000. Many people (including South Africans) left Oshakati immediately after independence in 1990, but the population grew again from the early-1990s. Population data from 1994 indicate a total

---

[2] Reliance on quantitative data does, of course, also raise a number of important concerns about the data themselves. Concepts and units of analysis that are central to much quantitative survey-based research, such as the household, household headship and formal and informal employment, are, almost by definition, distortions of a complex reality of processes and relationships. Having said this, it is necessary to draw some kind of analytical boundaries if one is to use and report on survey data on population and the material distribution of poverty. In presenting data from my survey, I have tried to balance the need for such analytical boundaries with using definitions as close as possible to the situation on the ground – while being keenly aware that quantitative data can never fully reflect 'reality'.

of 35,000 people, with approximately 57 percent or 20,000 living in eight informal settlements (OHSIP 1994, based on estimates from OTC). For 2002, the Oshakati Town Council operated with a total population of 42,000 people of whom 73 percent (approx. 30,000) were understood to be living in ten informal settlements (OTC 2002). This gives a population increase for Oshakati as a whole of 2.3 percent per year between 1994 and 2002. [3]

Despite uncertainty about the accuracy of available population figures, it seems safe to state that the main population increase in Oshakati has taken place in the shantytowns, as land and formal housing have been expensive and largely unavailable in the formal part of town (Urban Dynamics 2001). Those settling have gone to Oshoopala, Uupindi, Evululuku and Oneshila, or the smaller shantytowns Sky 1 and Sky 2, Kanjengedi, Eemwandi, Oshimbangu and Ompumbu. My own observations (see also Tvedten 2004) show that the large number of post-independence migrants coming into the shantytowns have been poor people from Owambo with a higher proportion of women than men – a migration that has also been described as "perhaps the most dramatic example of post-independence urbanisation in the communal areas of Namibia" (Frayne and Pendleton 2003:8).

As we shall see below, professionals and small-scale business people who have come to Oshakati from other parts of the country with the economic boom and extension of public services have also settled in these shantytown areas, primarily because of lack of alternatives. The result has been both a substantial increase in the population, with increasing density of settlement, and increasing socio-cultural complexity and internal differentiation between the poor and the less poor within the shanty areas.

Oshakati as a whole is densely settled, with 1,344 persons per km^2 on the usable land in the town. Annual flooding through the *cuvelai* drainage system renders up to 50 percent of the town's 61km^2 area uninhabitable (OTC 2002, see also Map 2). Flooding encroachment is the main reason why the four original and largest shantytowns that are the focus of my study are geographically confined, and why they have seen population increases manifesting as ever higher density of settlement. As seen from Table 1, the estimated population in these four areas has increased from 13,000 in 1994 to approximately 24,000 in 2002 (OHSIP 1994, OTC 2002). This suggests that the bulk of population growth in Oshakati has been concentrated in Oshoopala, Uupindi, Evululuku and Oneshila.

---

[3] To add to the confusion about real population figures, the most recent census (GoN 2003) puts the Oshakati population at 24.000 - apparently by defining large parts of the shantytowns outside the town boundaries.

	Uupindi	Evululuku	Oshoopala	Oneshila	All four shantytowns
1994	5057	2428	2286	3186	12957
2002	9474	5378	3167	6066	24085
Annual increase (%)	8.2	10.5	4.2	8.4	8.1

Table 1: Population in the Oshakati Shantytowns, 1994 & 2002

The population of the four settlements is relatively young (Table 2)[4]. 77 percent are 34 years or younger, and only 5 percent are 50 years or older. A distinct feature of the informal settlement areas is the relatively low proportion (22 percent) of youngsters from 5-19 years, reflecting migration patterns as well as the system of sending children away to relatives in rural areas to which I will return later. There is no noteworthy difference in age structure between the four shanty areas. The domination of young people in the shantytowns reflects the historical trends of migration, as well as the flows of the state and the market particularly in the form of rural and urban employment opportunities discussed earlier.

Years	Uupindi	Evululuku	Oshoopala	Oneshila	All four shantytowns
0-4	12	15	19	14	14
5-19	23	21	27	20	22
20-34	40	41	38	49	42
35-49	20	19	13	12	16
50+	5	4	4	5	5

Table 2: Age Structure of Oshakati Shantytown Population (Percent), 1994[5]

Furthermore, there is a majority of females in all the shantytowns except Oshoopala, which historically has been the most militarised area (Table 3). The overall distribution is 52 percent females and 48 percent males. By way of comparison, the last Census (GoN 2003) showed that those ratios were 54 percent females and 46 percent males in the Oshakati population as a whole (i.e. indicating an increase in the proportion of females if we employ the assumption that the census-figure is relevant also for the Oshakati shantytowns). The

---

[4] In the survey on which the following tables are based (Tvedten and Pomuti 1994), a seven percent sample was randomly selected from the households in each shantytown. This was done by selecting every 14th household from lists originally made by the OHSIP project in each shantytown. It produced a total sample of 178 households with a total of 907 individuals in them. According to economists Devereux and Hoodinott (1992 and personal communication) a seven percent sample is sufficiently large in a population of that size for one to draw generalised conclusions

[5] Due to the rounding process, the totals may add up to 99 percent or 101 percent

trend toward an increasing proportion of females in Oshana and Oshakati is underlined by preliminary data from a Household Income and Expenditure Survey from 2006 (NPC 2008), showing a ratio of 56 percent females and 44 percent males or 100 females for every 79 male – which is the highest proportion in the country. That in turn reflects an increase in the proportion of women in the Oshana region as a whole due to continued male migration to the south (Frayne and Pendleton 2003); an influx of women from rural Owambo to Oshakati with the town's economic boom and its improved options in the informal economy (Tvedten 2004); and, as we shall see in the second part of the study, an increasing responsibility among women to have to provide for their households and extended families.

Sex	Uupindi	Evululuku	Oshoopala	Oneshila	All four shantytowns
Male	46	49	52	48	48
Female	54	51	48	52	52

Table 3: Sex Structure of Oshakati Shantytown Population (Percent), 1994

The level of education in the informal settlements is generally low (Table 4). 16 percent of the population of more than six years of age have no education at all and 24 percent of those who have gone to school have Grade 4 or less, making the functional illiteracy rate 40 percent (Amukugo 1995). Only 9 percent have Grade 11 or higher. The level of education is higher among women than men: 19 percent of males have no education, with the equivalent proportion for females being 13 percent. Moreover, 42 percent of the women with education have obtained Grade 8 or higher, as against 23 percent for men. As I shall return to, many parents (or maternal uncles) have come to see girls as better prospects for future support than boys and therefore prefer to pay for the education of girls. The population in Oshoopala has the lowest level of education, while Oneshila has the highest.

Education	Uupindi	Evululuku	Oshoopala	Oneshila	All four shantytowns
No education	10	14	28	20	16
Grade 1-4	25	21	29	22	24
Grade 5-7	28	34	26	16	26
Grade 8-10	27	27	13	27	25
Grade 11-12	9	4	4	11	7
Diploma	0	0	0	3	1
Other	1	1	0	1	1

Table 4: Levels of Education of Oshakati Shantytown Population (Percent), 1994

I have no quantitative data of my own on the health situation in the shantytowns, but surveys carried out by UNICEF (1995) and the Ministry of Health and Social Services (MHSS 2001, see also MHSS 2008) in the "peri-urban areas of Oshakati", as the Government calls them, reveal a serious situation (Table 5). Infant and child mortality rates are high; children are frequently sick; nearly 40 percent of women under 20 have children; and the HIV/AIDS prevalence rate is 31 percent – well above the national average of 21 percent (UNDP 2000 and 2007). As we shall see, illness in general and HIV/AIDS in particular have considerable implications for the types of strategies and relationships pursued by the poor in the shantytowns, sometimes affecting the ways that households are constructed.

Health Indicator	Oshakati Shantytowns
Infant mortality rate	70/1000
Child mortality rate	106/1000
Life expectancy at birth	60 years
Maternal mortality rate	552/100,000
Sick children *	68 %
Under nutrition **	35 %
Women under 20 with children	39 %
HIV/AIDS affected	31 %
HIV/AIDS affected	31 %

* Percentage of children being sick (cough, fever, measles, diarrhoea) within the past 14 days of the interview.
** Under nutrition among children 6-60 months (reflects both recent and long-term malnutrition).

Table 5: Health Conditions of Oshakati Shantytown Population, 1995 & 2001

Moving on to a profile of the household, the definition of household units that I employed in my survey counted as members of a household every individual who had stayed in the enumerated household unit for six months or more in the preceding year and who was considered, by the household head, to be a member of that household.[6] The definition was explicitly drawn up in order to recognise the fact of migration and that household resources often derive from persons living away from the homestead for extended periods of time. It also recognised the possibility of oscillating urban-rural migration.

---

[6] This gives a somewhat different picture than the census definition, which defined a household as "[A] group of people related or unrelated, who live in the same household unit and share or have common catering arrangements" and only counted individuals who had spent the census night in the same household in a context where particularly men are frequently absent.

In my 1994 survey, 72 percent of the households in the informal settlements were identified by respondents as being male headed and 28 percent as female headed. Male-headed households were understood to be households with a man living alone, or where there was a man with dependants or with a female partner and where the man was considered to be the head by the other members. Female-headed households were understood to be either *de jure* (single mother, divorced or widowed) or *de facto* female headed (where a woman has the main economic and social responsibility and is perceived as the head by the other household members).

More recent data indicate a dramatic increase in the proportion of female headed households to around 50 percent (GON 2003, NPC 2006, see also MHSS 2008)[7]. This seems to confirm the increasing proportion of women in Oshakati referred to above, as well as what I will demonstrate in the second part of the book: a growth in the extent to which poor women have had to shoulder the burden of social reproduction and have therefore become household heads, while poor men in the shantytowns have been increasingly marginalised and attach themselves temporarily only to more stable households or else find themselves completely detached.

According to the 1994 survey, the average shantytown household had 5.1 members, with a household size range of one to 13 members. There were only small differences in average household size between male and female headed households, with averages of 5.2 and 5.0 respectively. My data also show that the proportion of extended- and non-relatives living in the household unit (i.e. other than core members of mother/father/ children) is generally higher for female-headed households (56 percent) than for male-headed households (46 percent), indicating a stronger social responsibility for women than men. As we shall see in subsequent chapters, many female headed households had a particularly heavy burden of young dependents (often children of AIDS-victims), and some had incorporated other adults (often female relatives or other women) into their household unit.

Finally, the educational level of household heads reflects the level of education for the population at large. 28 percent have no education at all, 22 percent have Grade 4 or less making them functionally illiterate, and only 8 percent have studied beyond Grade 10 which is necessary to continue with tertiary education. Female household heads showed a larger variation in terms of education than their male counterparts: Whereas a higher

---

[7] The definition of household and household headship employed in the census (where only people present in the dwelling the night before the census interview were counted) is likely to have inflated the proportion of female headed households, particularly in poor urban areas due to the frequent temporary absence of men from their dwellings revealed later in this study. Still, however, the figures do verify a significant increase in the proportion of female headed households – which is a process also found in other parts of Southern Africa (Chant 2007; World Bank 2008).

proportion of female household heads (34 percent) than male household heads (26 percent) had no education at all, as many as 36 percent of the female headed households had Grade 8 or higher, the equivalent figure for male household heads being 21 percent. This reflects a general trend revealed in my survey: The female headed households in the shantytowns who have 'made it' are often better-off than the male headed households in similar socio-economic positions (see below) – a point which confirms the importance of focussing on intra-household resource allocations.

As already noted, there are no directly comparable data from other urban shantytowns in Namibia on population and household composition. However, there are some demographic data in the national census that highlight the conditions of poverty and vulnerability in Oshakati's shantytowns. The infant mortality rate in Oshakati of 70/1000 is higher than the national infant mortality rate of 49/1000 for female- and 55/1000 for male-infants. And Oshakati's shantytown functional illiteracy rate of 40 percent is considerably higher than the national average of 19 percent (GON 2003).

The census also reveals two recent trends that are likely to also have affected the Oshakati shantytowns. One is the difference, referred to earlier, in the proportion of female headed households in my 1994 survey figure of 28 percent and a figure of 54 percent in the Census (GON 2003). As argued, this difference probably reflects a general growing dominance of women in the Oshana region, resulting from migration trends. It also points towards current gendered processes of impoverishment and marginalisation that will be a central focus in the subsequent chapters: an increasing responsibility of poor women for household reproduction, and a concomitant marginalisation of poor men.

The second trend relates to life-expectancy at birth. Set at 60 years for the Oshakati shantytowns by UNICEF in 1995, national figures were set at 50 years for females and 48 years for males in the census (GON 2003) - primarily reflecting the HIV/AIDS pandemic which has been particularly serious in Oshakati. This will clearly have strong implications for the demographic characteristics of Uupindi, Evuluolku, Oshoopala and Oneshila in the years to come, most likely by increasing dependency ratios and further impoverishing the shantytowns.

Material Conditions

Material conditions and poverty reflect the historical development and flows producing the kinds of oppression and marginalisation accounted for in the first part of this book: The Oshakati shantytowns and their inhabitants were marginalised by colonialism, war and apartheid, and oppressed by the cultural flows of the state and the market and their material implications.

Let me initially outline the differences between the four shanty-areas Uupindi, Evululuku, Oshoopala and Oneshila, in terms of levels of material poverty (Table 6). As shown earlier, the differences between the four shantytowns reflect differences in origin and history: Oneshila and Uupindi were parts of existing villages at the time of the establishment of Oshakati and, as more settled communities, they developed more extensive economic activities. This is reflected by the fact that 37 percent and 21 percent of the households in those two shantytowns were in the N$1000+ income bracket, as compared with Evululuku and Oshoopala where those figures were 11 percent and zero respectively. Since the latter two settlements later attracted men and especially women from diverse rural areas, of whom many women were without income and ended up in dependency relations, they have maintained their position as poorer and more violent than the two former areas. The general levels of poverty and the potential to construct mutually supportive social relationships has, I will argue and illustrate in subsequent chapters, implications for the sense of community and the type and nature of social relations of poverty in these areas.

Household Income	Uupindi	Evululuku	Oshoopala	Oneshila	All four shantytowns
N$ 0-250	35	35	63	21	37
N$ 251-500	26	24	17	21	23
N$ 501-1000	18	30	20	21	21
N$ 1001 +	21	11	0	37	19

Table 6: Monthly Household Income by Shantytown (Percent), 1994

Just as distributions of households by income bracket show significant differences between the shantytowns, so do distributions of employment figures. Oshoopala, where 63 percent of households were in the lowest (≤N$250) income bracket, had only 11 percent of its adult population 16 years and over in formal employment, compared with over 20 percent in each of the other three shantytowns (Table 7).[8] But that did not mean that there were not significant proportions of people in all four shantytowns who were dependent on informal income generating activities (33 percent of adults across the four) or were unemployed (31 percent) and, as we shall see later, dependent on entering social relationships with others

---

[8] Formal employment is based on formal contracts and/or a regular and fixed salary. Informal employment has no formal attributes related to contract or wage (normally, but not necessarily, self-employment). Unemployment is defined as people with neither formal nor informal employment, and hence with no income. Pensioners are people receiving a monthly state pension (N$ 120), either due to old age or physical disabilities. And the category "student" includes people over 16 years who are still studying.

for survival. The low level of formal employment was, as shown in Chapter 3, a combined outcome of limited public and private employment opportunities and of the inaccessibility of formal employment for a shanty population characterised by low levels of education and of urban cultural competence.

Employment status	Uupindi	Evululuku	Oshoopala	Oneshila	All four shantytowns
Formal	20	23	11	22	20
Informal	27	28	44	40	33
Pensioner	2	1	0	2	1
Unemployed	37	35	30	20	31
Student	12	7	9	10	10
Other	2	6	6	6	4

Table 7: Employment Status by Shantytown Population (Percent)

There were also marked gender differences in employment rates among the shantytowns' adults (Table 8). 29 percent of men and 11 percent of women were formally employed, with the equivalent figures for informal employment being 26 and 49 percent respectively. Equal proportions (31 percent) of men and women were unemployed and therefore lacked income. As I have shown, differences in types of employment and income for men and women are related to the historical and structural genderisation of the labour market in Oshakati, a process that has left the informal economy as the main option for women. While this may pay less than formal employment, it is flexible, something that women in particular seem to value, as we shall see in later chapters.

Employment status	Male	Female	Total
Formal	29	11	20
Informal	26	41	33
Pensioner	1	2	1
Unemployed	31	31	31
Student	10	11	10
Other	4	5	4

Table 8: Employment Status of Adult by Sex in Shantytown Population (Percent)

A correspondence between employment status and household income reveals itself in the distribution of income appearing in Table 9.[9] As seen, both male and female headed households in which the head's main source of income was derived from formal employment were in higher income brackets than households where the heads depended on informal employment as their main source of earnings (defined as the source providing the most income six months prior to the survey). Among formally employed male and female headed households, 70 and 60 percent respectively headed households earning more than N$ 500 per month, while among informally employed male and female headed households 67 and 56 percent respectively headed households earning N$ 250 or less per month.

Monthly income	Formally Employed		Informally Employed		Formally and Informally Employed
	MHH	FHH	MHH	FHH	All HHs
N$ 0-250	3	10	67	56	37
N$ 251-500	26	30	20	21	23
N$ 501-1000	67	20	3	21	21
N$ 1001+	3	40	10	3	19

Table 9: Employment Status and Sex of Household Head by Income (Percent)

Referring back to my discussion about the defined poverty line of N$ 662 in Chapter 1 and the distinction made between the less poor/better-off, and the poor/very poor households, approximately 30 percent found themselves in the first category and approximately 70 percent in the second category.[10]. The proportion of very poor households with a monthly income of less than 40 percent of the poverty line or N$ 250 was 37 percent. My survey also shows that the proportion of female-headed households in the 'very poor' category was 47 percent and of male-headed households 33 percent. This represents a very low household income in an urban setting like Oshakati, equivalent of N$ 8.33 per day and N$ 1.63 per person per day (assuming an average of 5.1 persons per household).[11] At the other end of the

---

[9] Households are defined with reference to their main source of income, and the monthly income reflects total household earnings. As all households have some kind of income, the unemployed do not represent a separate category but makes up non-income earners of household units. 61 percent of the households have more than one income earner, including children.

[10] As the income categories were defined prior to the poverty line, an estimated line has been drawn in the middle of the N$ 501-1000 household income category.

[11] The equivalent figures in USD are USD 38.46 per month, USD 1.28 per day and USD 0.25 per person/day.

scale, the proportion of male-headed households earning more than N$ 1000 is 22 percent and for female headed households 10 percent.

The significance of these differences for the analysis of processes of impoverishment and marginalisation in the context of the Oshakati shantytowns is that the employed and less-poor/better-off households are in a position to make strategic choices about whether to spend, invest or save – and, when spending, about what to buy. The poor/very poor households have much more limited choices by being compelled to spend most of what they earn on food and other basic necessities. The very poor households depend on establishing social relationships of employment, income or support outside the household unit to be viable – or they will remain in, or sink ever more deeply into, a situation of abject poverty and despair. At the same time, I will later show that while economic position does have significant implications for coping strategies, the relative material disadvantage of poorer female headed households is partly counteracted by their ability to create close female focussed networks that stretch across households.

The 1994 survey also showed a striking correspondence between type of employment and income, on one hand, and access to other basic means of livelihood, first and foremost land and cattle, on the other. As shown in the preceding chapters, colonialism, war and apartheid pauperised, impoverished and marginalised many Owambo from their family and rural possessions. Claims of rights to rural land are important for subsistence and income, as well as for social relationships and what I shall later call "double rootedness" in the urban and rural socio-cultural formations.

88 percent of the shantytown households claimed access to land. However, having access to land did not necessarily mean that residents in these households were actually in a position to produce crops. Rather, production depended on such people's ability to establish and maintain relationships with rural relatives or others who might help with ploughing, sowing, weeding and harvesting. Fully one-third of the households had no access to land or else had such access but did not produce any staple crops at all; one-third harvested or received between one and 20 bags of approximately 15 kgs – enough to contribute to subsistence needs; and one-third produced more than 20 bags which, for an average sized household, would, according to Frayne (2005) have left something for distribution or exchange. The better-off households in terms of income receipts (and in particular those headed by formally employed women) generally had significantly better access to land and agricultural products than the poorer households, indicating more limited relationships with rural areas for the latter category.

In addition to rural grain production, cattle too were important, not only for consumption and income, but also for saving, social security and social status. 61 percent of the households in the four shantytowns reported having no cattle. These were predominantly the poorest households in terms of income, and included both male and female headed households. Some 21 percent of households owned or had access to small herds of one to ten beasts while the remaining 18 percent had larger herds that had the potential to be of commercial value. This last cohort was primarily made up of formally employed better-off male-headed households (31 percent of the households headed by formally employed men had eleven or more cattle), although 10 percent of the households headed by formally employed women also had herds of eleven or more beasts.

My fieldwork also revealed correspondences between employment, income and other expressions of material poverty, such as housing and physical infrastructure. A proper brick dwelling tended to be important not only for the well-being of household members as a social unit and for their economic security, but also as a productive asset. Whereas some three fifths of all dwellings were used for producing food for sale (*okapana*), sale of alcoholic beverages (*cuca-shops* and bars), tailoring or other informal activities, all larger outlets and enterprises were run from brick-houses. Perhaps most importantly, a brick house implied better security of tenure, as non-permanent structures (such as iron shacks) were always the first to be moved during periods of eviction. Yet nearly two thirds of households in the shantytowns occupied iron shacks, traditional homesteads or tents, the remainder having access to at least one brick house. The former all tended to be smaller and to have fewer rooms than did the masonry structures. Broken down by sex of household head, some 71 percent of all female-headed households had poorer quality housing compared with 64 percent of all male-headed households. At the same time, a larger proportion (50 percent) of formally employed and better-off female-headed households had invested in brick houses than similar male-headed households (42 percent).

Other physical infrastructure also revealed a situation of structural poverty and differentiation. Three quarters of the shantytown population depended on water from communal taps that were often broken so that they had to rely on poor quality often contaminated water from the Okatana Canal, or from stagnant water pools. Close to 90 percent of the shantytown population had no access to gas or electricity and depended on wood for cooking and candles for lighting. Finally, two thirds of the population used the "bush" as their toilet, with serious implications for health conditions.[12] Interestingly, households headed by formally employed women (both in brick houses and in shacks) had the highest proportion of flush toilets/ pit-latrines indicating a stronger emphasis in such households on hygiene and health.

---

[12] Improved infrastructure (water taps, pit latrines or water-borne sewage and electricity) has become more available the past few years, but the costs of utilisation (water and electricity) and maintenance (pit-latrines) have inhibited any wider use particularly among the poorest parts of the population.

The extent to which the poorest households are chronically poor, in the sense of remaining in poverty over time, is indicated by the OTC (2002) survey – i.e. nine years after my own survey (Figure 4). As shown, the proportion of households with incomes below the poverty line of N$ 662 was by then approximately 47 percent and the proportion of very poor households earning less than N$ 250 was approximately 22 percent. With consumer inflation ranging from 8.6 to 11.3 percent per annum since the definition of the poverty line in 1999 and 2002 (Africa Research 2003), however, approximately 74 percent of the households would by now fall under an adjusted poverty line of N$ 958, leaving only 26 percent above it, and approximately 35 percent of the households would by now be earning less than 40 percent of the adjusted poverty line or N$ 383 per month. This is primarily an expression of continued unemployment and low income in the Oshakati shantytowns in a context of increasing costs of living – as well as continued economic inequalities.

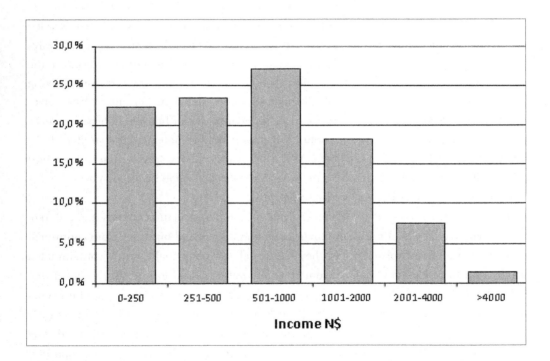

Figure 4: Monthly Household Income Distribution 2002

Conclusion

I have shown how historical processes of colonialism, apartheid and war, and the contemporary dominating forces of the state, the market, the media and social movements, have formed and shaped the Oshakati shantytowns and the general characteristics of their residents. The central theme of those historical processes has been one that has led to the oppression of those shantytown residents and their marginalisation, from rural as well as from urban social formations – largely making the shantytowns the antithesis of both. I have also outlined the demographic and material conditions following from these processes, conditions that are best characterised as deep material poverty that is nonetheless marked by internal differentiation along lines of class, gender and geographical space. Structural analyses and quantitative expressions of poverty of this type is where most development-oriented research ends. What such analyses are not able to reveal are the processes of social and cultural continuity and change that are to be found within shantytown populations themselves. Living in the same setting and apparently under the same conditions, some households and individuals in Oshakati's shantytowns appear to have been trapped in poverty and destitution and seem to have become marginalised and socially excluded, while others, it appears, have been able to strive to make a living and to improve their situations. To ascertain why this should be – why there is this differential experience of and response to conditions of poverty and marginalisation – we need to focus on the everyday practices and social relationships of people living in the shantytowns.

5 Social Relations of Poverty

Filemon Shiimi was born in a village in the district of Oshana, but moved to a village in Ohangwena when he was 12 years old to help his uncle with the cattle. Moving around so much made it difficult for him to go to school, and Filemon completed only Grade 3. In 1997, he left for Oshakati ("that was the saddest moment for my uncle. He gave me a talk on how to behave in town"), stayed with an aunt and subsequently got a job through her in a security company in Ruacana. Returning to Oshakati after one year, he found that his aunt no longer had room for him. He moved in with his brother, a taxi driver, and his brother's wife, who worked in a local store. There were eight people living in the house altogether. Filemon worked for another security company in Oshakati.

> It is a very new company and I was the first to be recruited. It is not easy to find a job here in Oshakati, but I was lucky because I knew people connected to this company. Even though I have a job, the problem is that the wages are very low and one cannot do much with the money. Currently I am earning (Namibian Dollars) 400 per month, but I am actually happy with that amount because most people start with 150 or 200. I am planning to have my own house soon, but I am happy here and I and my brother understand each other well. The house is a bit overcrowded, but my brother is happy about it. ... I also have very good relations with the rural area. Whenever any livestock gets lost, my uncle will call me to go to the village because I am the oldest at home. I think the rural area is a nice place to stay, the problem is just that there is no employment. ... At the moment I think I am in a good situation. I believe myself to be very fortunate because I get jobs easily through family and friends. There are others who have been looking for employment for years but cannot find any.

Emilia Uushona is a 60 year old grandmother who lives in a small run-down shack made out of tent material, and seems very poor, not only in her physical appearance, but also judging by the way she moves and lowers her head when she speaks to others. She grew up in a village in Oshikoto with a mother and father and 15 brothers and sisters, of whom only four are still alive. Her mother still lives in the village, but, Emilie says, she is "overloaded with grandchildren and cannot take any more". Since she came to Oshakati 20 years ago Emilia has lived with many different partners, and in her lifetime has had ten children. Only three children are still alive, and she does not have much contact with them, with the exception of a mentally ill daughter and a grandchild with whom she lives. Her last partner was, as she puts it: "a no-good alcoholic. He beat me and I had to tell him to leave". Her situation is very difficult, and she does not have the strength any more to sell *okapana* as she did before.

> I wonder if I will ever get out of this situation. I am living in poverty, I mean severe poverty. Look at my grandchild. He cannot walk even though he is now two years and nine months.

> His mother is mentally disabled and just goes to drink *tombo* the whole day. When she comes back it is dark and she does not eat – she does not even give her child attention. ... In order to eat we have to borrow food from people. I am even ashamed to be in our location these days because people are getting tired of us borrowing, borrowing every day – even though I mainly borrow food from people I know who are not from the neighbourhood. If you borrow from neighbours then everybody will start to talk about you. Neighbours are not good people. I do not talk to my neighbours because they abuse my daughter – beating her.

Filemon Shiimi and Emilia Uushona both live in the Oshakati shanties, but their economic positions and social relations vary greatly. Filemon has small but steady income, while Emilia has none. And while Filemon has managed to maintain relations with rural and urban areas outside the shantytowns and fill them with material as well as social content, Emilia has not and is largely trapped in the shantytown, barely making ends meet. Without such relationships, her impoverishment is not only related to material assets but also to social marginalisation and exclusion. In her words, "Poverty is the same as death (*oluhepo noosa shimwe ashike*). When you are poor, you are like a dead person." – a clear reference to her social isolation and an indication that she has given up making much of her life.

The history and structural conditions treated in the first part of this book, I have argued, have not only brought about poor and marginalized shanty neighbourhoods, but are internalised experiences that directly affect people's economic positions, their identities, their relations to each other and hence their actions. Even though structures do have a powerful effect upon human action and the shape of events, however, there is room for social mobility and people in the Oshakati shantytowns experience upward as well as downward shifts in their social position. Actions are types of critical reflections that involve conscious strategising within the confines set by the structuration of poverty (Bourdieu 1977 and 1990; Ortner 1984 and 2006:129-153) – either in the form of a longer-term strategic planning perspective requiring a minimal level of economic resources where motive and action are shaped by images and ideals of what constitute goodness in life (as in the case of Filemon), or as *ad hoc* and short-term decision-making instigated by abject poverty as emergencies (as in the case of Emilia).

In the second part of this book, I take a closer look at practice in terms of specific social relations of asymmetry, inequality and domination – as well as cooperation, reciprocity and solidarity – and explore how this is embodied through repetition and enactment over time (Ortner 1982 and 2006; Bourdieu 1990; Moore 1994). The dominant theme considers how material poverty influences the options and abilities of people in the shantytowns for establishing and maintaining social relationships that are vital for their individual and household reproduction (Moore 1994:71-85). I show that people who do not manage to establish and maintain such relationships over time are further impoverished and marginalized in the shantytowns, and they ultimately succumb to their fate as chronically poor and destitute in ways that "effectively contribut[e] to their own domination" (Bourdieu, quoted in Wacquant 1992:24).

To set the stage for my analysis of the coping strategies and processes of marginalisation and exclusion among the Oshakati shantytown population, I will show how a group of shanty-dwellers have chosen to present their shantytowns by way of photographs. The photographers were a mixture of young and old, men and women, and were given the task of taking pictures that they felt reflected shantytown realities.[1] The pictures turned out to centre around employment, income, education and housing, all of which, I showed in Chapter 4, are central external expressions distinguishing the less poor from the poor. Yet the pictures they produced did not include the best-off and the very poorest shanty-dwellers: According to the photographers the former did not want to be associated with shantytown life – pointing towards a central argument in the coming pages of the best-off residents focussing their attention and relationships outside the shantytowns. The latter, I was told, were – as one of the photographers put it – "too ashamed of the conditions they live in to want their pictures taken". The comment reflects Mary Douglas's [1982:17] argument that poverty is not merely a question of a lack of goods nor even a lack of money, but also a matter of loss of *dignity* – pointing towards an aspect of the lives of the very poorest that I will come back to in the end of the study.

Relinquishing for a moment the "right" to represent others and giving these "others" the means to present themselves seems a fitting thing to do through a mode of representation that until recently has been conducted exclusively by outsiders. Even in the second half of the twentieth century, Rohde (1998:188) argues, photographic production in developing countries, whether practised as "art", "social documentary" or "scientific ethnography", has been predominantly a middle-class activity, involving observing and making products that the people who have been photographed will never see.

I thus let the photos and captions written by the photographers speak for themselves and serve as an introduction to my subsequent analysis of the social relations of poverty in the shanty communities and beyond. Let me here simply emphasise that the photos and their accompanying texts – meant to illuminate shantytown life – reflect small local incidents and commentaries rather than larger political and existential issues. People find themselves in positions defined by the history and political and economic processes of oppression treated in the first part of this study; and they relate to these through everyday and

---

[1] People in the shanty communities were given a short course in photography, and were free to choose their motif. The pictures and their accompanying texts were originally exhibited in the shanties themselves, and later in Windhoek. The pictures shown here were selected for the purpose of this study in cooperation with the photographers, and are reprinted in their original form and with their original texts, with the photographers' permission.

grounded acts and relationships that are equally important as those broader processes for understanding the experiences of marginalisation and social exclusion that I have set out to explain. Such acts and their interpretations provide both meaning and order for people in the community – while at the same time being both constituted by, and contributing to the reproduction of, enduring structures of social inequalities in larger society (Ortner 1991:167, with reference to Willis 1977).

In line with this, Maria Nangolo in Figure 5 is surrounded by signs and symbols of the *market* dominated by loudspeakers belching out western music; cheap alcohol representing a serious social problem in the shantytowns; and Coca Cola as the ultimate sign of the global impact of free market enterprise. Yet Albertina Abiatar's comments focus on immediate conditions reflecting on everyday life: Maria is 25 years old and still not married, she has a child, and although "she is small" (violating the mediated ideal of beauty?) she is still "good looking".

The two children in Figure 7 are victims of an unwillingness or inability of the *state* to deliver proper educational facilities to the Oshakati shantytown, with serious implications for the longer term options for social mobility. Instead of a text highlighting this, Lydia Uudhigu, who created the image, emphasises how difficult it is to teach inside makeshift shacks, especially during the rainy and winter seasons that effectively make up the major part of the year.

The *social movement* of the NGO Ibis came with promises of democracy, equality and improved facilities for all – eventually primarily reaching the better-off with sufficient funds and social relationships to take part in it. Anton Silveira's text to Figure 11 showing a "poor quality bathroom and toilet" does not dwell on the exclusion of the poorest, but simply states that the man cannot afford a real bathroom but uses one made of "plastic, cutdrums and boxes".

Daniel Indongo, one of the few in the Oshakati shantytowns who has openly declared himself AIDS positive, has not benefited from his fulfilment of the importance of being open, as advocated by the state and the *media* alike. He has, Karen Shiimi tells us in Figure 17, stopped practising a life-style that can slow infection: "Drinking locally brewed *tombo*-liquor with friends at local shebeens is his every-day routine".

And finally, the little girl pictured fetching *tombo* for her mother "around 12 o'clock" in Figure 10, and the boy in Figure 20 gathering food in the dust-bin in the middle of the day who do not go to school because "his parents don't have money to pay his school-fees", indicate a bleak future with a state that does not provide education and parents who cannot afford to invest and make choices that will help their children get out of the poor and violent shantytowns one day.

Figure 5: "Maria Nangolo is a shopkeeper at the "Three Sisters", a Cuca-shop in Oshoopala location. She is 25 and still unmarried. She has one child though. She is small but quite good looking. I think."

Figure 6: "38 year old Lahia Endjala from Oneshila location slaughter a goat and sells the meat."

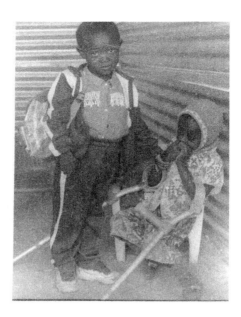

Figure 7: "*Some parents construct kindergarten classes in their community to give their children the opportunity to learn. Most kindergartens are made out of iron zinc to give shelter to the children. It is always difficult to teach inside them during the rain and winter season.*"

Figure 8: "*This is my family having dinner – my father Indongo and my sisters Loina, Laina and Toini. The little boy Mathew is laina's son. We are having oshifima, the traditional Owambo porridge. We have that every day.*"

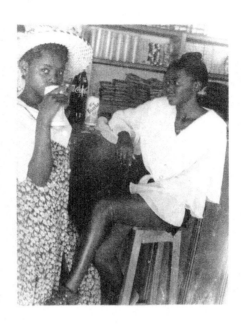

Figure 9: "Mamai (right) doesn't go to school, Lily does. They meet every day at this Cucashop once Lily is off school. They mostly talk about their boyfriends and what has happened at club Fantasy over the weekend."

Figure 10: "I met this girl in the location one day. She had been sent out by her mother to go and get some tombo, the traditional Owambo beer. It was around 12 o'clock, I think."

Figure 11: "This photo shows a poor-quality bathroom and toilet. People who cannot afford to build good quality wall-bathrooms for themselves build their own using plastic, cut-out drums and boxes. Here, this man is busy taking a bath in his bathroom."

Figure 12: "This photo shows these kids playing a game called Ndilimani. You play the drum and sing while playing it. I don't know the words but at one point the kids sing "PW Botha should be ashamed."

Figure: 13: "This photo shows 34 years old John Nandjembo Ndaunda-Onya practising the art of singing and playing the guitar. People interested in listening to his music have to pay some money in order to listen to his playing. He uses the money he earns to buy food and also to support his six children, of which three go to school."

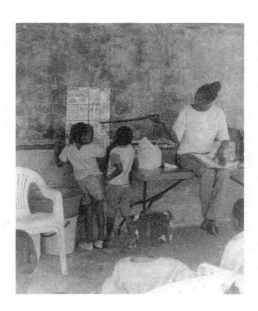

Figure 14: "This photo shows a kindergarten teacher teaching her young pupils names of different things on the picture and also how to count numbers."

Figure 15: "Small-scale business is the main source of income to many people living in informal settlements. This picture shows kuku Johanna selling apples at the Okamukuku Open Market at the Oshakati main road. This gives her money to help herself and her family."

Figure 16: "This is one of the houses built through loans from the Build Together Programme in the informal settlements."

Figure 17: "Daniel Indongo who is a self-declared HIV carrier sees no bright future ahead of him. After breaking the wall of silence about his HIV-status this year, Daniel lost hope and stopped to practise a life-style that can slow infection of various diseases which in the end can lead to full-blown AIDS. Drinking locally brewed tombo-liquor with friends at local shebeens his his every-day routine."

Figure 18: "Her name is Elisabeth Vilho, she is from the Oshoopala Location and she makes a living from doing these baskets. They are made of dried palm-leaves and sown with needles and a wet string from a leaf. people use them for carrying things and storing mahangu and things like that."

Figure 19: "Mamy uses Revlon to stretch her hair. many do that. You get it in three different colours – the blue one is very strong. You don't want to get it in your eyes, and you can't hold a baby when you have just used it. The skin gets all dried up. You shouldn't wash your hair beforehand, just put it and let it stay a while. Then wash out with hot water. If you let it stay too long, your hair will fall off."

Figure 20: "A lot of children in the location don't go to school. They spend all day playing in the streets or begging or, like this one, gathering food in the dustbin. Most of them have parents; the parents just don't look after them. This kid told me he doesn't go to school because his parents don't have money to pay his school-fees. For a child his age the fee is around 10 Namibian Dollars a year."

6 Rural Links

I will start my endeavours to understand social relations of impoverishment, marginalisation and social exclusion among the Oshakati shantytown population by exploring their relationships with rural areas and the extended family. These relations are central in people's daily lives as well as at decisive moments such as birth, marriage, sudden illness and death, and may encompass important economic resources as well as deep emotional sentiments of kinship and tradition. As such, rural relationships have a strong influence on economic position and general well-being, and their absence may contribute to the impoverishment and marginalisation ultimately trapping poor people in the shantytowns.

In an earlier chapter I showed that migration to towns in Owambo is a relatively recent phenomenon with Oshakati having been established in the mid 1960s and populated throughout the 1970s and 1980s, implying that most adult shanty-dwellers there have rural experience and village-based families. I have also argued that the special characteristics of urbanisation in Owambo, in a context of pauperisation, apartheid and war, implied a weakening or even termination of rural and extended family ties for many who became shanty-dwellers. Recent post-independence migrants to town are, as we have seen, a more mixed group: some have education and employment and have settled in the shantytowns because there are no alternatives in the formal town, but most are poor people who have been "pushed" by a deteriorating rural economy, or "pulled" by possibilities of employment and an urban life-style. As pointed out earlier and underlined in other studies (Peyroux et al.1995; Frayne 2005), however, the possibilities of urban employment for those who move to town is often an illusion, with most urban migrants ending up in poverty-stricken slums or shantytowns.

The contemporary rural crisis in Owambo is usually associated with poverty, social breakdown and environmental degradation (Fuller and Prommer 2000; Adongo and Deen-Swarray 2006). As shown in Chapter 1 the average income in rural areas is considerably lower than in urban areas, albeit hiding the income differentials between formal and informal parts of towns. There is also an increasing differentiation between better-off households and poorer ones in rural Owambo – the distinction being primarily related to the vicinity to markets and privatisation of land (Frayne 2005; NPC 2006). As socio-cultural space, moreover, rural Owambo stands in sharp contrast to the formal town of Oshakati as well as its poor and crowded shantytowns: rural village "centres" are normally very small and made up of a water-post, a small open market, a *cuca*-shop and informal church structures supplemented by a school and a more formal store in larger villages. And rural homesteads, often with several dwelling-units, are located in the middle of large, extensive fields frequently separated by several kilometres from the nearest neighbour.

National migration surveys (Pendleton and Frayne 1998; NPC 2006) as well as localised studies (Graefe et al. 1994; Frayne 2005; Greiner 2009; Schmidt-Kallert 2009) maintain that urban-rural relations are frequent, intense and important in the current political economy of Namibia. On the face of it, my data from the Oshakati shantytowns underscore the close linkages between the urban and the rural: 86 percent of the households have access to a rural dwelling, 88 percent have access to agricultural land and 39 percent have cattle in rural Owambo (see Chapter 4). Moreover, in 54 percent of the households in the Oshakati shantytowns at least one member of the household visits rural areas often (once a month or more), 31 percent visit rural areas sometimes (less than once a month but more than once a year), and only 14 percent visit such areas seldom (less than once a year) or never. There is a larger proportion of households who seldom or never visit rural areas among the poor households (21 percent for male- and 18 percent for female headed units) than among the better-off households (9 percent for male- and none for female-headed households).

In the following pages, I will argue that in the case of Oshakati and Owambo the practical implications of such urban-rural relationships are considerably more arbitrary than is often assumed, varying with economic position, gender and age and perceived differently at the urban and rural ends of the relationships. The key aspect of such relationships is that to be sustainable in a context of generalised poverty they have to be reciprocal – first and foremost in the form of exchange of money or urban commodities for agricultural products – and thereby contribute to the well-being of the rurally based extended family as well as the shanty-based households and individuals. For Oshakati's shantytown dwellers, fulfilling expectations in rural relationships requires employment and income. Poor people who cannot fulfil these expectations are easily marginalised from rural relationships – not necessarily by discontinuing relations altogether but by limiting their material content. Having said this, expectations are lower towards women than men for contributing materially to their rural relatives, and children still represent an important link with the extended family in matrilineal Owambo – which makes the maintenance of urban-rural relationships easier for poor women and female-headed households than for poor men and male-headed households.

I will pursue the extent and content of the shanty dwellers' rural relationships by assessing their perceptions and practises as revealed mainly in focus group interviews and individual case-studies. I have related to the methodological challenge of observing urban-rural relations by accompanying some shanty-dwellers on visits to rural relatives and friends. And to better understand the rural end of the relationships, my colleagues and I have spent time and carried out a small survey in two Owambo villages with significant differences in levels of poverty. Arguing that relations with rural relatives are central not only for economic well-being but also that they have deep emotional connotations, I end the chapter by discussing the implications of the uncertainty and vulnerability following from the dearth of such relationships.

Urban-Rural Links

People in Oshakati's shantytowns relate to their villages of origin and their rural extended families as best they can from their positions as urban slum dwellers. Rural areas and extended families are generally seen as important localities and relationships, both from an emotional point of view and as part of people's coping strategies. In line with this, "double-rootedness" (Bank 1996:40) – in the form of employment and income in town and a homestead (*egumbo*), cattle and land in the village – is seen as the ultimate sign of success by most of the Oshakati shanty-dwellers. Most of the better-off shanty-dwellers I have come to know have village-based family members, land and cattle in their rural area of birth. And they all make a point out of going there at central times of the agricultural season to prove their rural rootedness and hence enhance their authority in the shanty as well as in the rural areas.

Yet people in Oshakati's shantytowns also see the rural and urban as worlds apart, through what Ferguson in the case of Zambia has called "cultural bifurcation" (Ferguson 1999:91): There are "village ways" and there are "town-ways", and the very rationale for moving to town is to get employment and income that is not obtainable in a rural area. People primarily see themselves as town people with rural connections, relating to this not by changing "style" to emphasise their rural embeddedness, as argued by Ferguson (1999) in the case of Zambia, but by playing out their urbanity in rural contexts the best they can. People with employment and income I have accompanied dress well, bring presents and talk about their work and urban lives. Poorer people may also act and dress "town like" and bring small tokens to try to prove their urban success – only to realise that it is near-impossible to escape their status as "urban failures". The following case-studies illustrate that difference and its consequences for the kinds of rural relations each is able to maintain.

Mateus Shonga and Johannes Martin are neighbours in Oneshila. But apart from that, their lives are quite different. Johannes lives in a brick house built with loans from the Government's Build Together Programme, is formally married, has four children and is permanently employed by the Oshakati Town Council. During my fieldwork periods Johannes went to his village at least once a month, and always took with him money, detergents, soap, sweets and other "urban" goods. He always wore a clean white shirt and jacket. He told me he had his own house there, as well as land and cattle looked after by his sister and her family. Johannes often had relatives and friends visiting from his village. They brought *mahangu*, spinach, meat and traditional brew (as custom, he said, demands), and tended to stay for long periods of time looking for work or just hanging around in town. Although they often became an economic burden, not taking them in, said Johannes, could jeopardise his position in the rural areas where he ultimately wanted to retire. "A house full of people is a rich house" (*waana omutanda kunongomba*) he told me once.

Mateus lives with his girlfriend and a child in a small iron shack where they barely manage to make ends meet through his occasional work unloading trucks, and from income from a small *cuca*-shop. Mateus was constantly in need of money when I knew him, and he told me he had tried to have his extended family support him through all possible means. He argued that it was not his fault that he could not find a job, and that they should at least make sure that he did not suffer. He had pleaded and threatened. At one stage he also moved back to his village, leaving his girlfriend and their child behind. He stayed with his old mother, and tried to open a field, get cattle to care for and build his own dwelling. But the extended family kept refusing to support him, according to Mateus himself, because they knew they would not get anything in return and were embarrassed by the situation he was in. He went back to Oshakati after only a couple of months. His rural relatives never visited him in town, even though "I know they are here from time to time" as he said. The last time I accompanied Mateus to his village was in 1999. In 2001, he claimed he had not been there since, because he knew his relatives would not help him and he found it too difficult to face them in his condition of poverty.

The rural relations of Oshakati shanty dwellers centre around extended family and kin, even though friends and other acquaintances also matter. We saw in Chapter 2 how kinship relations have become fluid and ambiguous with colonialism, war and urbanisation. The matrilineal system, vesting rights and obligations with the mother's lineage, is under pressure with changing residence patterns and perceptions of rights and obligations in people, commodities, land and cattle (Hakulinen 1992; Hinz 2002). When I discussed these issues with informants in the shanties, people argued emphatically for the continued importance of the extended family. However, heated discussions arose when the more specific distribution of authority and responsibility was on the table.

Nowhere is this ambiguity more apparent than in cases of inheritance, which traditionally took place with reference to cultural rules – with a man's principle heir being his uterine brother or (if no brother) the eldest son of his eldest sister, and a woman's principle heir being her eldest son or (if no son) her eldest brother (Estermann 1976; see also Becker and Hinz 1995). Dramatic scenes often follow the death of people in the Oshakati shantytowns, with family members not seen for years appearing to claim their shares. I have seen beds, tables, chairs and corrugated iron plates disappear even before the deceased is buried, at the same time as other family members have searched for bank cards and savings accounts.

Julia Lameka from Uupindi described the aftermath of her father's death as the hardest experience in her life:

> My father was rich when he died, and what struck me was how his wealth was distributed. People came and took everything. My father's cattle, our furniture and our car were carried away while we as children were watching helplessly. There is no law on our side. They even wanted to take the *mahangu* field, but the king of Uukwaludhi intervened.

For people in the Oshakati shantytowns, relations with rural areas and the extended family have become a matter of specific social relations of asymmetry, inequality and domination, or cooperation, reciprocity and solidarity, within a kinship system that is contested and ambiguous. In the following, I will pursue the rural relationships of the better-off and the poor shanty dwellers, as well as cross-cutting differences related to age and gender.

The Better-Off

For better-off people with employment and income, relations with the rural areas and extended family are vital parts of a longer term strategy shaped by images and ideals of "double-rootedness", as the following case illustrates: Vitus Nangalo was 45 years old in 2001, and was born in a village in Oshikoto. He came to Oshakati in the mid-1980s with a wife and a small child, settled in Oneshila and established a small tailoring shop. Making shirts and trousers for soldiers in town and traditional *kuku* dresses meant for rural women, he maintained relations with his village both in the last part of the war and after independence. His mother and a sister helped with selling the dresses in villages in Oshikoto. And in the mid-1990s Vitus Nangalo set up a small tailoring shop there, employing three women in addition to his sister. By that point he had himself stopped making clothes in Oshakati because of competition from imported (new and second hand) clothes, and had built a lodging place for people visiting Oneshila. Thus he maintained relations with his village, not only through the tailor-shop he had established there and weekly visits, but also by building a small house there for himself and investing in cattle. He said that he was not sure he would ever move back permanently, but added that the visits did him well and he liked to have the option of moving back "if Oshakati becomes difficult".

Better-off households like that of Vitus Nangalo, then, maintain relations with their village of origin and prove their rural rootedness by maintaining an *egumbo* and investing in land and cattle. Some also establish small *cuca*-shops and other commercial outlets in their village, which is both a point of contact and proves their urban success. The village-based part of the family often works the land and takes care of the cattle against payment in cash or kind (including grain at the time of harvest, or milk or offspring). Such relations are seen to root the shanty-dwellers in their villages in a different way than only exchange of rural and urban goods, as it shows a long-term commitment to the rural area. A teacher from

Uupindi took every Friday off to drive to his village and stock the *cuca*-shop he had built there, arguing that the main reason was to "help the village develop" rather than to manage the money the shop earned.

Maintaining rural ties thus makes it necessary to undertake regular rural visits, in order to nurture social relations and to ensure that one's rural resources are well taken care of and properly maintained. As a man in his mid-40s from Evululuku told me:

> I have to keep very strong ties with the village. I have an *epya* [field] at Oshaanga, and my second wife is taking care of everything there. My two wives cooperate well and do not fight. A house will fall apart if the husband does not make sure that these relations are strengthened by visiting.

Better-off people I have seen or accompanied going to a rural village dress up in their best clothes to prove their urban success; bring money and urban goods (still largely associated with clothes, blankets, soap, sugar and sweets as in colonial times but augmented by more recent commodities such as plastic utensils, body lotions, mosquito nets, torches and SIM cards for the few with mobile phones); and stay for the weekend when people are less busy and have time to talk. They not only stay in their *egumbo* with their closest kin, but also make sure to visit church, the local store and the local *cuca*- shop or bar, all in order to maintain a broad set of relationships and exchange news with neighbours and friends.

Maintaining and nurturing such rural relations also makes it necessary to receive people from the village in town. It is, in fact, nearly impossible to escape responsibilities for people who come to town from the village without jeopardising the relations one has built up. This not only concerns close kin, but also more distant rural relatives, friends and neighbours. While often a heavy burden on their resources, many of the better-off households in the Oshakati shanty-towns continuously house rural visitors. They are expected to bring rural foodstuff in the form of the staple millet (*mahangu*), dried spinach (*ekaka*) and meat and rural brew for more special occasions, but otherwise they leave it to the urban household to prove its hospitality. For more distant relatives and friends staying for a longer period of time this may be subject of negotiation.[1] A reputation for being uninviting in town may, in fact, be as damaging for urban-rural relations as a reputation for being stingy in transfers to the village as the following two cases show.

Frieda Shigwedha is a nurse and Naatale Shilimonula is a teacher. They both moved to Uupindi after independence, and they are both in positions to relate to their rural kin through "double-rootedness". Frieda (a woman in her mid-30s) had for years made every

---

[1] However, clear distinctions are made between visitors (*aatalelipo* or *aamenekeli*) expecting to be treated like household members, and tenants (for which the Afrikaans word *huurder* is used, as there is no word for "paying guests" in Oshiwambo) who pay for room and board and have no additional claims.

effort to visit her extended family and the village, and host rural relatives in town. She had also helped and cared for many people from her village who have been admitted to the hospital where she works. Her two children – both below school age – lived with her mother and father in the village during periods when Frieda worked late shifts, and Frieda provided them with money and food to avoid being a burden to her old parents. She didn't have any immediate plans to return to the village "because there is no work for me there", but she insisted that her home is in rural Ohangwena and that she will eventually move back. Nataale (a man in his early 30s) comes from the same region, but hardly ever went to the village, claiming that it was too far and that he didn't have time. "I have nothing to talk about there", he said. "They don't understand urban people like me". People from the village visiting him in town bitterly complained that he did not treat them properly and with respect, and never shared anything with them. On one occasion Nataale became seriously ill over a long period of time, and stayed alone in his house in a situation where most better-off shanty-dwellers would have gone to the village or called on relatives for help. Although not admitting it, he was clearly disturbed by the lack of care and attention from his kin.

The Poor

For poorer households in the Oshakati shantytowns, with no employment and few means of filling urban-rural relationships with material content, extended family linkages take on a different form. Shilongo Nampila was around 35 years old when I got to know him in 1999. He had come to Oshakati from a village in Oshikoto immediately after independence to look for employment, and lived in a shack at the "mercy" of a friend when I met him. In the village he had stayed with his old mother and an older sister with two children. The former died just before he left, and the father of the sister's children had moved in with her making him feel unwelcome. In Oshakati, Shilongo Nampila had never managed to get employment, and primarily worked as an occasional labourer in construction work which implied intermittent income. In longer periods of unemployment, his main potential source of support was his sister and her husband. He visited them in the village several times bringing sweets and other small tokens, but always came back empty-handed and disappointed. He blamed his brother-in-law "who does not really want me there".

Poor households like that of Shilongo Nampila from the outset do not fulfil the criteria of rural rootedness by owning a rural homestead, land and cattle, and they thus limit their options for longer-term strategies in their relationship with rural areas. They may have access to a dwelling and land through rural relatives (as younger unmarried men and unmarried women often have through their father, mother or matrilineal kin), but they still need to maintain relations with people who will help work the land and who expect something in return. The rural relationships of the poor are governed primarily by immediate problems to be solved, often in connection with acute needs for food or money. However, reviving their rural relationships only occasionally and in times of need does not fulfil the expectations of their rural kin for rural rootedness. As an older man in the village of Oniihende lamented:

> People who go to town say that it is boring here [i.e. in the village], and that they will go to town to work and make money. But what happens? They don't get a job and they don't have money. Then they expect us who live in villages to support them, but when we visit them they don't accept us. They think we are intruding in their family lives and expect us to pay our own expenses, while they do not pay anything when they come here.

For the poorest shanty dwellers, just travelling to the village may be an obstacle due to high transportation costs. They also know well that they will not be able to bring the type of urban goods that are expected from town people. Visiting the home village thus easily becomes a question of asking for rather than giving favours, with the consequence that they are marginalised in relation to old rural neighbours, friends and more distant relatives. One of the poorest residents in Kanjengedi (a small shanty-town neighbouring Oneshila) with the name of Erasmus Negonga had come to Oshakati in the mid-1980s to join the military. He described his life at that time as "good", but also admitted that life after independence had been very difficult. One time he had walked the 25 kilometres to his rural home village, Ompundja. I asked him on his return whom he had seen. He said he had visited his mother and half-sister where he had been given some food. He had been to neither the church nor the *cuca*-shop, he told me, explaining that he did not have anything to contribute and that it was difficult for him because people always asked what he did in town. "Since I don't have employment and income, it is difficult for me to know what to say".

Even close kin – mothers, fathers, brothers, sisters and matrilineal relatives – may eventually weaken or cut ties with their poor urban kindred. This does not mean that there is no affection when poor and destitute shanty-dwellers manage to visit their kin in their village, but the relationship is affected by poverty. I have seen old people in villages overburdened by grandchildren and requests for support from children in town crying when they meet or talk about children who they are not able to support. They cannot afford to provide food and other rural resources in a depressed and poor rural context, and the burden of having close relatives having ended up as poor urban dwellers easily becomes heavy to bear. I also know poor shanty-dwellers who have spent their last Namibian dollars on clothes, sugar, soap and sweets and gone to their village to try to re-establish relationships, only to be met with suspicion.

In one case a shanty-dweller I travelled with at the time of harvest in 1995 did not even get to see his sister and her family on arrival to his village. Paulus Abiatar was very poor and had no income in town except for occasional piecemeal work, and though not saying so outright I knew he was going to the village to try to get *mahangu*. He himself brought nothing. When arriving at the dwelling, his sister, her husband and their four children were not home but working in the field of a wealthy farmer, and Paulus Abiatar went to wait at a friend's place a couple of kilometres away. After a while a boy arrived, and told Paulus Abiatar that his sister could not see him (as in most villages in Namibia, news spread fast...). Paulus Abiatar said that this had happened before: Her husband suspected that his wife gave her brother food and money from their own meagre resources, and refused her to see him. Going back to Oshakati with only a small bag of *mahangu* that he got from his friend, Paulus Abiatar complained about the lack of support from his sister but also admitted that it was difficult for her to help him as she and her family were so poor themselves.

The problematic relationship between the urban poor and their rural relatives is often exacerbated by the inability of the former to host even their immediate family in town. Living in small shacks, tents or even in the open air, they simply cannot accommodate visitors from rural areas, let alone feed them. Rural visitors also find it problematic to stay with people who have failed in their urban lives, violating, again, the very rationale for leaving the rural areas which is to find employment and earn money. In fact relatives of poor urbanites often end up lodging in one of the room-for-rent places in the shanties, which may be cheap but that are also noisy and violent. This is seen as an additional confirmation of the failure of the urban partner in the relationship to live up to expectations. As Dhimbulukweni Floriana related:

> In 1990 my husband lost his job, our income shrank, and we did not have money any more. I started to feel how my house was becoming poor. Before independence we used to eat three times a day, but that was reduced to one meal per day. During the good years [*omvula ombwaanawa*] we used to send money to our relatives in the village. Although they did not come to visit us in town there was always good communication. When we became poor, they stopped contacting us ...When my husband died in August 2000, I was deeply disappointed by our extended families. None of them came to the funeral, and if your family members fail to come to your husband's funeral then something is wrong. I suspect the reason is that he died a poor man. Not even a single cow was slaughtered, and he was buried the same day [rather than after a period of wake].

The weakening of urban-rural ties among the poorest section of the shanty population is experienced as highly painful and problematic. People in the shantytowns are acutely aware of the importance of these relationships for their own well-being, but there is often simply no choice. They cannot fill the relationship with material content over time, and their extended family members who control resources in the rural areas (be they land, cattle, pensions or other means) have to favour family members who are in a position to preserve viable urban relationships for them. Perhaps the most distressing expression of failure to maintain urban-rural relationships in the Oshakati shanties takes place at the height of each agricultural season: A local entrepreneur based in Uupindi employs people who are in desperate need of money and transports them to nearby farms to work as agricultural labourers under hard conditions and for very low pay. For the poor shanty-dwellers this embodies their failure to get proper urban jobs, as well as their failure to maintain reciprocal relations with rural kin and having to revert to agricultural labour.

Age and Gender
The nature of relationships with the rural areas and the extended family vary not only with economic position and poverty, but also with age and gender. Old shanty-dwellers have a personal history and a personal attachment to the rural areas, and not being in a position to go back to these areas during old age is a sign of their having fallen into utter destitution in town. For old Angolans in the shantytowns this seemed particularly hard, as they knew they would not only end their days in an "alien" setting like a town but also in a foreign country. Carlos Mendes and his wife Maria Conceição were more than 70 years old when I met them in 1995. They had come to Oshakati in 1975 together with other refugees from the war in Angola in which their only two sons died in the late 1980s. Carlos and Maria had made ends meet by hosting Angolan visitors in an extra shack they had built, and by reselling Angolan foodstuffs brought by regular visitors (including the very strong Angolan version of chilli called *gindungo*). Through regular contact with people who had news from their village in the Cunene province across the border, they kept informed and attached. But when they lost their extra shack and hence their main source of income in a fire in 2000, they had no way of getting the money to return. With less contact with the home district as visitors failed to appear, moreover, they became uncertain about whether they would find relatives to take care of them if they should manage to go back.

Many younger poor people and their children have little or no direct personal experience with village life and know few if any extended family members. Young people often use the Oshiwambo expression "*iinyakwi*" about things rural, which literally means "old things" or "dirt". And children in the shantytowns often demonstrate their distance from rurality by role-playing the part of rural people through walking, looking and acting strangely, pretending to bump into people, cars and buildings being a favourite stunt that always stirs laughs. Samuel Nambadja was 15 years old when I met him in 2001. He had been born in Oshakati, and had grown up in one of the poorest households in Evululuku. He still lived with his parents. With several convictions in the local traditional court for theft and burglary (and "one visit to the police station" as he put it), he seemed to be on his way to a life in poverty and difficulties. Samuel told me he had been to a rural village only once in his life, for the funeral of his mother's uncle in Oshikoto. Perhaps influenced by the event, he argued strongly that he would never live in a village as there was "no work" and "no shops and restaurants" – apparently forgetting that both were out of reach for him also in town. For many poor young people having been born and living in the shantytowns, potentially vital rural relationships are never established.

Women do not have the same expectations vested in them to become employed, to earn money and to support their rural family as men do (see Chapter 2), making the failure to live up to such expectations less dramatic for them than for unemployed men and male-headed households. Children also provide a critical conduit for the maintenance of social relations between the urban and the rural socio-cultural settings. They are still considered the "property" (*aakwanezimo*) and responsibility of the matrilineal extended family, and contribute to making it possible for women to visit their village and relatives without bringing money and urban goods. Again seen from the vantage point of my trips to rural areas in crowded mini-buses, many women's insistence on bringing their small children along is exactly to deepen and cement relationships with rural kin and friends. We have seen that the better-off female headed households are the most frequent visitors to rural areas and, as the following case shows, they often make active use of their rural relationships as a means of ensuring a livelihood for themselves.

Lucia Mbunde lived in a two-room iron shack in Uupindi, and her immediate circumstances offered little evidence as to how she could make ends meet other than from selling home-brewed beer and *okapana*, which she appeared to do most of each day. Lucia seemed always to have lots of children around, though no man was to be seen, and she always displayed a sense of self-confidence. One day she was unusually nicely dressed, and I greeted her in the normal urban fashion (long enough, but not nearly as long as the full rural version):

> *Wa lala po, Meme? – Ee – Onawa ngaa? – Ee. Ngoye wa lala po, Tate? – Ee – Onawa ngaa? – Ee* – You look nice today. Are you going anywhere? – Yes, I am going to Cape Town on a business trip – You are what? – I am going to Cape Town on a business trip – What do you mean? – I am going down with relatives and friends from my village in Ohangwena. We hire a bus and a driver three or four times a year, bringing down baskets made in the village to sell, and buying second-hand clothes that we sell in the rural areas when we come back. To make it cheap we sleep in the bus. The whole trip takes about three weeks, and I make a profit of about 1500 Rand each time. It helps me a lot, and I keep contact with my village. It is a long trip, and my job is mainly to arrange practicalities. They tell me I am an expert because I live in a town!

Despite the importance of matrilineal relations and children for maintaining rural relationships, however, also women's relationships with people in rural areas have to be filled with some material content over time in order not to be jeopardised. As the following case shows, poor shantytown women with poor rural relatives have few options of rural support.

Sofia Kallo was among the very poorest female headed households in Oshoopala, living in a one-room shack and showing signs of under-nutrition. She had come to Oshakati in the late 1980s in search for work and money to house and feed herself and her two children (and a third which was on its way). With a mother, a sister with a child and a handicapped brother in the village, and few prospects of getting married with three children from three different men, she told me she had really had no choice. She managed well in Oshakati as long as there were "soldiers here with money" as she put it. But since independence her life had been a constant struggle to make ends meet, with a meagre income from selling *okapana*. Her relations with men had never lasted, and two of her children had died. When I first met her in 1995, Sofia Kallo told me she had travelled to her village to seek help several times after life turned difficult. Her mother, she claimed, had a small income from selling tombo and she and her daughter still living in the village had a small field. But her mother had given priority to supporting her son and to helping her other daughter's children. When I last met her in 2001, Maria Kallo told me she had not visited her mother for two years. Though she claimed that their relationship with her was good, I could see that her inability to maintain the relationship with her relatives in the village troubled her greatly.

While better-off shanty-dwellers actively use rural relationships as part of their coping strategies as urban dwellers and in order to maintain the option of retreating to their rural area of origin, then, the poorest shanty-dwellers do not manage to do so and easily become marginalised, or marginalise themselves from, such relationships. The poorest men and women without active kin relationships and access to agricultural resources not only find themselves in a difficult material situation, but also violate deep cultural sentiments of being Owambo. In the language of Hiltunen (1993:34),

> [an Owambo] without descendants is nobody and the flowing power of lineage is terminated in him. Life is understood as an endless continuum encompassing past generations, the present and the generations still to be born. This implies the collective nature of life. An individual is significant only as a member of his own community (family, kin, clan, subtribe).

Rural-Urban Links

To better understand the rural end of the urban-rural relationships, my colleagues and I have spent time in the villages of Ompundja and Oniihende. Ompundja is situated in the Oshana region, only 15 km from Oshakati. It is a large village by Namibian standards with 200 households, and boasts a primary school, a church, a clinic and a small shop. Oniihende is a small village of only 51 households, located in the Ohangwena region towards the Angolan border. The village is situated 30 km from the nearest proper road and 105 km from Oshakati, and has no shops, schools, clinics or other facilities. Albeit largely similar in appearance, with *egumbos* located in the middle of agricultural fields, differences are evident in the way people speak, dress, greet and eat, as well as in more external signs: In Ompundja, cars, bicycles, radios, bottled beer, cell-phones and other signs of modernity are visible all over. In Oniihende these are hardly present at all.

In both villages, most households consist of older people staying with their younger children, grandchildren and other dependants.[2] The average household size is 5.3, which is close to the average in the Oshakati shantytowns even though the composition is different: 18 percent of the population are more than 45 years and 31 percent are children below ten years of age. The people absent mainly belong to the economically active group between approximately 20 and 40 years of age. 57 percent of the households are male headed and 43 percent are female-headed.

There are differences between the villages in terms of income and expenditures. Household income is higher in Ompundja with 55 percent of the households earnings more than 250 NAD per month and 15 percent earning more than 3000 NAD per month (at least partly a reflection of the vicinity to employment and markets in town), and lower in Oniihende with *no* household earning more than 250 NAD per month. Ompundja is also better off than Oniihende in terms of agricultural production and livestock: in the former village, households harvest an average of 140 *oorata* (i.e. bags of approximately 15 kg) and 85 percent of the households own cattle, while households in Oniihende harvest an average of 34 *oorata* and only 47 percent of the households have cattle, most of them with small herds. Old-age pensions are, as I shall return to, the most important source of income for 53 percent of the households.

Differences in geographical locations and in levels of well-being and poverty between Ompundja and Oniihende find their expressions in differences in the frequency of relations with urban-based relatives and friends as well as in different perceptions of urban life.[3] Looking at rural-urban relationships, in Ompundja 50 percent of the households have members who visit urban areas often (i.e. at least once a month) and only 15 percent visit seldom (i.e.

---

[2] All figures are from a survey carried out for this study by Selma Nangulah, Martha Naanda, Frieda Iigonda and Gabriel Daniel from the University of Namibia (see Tvedten and Nangulah 1999).

[3] In our case, these differences are exacerbated by history (see Chapter 2). The villages around Oshakati were the most important recruitment areas for the South African Defence Force and young women seeking income, giving people closer contact with urban life. Villages such as Oniihende, on the other hand, were not only located in areas where recruitment to Swapo was high but which also suffered the most from South African atrocities, giving Oshakati strong negative connotations as an urban place. When people are moving to town from Oniihende they are still taken aside by the village elders and told about the dangers of urban life and the importance of maintaining a good relationship with their kindred and their village. In Ompundja, going to town is more of an everyday and privatised affair.

less than once a year) or never, with the equivalent figures for Oniihende being 15 and 53 percent. Discourses about towns and urban life are of two main types, both expressing perceptions of emic dualities between rural and urban socio-cultural space: For many people in Ompundja towns imply employment, income and access to goods and services that are not available in the village. According to our survey there, the main advantages of living in towns are seen as job opportunities, less hard work, availability of shops and markets, closeness to hospitals, better educational facilities, and "options for meeting many different people".

In contrast, for many people in Oniihende, urban areas are stigmatised around topics of crowdedness, violence, immorality and loss of culture. "Why do our women go to town?" an old woman lamented. "It is a place for prostitutes". "I don't think it is good to live in urban areas, because people there are only going from place to place; when poverty strikes they turn into thieves and have nowhere to turn to, and once they are back here they bring trouble with them," a man complained. "I cannot get used to the noise in urban areas, and recently one of my relatives was stabbed to death in Evululuku. I think there is more misery in urban than in rural areas," a woman argued. And, according to an older man,

> [i]n rural areas one has the advantage of having one's own fields to cultivate. Friendship in rural areas is also better than in towns. There a person cannot eat with a neighbour if he is hungry. Here neighbours who have ploughs can plough your field for free. In town nothing is done without charge. Friends who help each other in rural areas do not expect any type of refund. *Ondolopa ondolopa ashike* ("a town is just a town").

For rural people without prospects for employment and income, then, urban life has little attraction, particularly as people gain increasing knowledge about urban poverty and hardships. Therefore, when people still move to town, this is an expression of the even harder conditions found in many rural areas (Norman 1996; GON 2003). According to a man in his mid-40s in Oniihende:

> [t]he youth are going to towns to sell *okapana*, and not to work on farms and in mines as we used to. We [the] parents are fed up with towns. You expect a person going to town to bring something useful, not only do *okapana*. Some who go to town write letters to their parents telling them that they have arrived, but others keep quiet. We only send food to those who have contact with us.

For rural families that have urban relatives with employment and income, the link to town is seen as an asset. Urban, modern commodities are coveted for the status they offer, and having successful urban relatives gives one prestige. Education ranks high, but formal employment and income rank higher. A man in Oniihende explains:

> Even in rural areas some traditional patterns are changing. Like in the past: neighbours used to cook and call up other neighbours to eat and celebrate, but now this is becoming rare. Now

the rich do not like to associate with the poor, and the poor envy the rich. People nowadays are even jealous of each other, especially if you have someone supporting you from urban centres.

When better-off and successful shanty-dwellers visit their relatives and their village, they are often given a full rural welcome in the guest section (*oshinyanga*) of the *egumbo*, with traditional drinks and traditional food in the form of *ondjuva* (chicken), *onyama* (beef) and *oshifima* (*mahango* porridge). Family members who have failed in town by not getting employment and who embody poverty and despair are pitied. They are still received by their closest family and given food, but the latter are normally less prone to invite other relatives, neighbours and friends and such visits are often what an old woman described as "sad rather than joyous moments".

The end of each month when pensions are paid out to the many older people, living in rural areas is a particularly tense period. Visits from town tend to intensify at those times, and many rural families know that the pressure will be considerable to share with their poor urban relatives. The headman in Ompundja told me that there are old people who leave for other villages at pension payment time, precisely to avoid the pressure for sharing their pensions with relatives and other acquaintances from urban areas. In any case, he pointed out, most of the money is used to support children whom relatives have sent to be cared for by the old pensioners.

Women and female-headed households are in a special position compared to men and male-headed households, also seen from a rural perspective. It has struck me many times how people in rural areas talk about urban based daughters, sisters, nieces and other female relatives in a more inclusive way than they do about men. Some people still define women who have left as part of the *egumbo* or household, in a way which they will not do about men. A woman in Oniihende states:

> The most important reason why people go to town is that they need money to support themselves. When they come back to the village they bring soaps, cooking oil and body lotions. My family lives in Oshakati and sends us money to buy maize meal flour. I think it is because she is a woman, and women are responsible people – unlike men. Men forget where home is, and never support parents. If there are two households with children in urban areas, one with a male and one with a female, the one with a female will be well-off and the other not.

In a matrilineal setting like Owambo, children are also still seen as an extended family responsibility and as a potential future investment in better times, particularly through education. Many better-off urban households send their children to villages like Ompundja and Oniihende at a young age to "learn Owambo culture" as they put it, in line with the notion of double rootedness.[4] They maintain close contact through frequent visits, and pay

---

[4] As we saw in Chapter 4 on population and household characteristics, there is a relatively large

for expenses for example related to food, clothing and education. A girl in Ompundja had lived with her grandparents throughout primary school (visiting Oshakati and her parents at least two weekends a month), and was on her way back to Oshakati and her parents to take secondary school when I met her in 2001. For the poorest rural and urban households, however, the options for this type of relationships are much more constrained. Most poor households in the Oshakati shantytowns do not have means or relationships to send their children to rural areas, and the poorer households who do manage to send children to the village often do so without any accompanying resources, leaving the children in precarious situations. Several of the street children I have met in the shantytowns have grown up with grandparents in a rural areas, where they told me life was very hard and they did not go to school. Coming back to Oshakati when the grandparents died or were too old to take care of them, they found themselves lost with little or no contact with the town-based part of their family.

In small-scale village communities like Ompundja and Oniihende, then, it is nearly impossible for unemployed and poor urban dwellers to escape the stigma of urban failure, and relatives and friends are unwilling to support people from whom they know they can expect little in return. In the harsh words of an older man in Ompundja,

> [w]e do not support people who have no contact and do not support us and we do not feel we have any responsibility towards them. The only time we have [responsibility] is when they die. We have to bury them.

For the poorest in the Oshakati shantytowns, then, rural life and rural connections do not present themselves as a "rural option" as argued by studies from Namibia referred to in the introduction to this chapter, by Ferguson (1999) and Hansen (1997) in the case of Zambia and by Bank (2001) in the case of South Africa's East London. That is because they cannot fulfil rural expectations of employment and income; they cannot fill their relationships with rural relatives with material content; and they tend to be marginalized from such relationships over time. Some also withdraw themselves, giving up making more out of the relationships and avoiding the humiliation of being urban failures in a rural context.

Dealing with Uncertainty

While rural areas and extended family relations may be important for daily coping strategies, they are absolutely vital at more critical times in life. The urban poor are usually able to find some way to cope in their daily lives, but their vulnerability as poor is determined by their ability to mobilise support and resources in extraordinary situations. There are

---

proportion of absent children from 5-19 years in the Oshakati shantytowns.

junctures in life when extended family is seen to have special responsibilities. These include important events like childbirth, weddings and funerals which people believe should be rurally rooted, and also critical occurrences such as diseases like AIDS and malaria (the second biggest killer in the Oshakati shanties). Other such crises include a sudden loss of dwelling and property, and criminal convictions involving compensation. Not being in control at such stages in life implies a basic vulnerability and *uncertainty* that is at the core of the selves of Oshakati's poor shanty dwellers.

My most vivid experience of how deep the responsibility of the extended family may reach, and how vital it may be, is from a court case that took place in the Uukwambi traditional court at Uukwangula in November 2001 (see also Uukwambi, n.d.). A poor white Portuguese farmer, speaking fluent Oshiwambo and living in the village of Olupale on the Angolan side of the border, had taken the relatives of an Uukwambi man to court. He insisted the relative stole 63 sheep from him in 1982, and the claim for compensation was 63 sheep or 6000 Namibian Dollars. The culprit himself died in 1983 in Uukwambi, apparently poisoned by his wife's relatives for having left her for another woman. The case had come a long way: The headman (*soba*) from the village in Angola sent a letter to the chief of Uukwambi more than a year prior to the court case, insisting that the case be heard and compensation given. The chief had located a poor household from the Uupindi shantytown as the closest family of the culprit.

At Uukwangula, all Uukwambi senior headmen (who included three women...) were present. The hall was filled with more than 50 relatives of the accused, who had realised that they could be made accountable. The suitor was there with two sons brought from Angola, a few of his Namibian wife's relatives living in Owambo, and the former wife of the alleged culprit and her relatives, who had been requested to take part as witnesses. The atmosphere was tense: Much was at stake, and each party gave introductory testimonies about the tragic implications of the loss of the sheep, and pleas that the case was too old and the culprit dead too long to make the extended family accountable. The deliberations lasted for several hours. Some put on angry voices, some cried, and some younger people seemed absolutely dumbfounded by such an encounter with tradition. The outcome was that the extended family of the culprit was sentenced to pay back the sheep or money, leaving it to an old family head to fulfil the obligations within a stipulated time. For the Uupindi family the verdict meant even further hardships.

The involvement of the extended family in central events like childbirth, weddings and funerals has a socio-cultural as well as a material side to it, and is seen as critical in cementing and confirming extended family relations and their boundaries. Affinal as well as consanguineal family members involving themselves in such incidents in practice say "yes, you are one of us, and we will support you and your household in times of need". That is why extended family presence is attributed such importance. Involvement by the extended family implies outstanding claims in a co-operative extended network, building cultural and emotional, as well as material and reciprocal relationships – the importance of which has been clear to me in a large number of incidents that I have heard of or taken part in throughout my years of visiting Oshakati. These include a young high-school student in Oneshila who managed to continue her education despite having had a child because her sister came from the village to take care of it; a young man from Uupindi who finally managed to convince the parents of a girl he had a child with that he would be able to take care of them when he managed to upgrade his shack with help from an uncle in Windhoek; and the extended family members who came all the way from Caprivi to take a relative, sick with AIDS, back to his village to let him die there when the disease was still highly stigmatised.

These ideals notwithstanding, the economic position of the poorest shanty households tends to limit the depth and range of extended family relationships in such important acts and events. I have described how relationships need to be maintained on a regular basis to be sustainable and how, for many poor people, their inability to contribute materially is difficult and painful and may lead to their social marginalisation. People in the shantytowns told me that many new-born children die because (often young) mothers do not have the resources to be able to call on relatives who can guide them. I also heard of several cases of young petty thieves (*botstsotsos*) who had been lynched or beaten in the shanties, precisely because they were men who people knew had no supportive relatives and hence could not pay compensation for what they had done. And there are frequently cases where poor people without supportive relatives have become sick and have been left alone because people in the neighbourhood cannot afford to take them to hospital or feel no responsibility for doing so.

Poverty thus puts even the role of the extended family at life crisis moments under strong pressure, often limiting people's extended networks to their very closest family members only. Among these, mother's brother (*otatekulu gwe a valwa nayina*) and brothers (*aamwayinamati awe*) take on a special importance. Mother's oldest brother has a special responsibility for the well-being of his nephews and nieces, particularly if they experience severe problems and for supporting their future through education. People in the shantytowns know well how important education can be for employment and an urban life-style. In the only case I know where a girl from one of the shantytowns made it all the way to the University of Namibia, she did so because of an uncle: The girl had grown up in Oshoopala with her mother, who had a low-paid job as a cleaner in a government office. The uncle was a teacher living alone without children in Windhoek, and he had supported his sister's daughter through her education. For him, his sister told me, her daughter was like his own child.

For poor children in the shanties without support from the extended family, however, making it through school is considerably more difficult. Many poor parents and their children know they will not be able to make it without such support. Taking part in their first day at a primary school in the outskirts of Oneshila, children from poor households (discernible by being poorly dressed on a day parents wanted to present their child the best way they could) seemed to enter with hesitation, stayed in the margins of the school-yard, and found seats in the back of the class-room. Teachers emphasised how the poorest children differed in their interest in learning and their ability to concentrate. On the particular first day of school I observed, the son of one of Oneshila's poorest women was first ridiculed for not having a uniform, then rebuked for making a noise in the class-room, and finally expelled for three days for fighting in the school-yard. When I met him two weeks later, he had still not gone back to school.

Brothers have special responsibilities for protecting and taking care of younger siblings in critical events such as domestic violence, sudden loss of income through unemployment; loss of property through damage or theft; and diseases such as AIDS suddenly making people into dependants. The most common explanation given to me for a number of severe cases of repeated domestic violence was that the women concerned had no brother to protect them. In one case, a visit by a brother was enough for a young woman in Uupindi to get out of a violent relationship that she had suffered in for a long time. He helped his sister move out with her things and settle in another shantytown, and simply told the boyfriend to stay away. In another case, two brothers severely beat the boyfriend of their sister and chased him away from her shack. "People who do not have a brother [from the same mother]", a young woman in Uupindi explained, "are the ones who are in real trouble".

But even key relationships with matrilateral uncles and brothers may be jeopardised: I have repeatedly asked very poor and destitute shantytown people whether they don't have somebody to help alleviate the critical situations they face; and many answer that while they do have a mother, a father, a brother, a sister or an uncle, those relatives cannot or will not help them. Usually they explain it by arguing that their family have always been poor, and that "there is nothing to share" as one put it. But there are also stories of disrupted relationships: Some argue that they have not had contact with their extended families since the war (admitting that they found themselves on the wrong side of that conflict and did things their family will not forgive)[5], and some have become increasingly marginalised or excluded over a period of time as the following case shows.

Akiser Kashupi was 19 years old when I first met him in 1991. He had grown up in a village in Onheleiwa close to the Angolan border in what he described as a "very poor family",[6]

---

[5] Often, this involved raids and killings in their own or close villages, which was one strategy by the South African military to make sure that Namibian soldiers remained on their side (Brown 1995; Erasmus 1995)

[6] As many people in that area (which historically has been under heavy influence from Angola-based Catholic missions), he spoke Portuguese and used the term *pobríssimo*.

with his mother and three younger sisters. He seemed lost and in despair when I met him, and said he had moved to town at independence (i.e. the year before) to find employment and support his family but found it very hard. He had secured a short-time job with a local entrepreneur as a cleaner the first few months, which had made it possible for him to build a shack and give a little money to his mother. When I met him he managed with a very small income from transporting goods for women working at Omatala, and food (mainly *mahango*) he received from his family in the village. The three or four times I came across him after that, he seemed poorer and poorer and more and more bewildered. He was still struggling to get by, and told me he simply did not manage to earn enough money to send to is mother and sisters in the village. He could only afford to go to there about once a year, and the last time I met him he had just come back from such a trip. He had gone there empty-handed, and he had come back empty-handed: For the first time his mother had not given him any food to take to town, and he told me that his inability to support her and her unwillingness to give him food from her own meagre harvest made him feel "useless" and "ashamed" (*inútil e vergonhado*): "But what can I do? I don't have a life here in Oshakati, and I cannot return to the village because we don't have a sufficiently big field and I cannot confront my family with nothing".

Weakened or disrupted rural links strike deep chords among most Oshakati shanty-dwellers, and are a constant field of contention, bitterness or shame. We shall see in later chapters that marginalisation and social exclusion have a number of implications for acts and events. However, being marginalised or left out by the extended family seems to make people feel particularly vulnerable, and witchcraft and sorcery are common ways to relate to such disconnections.[7] Contemporary witchcraft represents thoroughly modern manifestations of uncertainties, moral disquiet and unequal rewards in the contemporary world (Comaroff and Comaroff 1999; see also Moore and Sanders 2001), and anthropologists have emphasised its importance in poor urban areas (Hansen 1995:178; Ferguson 1999:158).

Community leaders in Oshakati's shantytowns say that there has been an increase in the use of witchcraft with urbanisation and increased poverty, with witchcraft having taken precedence over "good magic" (Hiltunen 1993). Still according to community leaders, the

---

[7] In Owambo there is a long tradition of witchcraft and sorcery as well as "good magic", as thoroughly described by Hiltunen (1986 and 1993). A witch (*omulodhi*) worked involuntarily without being aware of her or his abilities, while sorcerers (*omutikili*) employed magical techniques and bewitched on purpose. Both caused misfortunes in the form of abortions, birth of twins, sickness and death. While witchcraft "dramatised and thus reinforced social norms" (Hiltunen 1986:55), good magic (*okuanekela*) was used to increase production, prevent misfortune from entering the family, and heal and reconcile through the use of diviners (*oonganga*).

most commonly accused are relatives, who are seen to revenge themselves on family-members who have "made it" or caused misfortune. José António is a case in point.

> Life in the shantytown [as a soldier] was good. Our *cuca*-shop was popular. All our Angolan friends who were in the army used to visit us, and they used to drink a lot of cold beer.[But] we were not clever that time, and did not imagine that one day we may be out of work. As you know God strikes without warning [*kalunga ohaa denge ina popya*]. I worked for the 101 Battalion until 1990, when our life changed. I was bewitched by my own family, who wanted my wealth. After I was bewitched I became mentally ill, and used to see people who tried to kill me. My wife started to support the house by selling at Omatala. I am now better, but our income situation is deteriorating.

Sitting in and observing in a community court in Uupindi in November 2001, I heard a woman claimed that her ex-husband's sister had made her lose a child and sink deep into poverty. She was advised by the old man presiding over the court to see a traditional healer[8] to resolve the problem, as he could not prove her ex-sister-in-law was to blame. There are also more private expressions of the perceived power of witchcraft. For protection many wear small amulets and ornaments that are well hidden (such as the *omagwe* that women wear around their waist), feeling uneasy about such expressions of traditional beliefs in an urban setting. And some old traditions have also been revitalised, such as a ritual known as *epititho* ("strong wind") to protect children against an urban and hostile environment and poverty. In the Oshakati shantytowns such revitalisation of witchcraft and rituals may be interpreted as acts to create some order in a confusing and oppressive urban world, where the weakening and discontinuation of relations with rural areas and the extended family are seen as particularly detrimental, not only for current survival but also for future social security.

Concluding this chapter on the relevance of rural relationships for understanding why the poorest in the Oshakati shantytowns seem trapped in poverty and destitution, urban-rural relations have been a central concern in Southern African anthropology, from the Copperbelt (see e.g. Epstein 1958, Gluckman 1961) and East London studies (see e.g. Mayer 1963) to the more recent studies by Tranberg Hansen (1997), Ferguson (1997, 1999) and Bank (1996, 2001). Central topics in the early studies were the extent to which migrants from rural areas became "permanently urbanised" and lost their "rural identity", and to what extent social relations were maintained between the urban dwellers and their rural relatives and friends. The later studies criticise old dualisms and problematise notions of "urban"

---

[8] Traditional healers (*ongangwa oshiludlu*) have become increasingly common in the Oshakati shantytowns, and are normally older people who know the herbs to use for treatment as well as traditional "vaccination" (making incision with sharp instruments) and "sucking surgery" (creating a vacuum and sucking blood) – often used in combination with manipulation of the spirit world.

and "rural" by pointing out that tradition and modernity are matters of degree both in geographical and cultural terms. Ferguson (1999:40) is struck by the prominence of the "rural option", and the extent to which the desperate conditions of the urban economy are leading even the apparently most permanently urbanised people to contemplate rural retreat. Hansen (1997:110) makes a similar point by arguing that as Lusaka's economy deteriorated, the involvement of Mtendere residents with the countryside increased and diversified. And Bank for his part emphasises the "double-rootedness" of most people in the East London shantytowns, with "patterns of circular migration and urban-rural mobility [being] deeply inscribed in the social fabric of Duncan village" (Bank 1996:43).[9]

While most current studies of urban-rural relationships in Southern Africa focus on continuities with rurality and tradition, however, I have argued that, in the case of the Oshakati shantytowns, maintaining such relations through investments in rural rootedness and the fulfilment of minimal cultural decencies in relation to kindred require economic means that the poor commonly do not have. For the poorest men and the poorest male-headed households, not being able to maintain such links strikes deep personal chords and further marginalises and encapsulates them as shanty-dwellers. For poor women and female-headed households, the expectations for filling these relations with material content are lower than in the case of men and their children represent a mutual bond with matrilineal kin, both making their rural relations more sustainable. For both, however, urban life and urban connections tend to take precedence in their daily struggle for survival. This is the subject of the next chapter.

---

[9] Similar points have been made for Malawi (Englund 2002); Zimbabwe (Anderson 2001) and the Democratic Republic of Congo (Devisch 1995).

7 Urban Connections

Continuing to explore my research question of why some people living in the Oshakati shantytowns seem trapped in abject poverty and give up making more of out of their lives, I will now look at urban-based relationships with neighbours, friends, workmates, employers, and agents of the state and the market. We saw in the last chapter how the poorest shanty-dwellers, especially the men among them, faced difficulties in maintaining relationships with the kin and others in rural areas. What this suggests is that urban-based relations are particularly vital for their well-being. Such relationships are vital for employment, income and material support. It is also important for enabling people to gain a sense of belonging in an urban context where we have seen that a divided town developed over time, with a formal centre and residential areas fulfilling conventional notions of modern urbanism and surrounding shantytowns being characterised by density of population, by inequalities and poverty.

While both parts of town are effectively the outcome of the same structural political and economic processes, people perceive and relate to the two kinds of area as distinct socio-economic and cultural entities. This reflects economic realities, as well as perceptions of the shantytowns being socio-cultural settings of and on their own. Instead of recognising a socio-cultural dichotomy dividing the "urban and modern" from the "rural and traditional", people in Oshakati's shantytowns add a third socio-spatial category, perceiving socio-cultural space as a *trichotomy* of urban and modern, rural and traditional, and the poor and violent shanty-setting. In line with this, the formal town is generally referred to by insiders as well as outsiders by the neutral Afrikaans word *ondoolopa* (from *"dorp"*); rural villages are referred to by the neutral Oshiwambo word *omukunda* ("area with houses built with poles"); and the shantytowns are denoted by the diminutive *uulukanda* ("little or dirty town") or the derogatory *obumbashi* which literally means "a blow out of diarrhoea" indicating uncleanliness and chaos. When I in the following pages denote the formal town and the urban life-style it entails as "modern" in contrast to the shantytowns and shanty-life, then, this echoes emic perceptions among the shanty-dwellers themselves.

My central argument in this chapter is that the structural oppression and the economic positions of the shanty-dwellers, as these were depicted in the first part of this study, have strong bearings on the types of urban-based social relationships shanty-dwellers become involved in. I show that only the better-off shanty-dwellers are in positions to link up to the formal town through employment and through their command of an urban life-style. The poorest, on the other hand, are marginalised from the formal town and its options for employment, and, as I shall show, are forced into shanty-based relationships that encapsulate them in poverty. Having said this, the argument is also here qualified by gender: With higher expectations vested in men for employment, provisioning and command of urban style, unemployment and poverty is experienced as more dramatic for them than for women. Female headed households and women, with the exception of the poorest among them, are involved in more extensive relationships and activities that often transgress the formal and informal town, primarily related to the informal economy.

To start probing into the complex sets of social relationships among Oshakati's shanty dwellers, I return to some early field notes from 1993 (translated from original text in Norwegian). I stayed for a whole day at a central place in Uupindi, the most congested of the shantytowns, observing and trying to make sense of what I was seeing and experiencing; and I wrote:

> It is early morning, at six o'clock, and already frantic activity. Women have started to cook porridge on fireplaces outside their houses or shacks; children roam sleepily around with some already playing with neighbours; and men come out of their shacks or houses – some miraculously nicely dressed given the shape of their dwellings, and some on their way to makeshift bathrooms to tidy up as best they can. Some people greet each other. Others yell at their children, husbands or wives. But most go about starting the day without saying much. By eight o'clock many men and women have left the shanty, apparently for work; and children have left for school, as is evident from their uniforms. Some women have also left with bundles of goods on their heads or in small wheelbarrows, apparently on their way to markets in town.
>
> People remaining, around a third of the dwellers I would estimate, seem to take things more easily. Women have started to cook meat and fish outside their shacks. The first men sit down in *cuca*-shops and order their first *tombo*. Young boys in small groups walk relentlessly from place to place stopping only to drink or play dice. And most young girls seem to braid their hair and work on their looks, while there are still children around apparently without much to do. I can also hear voices inside shacks that had seemed empty (closed, as they are, with all kinds of gadgets to avoid nightly visitors), meaning that some people delay the start of their day as long as they can. In between, the tranquillity is broken by loud and exalted voices: there are quite a few men drunk or with mental problems making much out of themselves; and I understand that there have been several attempted burglaries and a rape in the immediate neighbourhood only last night that are eagerly discussed. The calm is also broken by cars and pickup trucks trying to find their way in the criss-cross of streets and dirt tracks while attempting to avoid hitting children, dogs and chickens .... One car carries police officers; one unloads corrugated iron sheets; and one delivers bottled beer to one of the few bars located inside the shanty.
>
> Around two o'clock people start coming back into the area, most of them children from school, but also men and women who seem to have finished their errands in town, and the occasional visitor, to judge from the reserved way they are greeted. Many of the men go directly to one of the many *cuca*-shops, and women centre around other women selling *okapana* outside their houses and shacks. A new wave of people coming back starts around five o'clock. People eat,

talk, and drink outside their dwellings, making the private more public than personal; and the shanties get hectic and rowdy again, as in the early morning, particularly around the many drinking places where loud music competes for attention with news from Radio Owambo. Then, as darkness arrives, it is like the shanties are switched off, with hardly anyone having electricity and the fireplaces and kerosene lamps not managing to compensate for more than a fraction of the day gone by. Still, however, the private is conspicuously public: noises and voices reveal heated discussions (with so many people in such small shacks, how could it be otherwise?); swearing when things go wrong (stepping on burning coal? chairs falling apart? missing pots and pans? stray goats eating the last seed of a would-be maize-plant?); and even acts of love (who says there is no universal language?). By midnight, everything seems quiet.

Such comings and goings of people from the shantytown are telling spatial expressions of their urban social relations. People leaving in the morning and coming back in the late afternoon represent one category: those with formal employment and income, being connected with the modern town. People leaving in the morning but coming back early represent a second such category: they are usually those trying to connect into that formal section of the town, in search of formal or informal employment or pursuing other ventures. And people staying behind represent a third category: those who have given up trying to make such connections and who are now forced to rely on shanty-based relations of poverty with few options for income generation or social mobility. The three socio-spatial categories I have identified above are, in fact, also conceptualised by people in the Oshakati shanties themselves who recognise differences between urban "cosmopolitans" (*oombwiti*); "straddlers" between the modern town and the shantytown (*omunyanganyanga*); and shanty "localists" (*omushiinda shiinda*).[1] Below I discuss each of these three ways of relating to the urban context, and their implications for processes of marginalisation and impoverishment among the shantytown population.

The Cosmopolitans

Being a cosmopolitan or *mbwiti* is first and foremost the outcome of having formal employment and income, as we have seen is the case for only 20 percent of the adult shanty population (Chapter 4). It also reflects having adopted an urban modern life-style in the sense of images associated with Western-style progress and development (Knauft 2002). Formal employment, I have reiterated, is not only a superior source of income, but also carries high

---

[1] These three types of relation and network conform with Hannerz's (1980:255-260) set of urban relationships and networks which he calls "segregativity", "integrativity" and "encapsulation": People engaged in segregativity have two or more segments in their networks which they keep well separated. In integrativity an individual's network is spread among domains without strong tendencies to concentration in any one. And the characteristic trait of encapsulation is that ego has one network sector in which he or she invests a very high proportion of time and focus.

status and brings one self esteem in a context riddled with unemployment. It is primarily people with reliable employment and income who are in a position to relate constructively to the flows of the state, the market, the media and social movements, and to fulfil notions of modernity in the form of dwelling, food, dress, language and other related signs and symbols.

Imanuel Kahweka was 40 years old when I first met him in 1998, and manager of a local hardware-store. He had a wife and four children between five and twenty years, and lived in a brick-house in the outskirts of Oneshila, towards the main road. Imanuel Kahweka was born in Ohangwena, where his father was a cattle owner who saw the value of education and sent all his children to a primary school run by the Catholic church. For his secondary school education, Imanuel Kahweka was sent to an uncle in Walvis Bay. Coming back to Owambo in the early 1980s, he worked as a clerk in the South African administration. At independence his administrative skills got him the job as manager of one of the locally owned department-stores in Oshakati. Imanuel Kahweka always left for work early in the morning, and was always nicely dressed (managing the store from behind a glass wall, he said: "everybody can see me"). He spent most of his day in town, eating lunch with colleagues at a local restaurant and often meeting friends in their homes after work to watch TV and talk (many lived in the formal part of town). His network was very much a man's world, and when I sat in on some of these occasions I heard topics of discussion centring around work and developments in Oshakati. As for most better-off *oombwiti*, rural possessions and relationships were also central topics of discussion since many had invested in cattle in rural areas. Imanuel's relations within the shantytown were conspicuously few. He usually came home late at night, and during weekends much of his and his family's time was spent visiting his village or in the Catholic Church outside the shantytown with services and social engagements.

The *oombwiti* in the Oshakati shanties include professionals such as teachers and nurses, small-scale businessmen, lower-level government employees and employees in the private sector – most of whom have moved to Oshakati since independence. Some are also people without permanent employment but who closely identify themselves with urban life and have the means to live up to an urban life-style, such as young and educated men and women who stay in the shantytowns while seeking work. People in this social-cultural category spend most of their days in the formal parts of Oshakati at work; they buy their meals at one of the new fast-food outlets or one of the small restaurants along the main road; and they often visit relatives, friends or workmates in their houses after hours. Being employed, and commanding urban cultural codes, also opens up a wide array of other urban connections for them as we saw in Chapter 3. *Oombwiti* have easy access to the new department stores that are the ultimate sign locally of modern consumption; they can contact the Municipality with greater authority and request and acquire special services; they often go to the English-language church services instead of the more common Oshiwambo services; and, being well informed through urban networks opens up for them reciprocal relations and contacts ranging from buying on credit to obtaining free rides from colleagues to Windhoek (an impossibly expensive journey to make for most shanty-dwellers). Perhaps most importantly for their longer term options for urban success and double rootedness, *oombwiti* tend to invest and save money for future utilisation (Chapter 4).

A status as *mbwiti* requires not only permanent employment and regular income, but also special types of occupations that fulfil notions of urbanism and modernity. As such, it does not include informal economic activities that are not really perceived as expressions of modernity (thereby excluding many women),[2] and it does not include non-permanent piecemeal work being, as it were, only brief guest appearances into the formally urban world (thereby excluding many men). Moreover, being an *mbwiti* requires consumption typically manifested in the form of modern dwellings, modern foodstuffs, modern clothes and modern bodies (thin and light-skinned to match posters like the one we saw in Chapter 3).

Most *oombwiti* or "cosmopolitans" have obtained their education and economic resources while living in rural or other urban areas, and moved to Oshakati to seek employment and an urban life-style. They originally settled in the shantytown because that was all they could afford – even though many emphatically emphasise that they only live there to save money – but their attention is directed towards the urban life outside the shantytowns. The few people I have known who have managed to move out of the shanty areas and into the formal town with expensive plots and serviced with water and electricity are mainly people in government who have been promoted to jobs involving government housing, and some people in the private sector who have earned enough to buy land and construct their own serviced dwelling. Among the latter I know only two original shantytown dwellers, who earned their money from informal enterprises in panel-beating and brick-making.

While the status of *mbwiti* and urban success is normally the outcome of a longer term strategy of having obtained education and working towards images and ideals of an urban life-style (as in the case of Imanuel Kahweka above), fulfilment of its ideals may also be the outcome of coincidence and of changes in the cultural flows of the state and the market as these were described in Chapter 3. This is illustrated in the following case:

Lavinia and Maria are sisters and daughters of Angolan refugees who came to Oshakati in 1975. Originally they had most odds stacked against them. Being poor, Angolan, Portuguese speakers, women and *mestiços* (i.e. of a white father and black mother), they violated

---

[2] As will be further discusses in the next chapter, few women married to formally employed men work in the informal sector, partly because their husbands do not want them to and partly because they do not need to (being, as it were, *ombwiti* wives).

the hegemonic culture of class, race, ethnicity and gender, both of the apartheid state and of the local Owambo socio-cultural formation. I originally got to know them in 1991, and throughout the first half of the 1990s their situation was extremely difficult. Their mother, who at the time was the only breadwinner in the household, could only carry out her cross-border trade to Angola for brief periods due to the war, and the sisters were stigmatised in post-independence Oshakati largely for the same reasons as in pre-independence Oshakati. From the mid-1990s, however, and with the opening up of the market described in Chapter 3, their luck changed. Marketing posters started to pop up with lightly skinned and lightly dressed African women being the main eye-catcher, and shopping centres were established with Angolan customers becoming increasingly important as relative peace came to southern Angola. Both Lavinia and Maria soon found permanent employment with the main department store in Oshakati, in a context where it had become legitimate to play out a Latin-style Angolan cosmopolitanism, which is markedly different from the Namibian style.

While directing their attention towards the formal town and a modern lifestyle, most *oombwiti* make a similar effort to limit their relationships with people in the shantytown, at least outside their immediate family and people in similar positions. Just living in brick houses, most of which are built on relatively large plots of land with a front or a back yard, limits their accessibility.[3] Some people have also built dividing walls to separate their houses and plots from the shanty community, walls modelled on the formal area prototype of smooth concrete topped with broken glass or barbed wire. *Oombwiti* also avoid social relations of asymmetry with shanty neighbours because, as I was told, they easily become one-sided with strong pressure on people with employment and income to support poorer shanty dwellers. *Oombwiti* also try to avoid other social arenas in the shanties, to dissociate themselves from shanty life and avoid commitments. They do not normally go to the shanty-based "African" churches; they avoid using informal shanty-based tailors, bakers, backyard garages or other slum-associated commercial outlets; and they tend to use the police and courts rather than local headmen and diviners for resolving conflicts and disagreements.

Perhaps the clearest sign of their segregated lives is that male *oombwiti* do not go to *cuca*-shops in the shanties, the most important male shantytown social arena, and where drinking is communal and committing. Instead, they drink in bars on the margins of the shanties or in town, bars where everybody pays for their own beer, wine or liquor and drinking is individualised. The differences are immediately apparent when entering these

---

[3] The link between employment, income and brick houses is not only one of market and money, but also necessitates relations with the State. The only realistic way to get a loan to build in the shanties is through the government's Build Together Programme (BtP 1992) on conditions of permanent employment and a minimum wage. Private banks and moneylenders do normally not give loans in shanty areas where tenure is insecure, and if they do the interest rates are exorbitant.

places. *Cuca*-shops are loud and rowdy places where a sense of community is evident and reinforced by people passing around plastic mugs of *tombo* and where money's presence is kept discretely under control by the *cuca*-shop owner or employee as outstanding claims on patrons. In bars, in contrast, patrons pay for their drinks individually and up front, and conversations between them are discrete and private – helped along by loud music broadcasts that hinder inclusive exchanges.

This all said, however, there are limits to the extent to which shanty-based *oombwiti* can become "truly and properly urbanised" to borrow an expression from Ferguson (1999:83). Living in an urban slum area, even if their dwelling is large and relatively costly and their style cosmopolitan, signals that they have not been able to take the final step into the urban and modern world. In their encounters with employers, local government employees or other agents of the state and the market, having to name a shantytown as home gives the *oombwiti* away and tends to change direction of the discourse and line of events – as the following examples show.

According to a secondary school graduate from Uuupindi who had applied for a position in one of the new department stores in Oshakati, he was turned down with direct reference to the fact that he lived in a "slum area" and did not have a proper address. Accompanying a teacher I knew who wanted to have electricity in his house to the local government office, he was told that people from the shantytown could not be connected with the explanation that people in such areas steal the poles and electricity-lines. And applying for a loan from one of the banks in town, a resident in Uupindi who ran a successful back-yard garage told me he did not get it as he could not produce a certificate confirming his ownership of land.

For shanty-based *oombwiti* themselves, their identification with the formal urban world outside is a constant source of tension: living in a shantytown jeopardises their sense of being *oombwiti*, whilst isolating themselves by not taking part in community relationships may lead to strained relations with other shanty-dwellers and thus jeopardise their own safety and survival. While robbery or burglary in the shanties usually lead to hectic activities to identify the *botstsotso* and bring the culprit to the community leader or police, robberies from the houses of *oombwiti* are commonly met with a shrug of the shoulders and comments such as "what else can you expect?" In fact, despite being residents in the area, *oombwiti* are regarded with suspicion by many poorer shanty dwellers who perceive them as visitors in the poor shanty context where they themselves are trapped.

For *oombwiti* who become unemployed, lose their income or do not manage to live up to their own and others' expectations of urban style, the downfall may be hard and brutal. A former government employee, considered arrogant and stingy and dealing with the collection of water fees in the shantytowns, lost his job in late-1999 and suddenly became just one of many shanty-dwellers. His downfall could literally be read not only in change of daily routines, clothing and other external signs, but also in his body language and speech as he became introvert and silent. But even that did not enable him to re-embed himself and his dependents in the shanty community. Indeed, some people in the neighbourhood made it so intolerable for him to live where he did – by talking behind his back, and refusing to help him as things became really difficult – that he and his wife and children were eventually forced out of the shantytown and returned to his rural village. Meeting him in Oshakati a couple of years later, I found he was still bewildered by his downfall.

People with employment, income and options for an urban lifestyle, then, tend to direct their attention outwards towards the formal town, often at the expense of shanty-based relations. The ultimate goal for most *oombwiti*, of moving out of the shanties, is pursued through conscious strategizing and long-term moves related to social relations and style, albeit also influenced by changes in structural conditions and coincidence as in the case of Lavinia and Maria. Being a minority in a shanty population otherwise characterised by poverty and vulnerability, they experience their shanty lives as deeply traumatic because they are at once socially distinct from the shanty population but spatially not so; and they are also not really part of the modern town. Yet the possibility for most *oombwiti* of moving out of the shanties and into the formal urban town is beset with difficulties, such as prices of land and housing. This makes the option of staying on and balancing the two segregated worlds most relevant for all but the few who have overcome the structural constraints, accumulated sufficient capital and established the right connections to move out.

The Straddlers

"*Okunyanganyanga* [literally to "search around"] and poverty are brothers", an older man in Oshoopala told me once. Being without formal employment, as we saw in Chapter 4 is the case for 80 percent of the adult shanty population, it is necessary to constantly search for social relationships, employment and income by trying to integrate one's shanty life with opportunities available in the formal town. The people from Uupindi I described in the beginning of this chapter, who left the shanties in the morning and came back again in the early-mid afternoon, were doing exactly that. They were old people, adult men and women and youngsters who left the shantytowns each morning in search of economic means to support themselves and their families and who commonly came back again with little to show for their efforts.

As I will show in the following pages, there is a clear gender division in the types of strategies the poor and formally unemployed men and women pursue, that is also reported from other urban areas in Africa (Hansen and Vaa 2004; Konings and Foeken 2006). In the Oshakati shantytowns, men primarily seek individuated wage work that represent (albeit only partial and intermittent) appearances in the urban and modern setting and are the object of fierce competition. Women, on the other hand, focus their strategies on the informal economy in close female-focussed networks where they sell items and services that may be seen as extensions of their shanty-based domestic work and responsibilities.

Men Straddlers

Unemployed men primarily seek piece- or occasional employment in the formal sector. The advantage with this, they told me, is that if they get work the pay is reasonable and they will get the money they are entitled to. The disadvantage, they maintained, is that they are frequently out of work with no income. They leave the shanties day after day, sometimes for weeks in a row, to appear up in front of the employers such as the Municipality, wholesalers, grocery-stores and other shops, restaurants, construction companies, the abattoir, brick-makers, mini-bus owners and garages where rumour says that there is work. There they queue up and try to get the attention of the manager or any other person with the authority to select the lucky few who will get work for a day, a week and in rare cases for several weeks.

There are also alternative sources of informal or occasional employment, but these are considered irrelevant by the large majority of the poor and uneducated male shanty dwellers: A limited number particularly of older men have the skills to do informal trades like tailoring, shoe-repairs, furniture-making and radio-repairs, but they acknowledge that the returns are low and decreasing as people with money get these services done in the new department-stores and other shops. A limited number particularly of younger boys are involved in selling consumer items such as videos, cassettes, 'jewellery', watches, perfumes and pens in streets and markets, but they admit that the profit is picked up by Chinese, Lebanese or other middlemen and that their returns are minimal. And security companies solely employ former soldiers ("who have fought and killed our people" as one shanty-resident unable to secure such employment bitterly put it), who work long and dangerous hours for very little pay. Among poor unemployed men in the Oshakati shantytowns, then, the employment career of Silas Litta is fairly typical:

Silas Litta had come to Oshakati in 1990. He came alone. Only having reached Grade 4 in school and hardly able to read and write, he did not manage to get employment. When I met him in 1995, he was staying with a brother who had been in the army and became unemployed at the time of independence. And, he told me, he had held a number of different jobs. He had been a cook at a restaurant; a labourer on the main road from the South; a guard at Oshakati town's first shopping centre and a cleaner at the town's pharmacy; he had sold watches, cassettes and other small commodities for a Lebanese trader; and he had constructed toilets for an international development project. The problem with all these jobs, Silas Litta said, was that they were difficult to get and short-term. Sometimes others took over the job because they knew the manager; sometimes people were so desperate that they worked for practically nothing; and sometimes, he added, he was "just fired". The long periods without work became especially difficult after 1995, when he had to support his new girlfriend's two children. He always kept looking but, he complained, it had become more and more difficult to find employment without his having the right contacts.

In fact, an increasing number even of short-term or occasional jobs in the formal sector seem to be passed on between family and friends with the consent of employers who like predictability; many require formal applications that illiterate shanty-dwellers miss out on; and an increasing number of jobs go to people moving into Oshakati with better qualifications and the right connections. A young man in Oneshila told me in 2001:

> I have worked for Shoprite two days a week since 1999 but I am not permanently employed. Those who come from the South – Namas, Damaras, coloured and whites – are permanently employed because they have connections with each other. Say, for example, there is a vacant post; they phone their friends to come and work. Our manager is still full of apartheid (*okatongatonga*); he does not like Oowambo.

When poor and formally unqualified men obtain employment, they guard it with the utmost care, knowing as they do that they may soon be out of work again if they do not follow the rules. Having accompanied poor shanty-dwellers to their places of work in government offices, shops and security companies, I have been struck by the diligence with which they go about their duties. Some show up far earlier than required; some work longer hours than what is expected and they get paid for; and even menial jobs that are difficult to control (such as cleaning streets and watching empty buildings at night) are carried out with great effort. Nevertheless, the pressure and temptation for short-term gain in a situation of extremely low pay and poverty are strong. With minimal job security and outstanding claims from family, neighbours and friends, embezzlement from the workplace is common and summed up by people in the shanties in the phrase *okupithika* (meaning "bring something out of"), alluding to the pressure from family, neighbours and friends for money and commodities.

With the problem of obtaining even piecemeal work in the formal sector, an increasing number of poor male shanty-dwellers have to resort to totally unregulated sources of employment. Since the late 1990s this has primarily been done by simply sitting at designated pavements and street-corners waiting to be picked up (denoted *aakongi yiilonga*) by people needing a hand for an hour, a day or a week – with the shanty dwellers having little or no control over the type of work or the pay they receive. Such work may be in construction, as gardeners for private home owners, as agricultural labourers, loading or unloading trucks or other seasonal or intermittent occupations. Young men receive as little as to five Namibian

Dollars for a whole day of hard work, knowing well how little it is but with nothing they can do about it.

João Dungo went to town several times a week when I met him in 2001 to seek work by sitting in the traffic island of the main street entering Oshakati from the south. He had come from Angola to Oshakati in 1996, and was desperate to earn money to feed himself and his family. He described his mornings trying to get work as *uma guerra* ("a war"), competing with other men sitting there for the attention of potential employers passing by. The few times he had managed to get a job it lasted only for 2-3 days, and it was usually hard manual work clearing fields or loading and unloading trucks. He was particularly upset about the low pay he received, and complained that sometimes he received much less than what he was promised or nothing at all.[4] He also explained how the feeling of returning to Oshoopala and facing his girlfriend and their two children with little or no money got worse and worse. He said he felt ashamed that he could not provide for his family, and did not know what to do to get out of the situation. The fact that they had come to depend on the girlfriend's income from braiding hair seemed to make matters even worse for João.

Most unemployed men leaving the shanties in the morning to seek short-term or piecemeal work, then, return empty-handed. Going back through the centre of town bustling with life and full of urban commodities they cannot afford is a constant reminder of their own poverty and inadequacy – affecting their self-esteem and personal dignity and making them feel marginalised in relation to the urban context of employment and modernity.

Women Straddlers

For unemployed women heading or being part of poor households, their attempts to secure employment and income is primarily done through close female-focussed networks in the informal economy (see Chapter 4). They sell flour, tomatoes, onions, apples and other agricultural products, fresh meat, bread, soft drinks, beer and liquor, firewood, second hand clothes, dresses of local design and food cooked, fried and prepared by themselves. And they do basket making, hairdressing, braiding, sewing and other arts. "Women", people in the shanties constantly told me, "move better than men [*oomeme oye na oonkondo ye vule ootate*]", as the following case suggests.

Ndeulita Henock lived in Evululuku when I first met her in 1995. She had come to Oshakati from Omusati in 1988 with two children, and moved in with a friend from her village who had migrated to Oshakati a couple of years earlier. Her friend was also alone with small children, and made fat-cakes in her house which she sold mainly to soldiers who had nobody to cook for them. Ndeulita Henock started to help her friend by watching over the

---

[4] As with many other Angolans João Dungo did not have Namibian citizenship or a residential permit, making it particularly difficult for him to go to the police or other authorities to complain.

children or selling the fat-cakes in the shanty while her friend sold in Amunkambya (now Oshoopola). Ndeulita's presence thus gave the business more flexibility and a larger area of operation. With independence, the soldiers gone and less money among people, however, the business deteriorated and Ndeulita Henock had to establish something for herself. She continued to share the shack with her friend, but now she started selling second-hand clothes obtained from Development Aid from People to People (DAPP) through another friend. When I first met her, she spent most of the time selling the clothes in Evululuku itself thus allowing her to look after her children. But at the end of each month (at the time of salaries and pensions) she left for town to sell clothes at bus-stops, markets and other places where there were many passers-by. The main advantage with her little business, she told me, was that she had a steady income. The main problem was that the returns were usually very low.

There are also women who seek piecemeal or short-term work in the formal economy, but many express that they cannot handle the fierce competition with men for such jobs and that they need the regular income the informal economic activities give even though it is small – often with reference to the needs of their children. For some younger women without domestic responsibilities, like Mondjila Shikololo living alone in Oneshila, attempts to enter the arena of formal employment yielded additional challenges:

> In 1997 when I left school, I used to hunt for work, but I could not find any. I went to the newly established shops, filled out the application form, posted and delivered it and, once done, waited for a letter starting with 'I regret to inform you that your application form is unsuccessful'. There is this 'me first attitude', which creates corruption and unfair treatment. Someone may not have the skills [for a job] that I have, but the person is put there because of connections, bribery and sexual favours. It happened to me once: I was told that if I wanted the job I had to provide sex – and walked out. I am not that desperate, and would rather die of hunger. Is this happening? Yes it is: I am a woman, I have friends who are women, and women talk.

For women involved in the informal economy the day starts early. They leave the shanties to pick up goods at trading points that may be spread around town, and cook the food to be sold to busy urbanites on their way to work. In an intricate network of social relations of co-operation and reciprocity that will be demonstrated below, women in the informal economy have their own places at street-corners or at one of the many markets in town, including the main market *Omatala* (see Chapter 3). The networks of these women are strongly matrifocal, with women being closer, as it were, to local flows of production and exchange.

Women in the informal economy do not really fulfil criteria for cosmopolitan style because informal trade is not considered "real employment" and the returns are too low. Rather they find themselves in an intermediate position between the urban/modern and their shanty lives. Their discourses centre around the immediate need to feed their families, partly because their low incomes from informal economic activities do not give room for longer-term investments; but also, as we shall return to, because women sit with an increasing responsibility for providing for their households.

Emilie Shonga lived in a shack in Uupindi with two small children when I first met her in 1999. Her working days started early. After having cleaned the shack, made breakfast and followed her children to a friend in the neighbourhood, she walked about three kilometres to Oshakati's abattoir, Meatco, to line up and buy meat outside the gate. On lucky days, when she managed to buy before the meat ran out, she transported the meat to Uupindi's "Bush-Bush" market, helped by a young boy with a wheelbarrow. When unsuccessful at Meatco, she bought cheap frozen chicken from a local wholesaler. At "Bush-Bush" she had a small stall next to two friends, one selling cool-drinks and beer, the other cooked chips, beans and rice. The problem, she told me, was that after people with employment and income had left for work, very few people remaining in the shanty bought anything. After a couple of months Emile and her friends managed to move the business to the main road going to Ruacana, close to the bus-stop, where there were more customers with money. There they reached an agreement with some mini-bus drivers to whom they gave free food while their passengers bought for themselves. Later they managed to buy a small table and chairs, and had regular customers both in the morning and for lunch and dinner. Their plan was eventually to move to Omatala, being a market area with better income generating opportunities.

Omatala is constructed with small marketing stalls in neat rows, and represents women-focussed social relations of cooperation and reciprocity. The market fills up with women traders from early morning, each having acquired a place on the basis of experience, contacts and a fee to a caretaker. Unwritten rules reign: vegetables, meat, clothes and small capital items are sold in different parts of the area; prices for the same goods are uniform (with some using lucky charms to attract potential buyers); aggressive advertising is banned (capturing regular customers through congenial relationships and good quality); and goods are by and large legally obtained (as exemplified by the head of a beast displayed next to meat that is on sale to make it traceable to the original owner).

The close matri-focal network at the Omatala market is also used for collective protection against outsiders. The Municipality has for years tried to move the market to a location further away from the centre of town and hence from potential customers (see Chapter 3), but has not managed due to fierce resistance from the women working there. Moreover, when leaving the marketing stall for a moment, other trading women take care of the business; when newcomers who do not follow the rules threaten the established order, they are effectively isolated; and if a trader is robbed or assaulted I have seen women risk their lives to capture the culprit on behalf of the collective. As one young saleswoman explained to me:

> *Botsotsos* are a problem, but they are afraid of stealing or pick pocketing somebody at our stalls because the traders will deal with them. If *botstsosos* rob a person at Omatala, the traders usually chase him and once caught he is beaten up and left lying in pain. We have decided that we will not take the *botsotso* to the police, for we can do all the punishing ourselves.[5]

Most of the women traders seem to have a remarkable capacity for knowing how much will be sold, despite daily fluctuations. But sometimes there are goods that are not vended, and they are brought back to the shantytown to be traded for a lower price or consumed in the neighbourhood, both of which activities strengthen female shanty-based networks. Lagia Lyapwa was an older, burly lady running one of the more successful *okapana* businesses in Oshakati. She had "monopolised" a place outside the Standard Bank along the main road through Oshakati, which was always full of people. She lived on the outskirts of Evululuku, in one of the few proper traditional homesteads to be considered part of the shantytown. Walking home with her one day she had not sold all her goods, she seemed to know half the people we met. Some stopped to buy (knowing that the time was right for bargaining), and some just to greet and talk. In her dwelling she sold the remains of her *okapana* cheaply to neighbours or acquaintances (such as other women re-selling the *okapana* in the shantytown itself), or gave it away to people with whom she had a special relationship (including a young man with AIDS she cared for) – all making her a prominent person in town as well as in her part of Evululuku.

Summing up this section, most poor unemployed men who leave the shanties in the morning come back to the shanties in the afternoon have at best obtained small piecemeal work but usually yet another confirmation of their poverty and failure as urbanites. Most poor unemployed women integrate their formal town and their shanty life through the informal economic activities in town with some income, some sense of being part of the urban and modern world and with a social as well as economic base in the shantytowns through their *cuca*-shops and *okapana*.

The Shanty Localists

Most of the shanty-dwellers from Uupindi described in the beginning of this chapter who stayed in the slum area during the day did so because they were unemployed and had no alternatives. Very few shanty-households can afford to have adult household members who do not constantly search for income or other means necessary to secure basic necessities.

---

[5] Outside the marketing stalls dominated by Oshakati shanty-dwellers, close matrifocal social networks are substituted by fierce competition between traders from other areas trying to take advantage of the crowding together of people. Angolans in particular - notorious among the Namibians for their trading skills – have their networks and loyalties elsewhere and buy and sell according to laws of the free market.

There the "shanty localists" become part of impoverished and vulnerable social relations and networks, but as we shall see in the following pages the strategies pursued by the men and women in such situations differ significantly.

Localised Men

Poor men having repeatedly failed in the quest for employment and income in the formal town tend to withdraw and focus their coping strategy of *omunyangayangi* on the shanties themselves, becoming encapsulated in the poor and vulnerable shanty setting. Being failures as proper urban dwellers by not having employment and income and not fulfilling notions of urban style, their options are limited: they clean yards, fetch water, do small repair work or guard property, with their main option being to establish and take advantage of social relations with other shanty-dwellers. Some also try to get money, food or other necessities by helping out in small shanty-based enterprises such as carpentries, tailors, bicycle-repairs, shoe-repairs, hair-salons and bakers.

Kauko Nkambale, who was one of the poorest men in Oshoopala living in a tent and on hand-outs, had a near-daily routine of visiting acquaintances early in the morning at the time of the first meal. When I met him, they included an old neighbour who lived alone, a friend who ran a small bakery, and a woman who was a friend of his mother and sold *okupana*. His objective was always to help out in order to get something in return, but he usually failed to maintain such relationships over time. One of his contacts, Mweshiika Haukongo, owned a carpentry shop on the outskirts of Oshoopala. He built beds, chairs, tables and cupboards, as well as other items on special request. When I first met him his shop was new, and Kauko Nkambale helped out by fetching materials, gluing pieces of wood together, cleaning the floor and other small tasks against small returns in the form of food, drinks or money. But Mweshiika Haukongo soon found himself in a position where he got much more "help" than he needed. When he stopped giving Kauko Nkambale anything in return, he disappeared and continued his frantic search for support with others in the shantytown.

What is being exchanged in male-focussed shanty-based relations of this type is money, food, drinks, firewood, clothes and other basic necessities against goods or labour. However, most of the poor and marginalised men do not have much to offer neither in the form of goods (as they, at best, have a small and irregular income) nor in the form of labour (as they tend to be physically weak and frequently sick). In the longer run, such reciprocal relations have to be more equal to be sustainable. Knowing that returns *have* to be made not to jeopardise relationships that are established, poor men in such relations often make *ad hoc* and short-term decisions to spend apparently conspicuously when they do have access to money or other resources through occasional jobs, favours in kind or illicit activities such as theft.

John Shitenya was one of the poorest men in Oneshila. He lived alone and was around 40 years when I met him in 1995; he had spent many years in exile as a detainee or suspected "traitor" (Groth 1995); and partly for that reason had never managed to get employment. He spent all his days in the shantytown, and sometimes managed to get a little money by helping people in the neighbourhood. Yet, instead of using such income to eat well, to buy things for himself that he desperately needed, or to save, he always spent it all within hours on friends and other acquaintances. This usually took the form of buying rounds of *tombo* at *cuca*-shops, but I have also seen him spend it on meals for friends and toys for children in the neighbourhood. Thus at the same time as he (at least for a moment) boosted his own self-esteem and position in the shanty he literally sank back into the type of poverty he said he wanted to get out of.

By far the most common social arena for men who withdraw to the shanties is the *cuca*-shops, found in every third dwelling in the shanties (see Chapter 4). The *cuca*-shops are closed, male-dominated arenas with unwritten rules of behaviour. The few women who frequent *cuca*-shops and stay on late are stigmatised as "loose girls" and marginalised, particularly if they drink and behave badly (or "as men" as one older lady put it). The mugs of *tombo* that circulate in such places are considered common property by the regulars, even though those in the most difficult situations may postpone their contribution to the purchase of such beverage for weeks or months without jeopardising their position; that is because their friends know that they may soon find themselves in a similar situation. While the *cuca*-shops may be important arenas of belonging for the poorest men, however, hardly anybody has money or other resources to support and share in times of need that surpass the few cents necessary to buy a mug of *tombo*.

Yet, that all said, there are limits to how long the unemployed and very poor men can rely on the goodwill of local powerholders, of neighbours and of friends, and the very poorest are gradually pushed out of shanty-based social networks. The transition from poor (*oluhepo*) to destitute (*omuthigona*) is a dramatic one. The very poorest are recognised through the way they dress and the shoes they wear, through bodily expressions of skinniness, furrowed and ashen skin or changing hair colour, or through withdrawn or aggressive behaviour and incoherent and disconnected discourses in cases where hunger has taken its toll, all adding to their social isolation. "I am a person on two feet, but dead" [*Ondi na amagule ge li gaali ihe onda sa*], a young man from Evululuku complained while telling me that he had nowhere to turn, with no relatives in the rural areas, no employment and no friends or other contacts in the shantytown.

For the poorest and most marginalized men in particular, theft and other illicit activities may present themselves as the only alternative "relations" of poverty to secure basic necessities of food and clothes.⁶ Yet, as *ad hoc* decisions, their doing easily further undermines their own positions by being further marginalised or caught. These activities include stealing food from neighbours; breaking into shacks to steal as many youngsters do; killing and eating pigs, goats, ducks, chickens or other animals roaming around in the shanties; or joining more sophisticated *botsotso* networks where gains may be higher but also where the danger of being caught by the police is larger. Crime riddles the Oshakati shantytowns, as in most other poor urban areas in Namibia.⁷

Experience and knowledge of such criminal activities tends to evoke a mixture of anger and fear in people, not only for their lives but for property and resources that are vital for them, as very poor people, to avoid destitution for themselves. A young man I met in Uupindi in 1999 had worked hard to build a shack with a separate room for his little barber business. Just a week after he finished it everything, from corrugated iron sheets to his scissors, was stolen; and when I came back to Oshakati next time in 2001 he had still not managed to get his own dwelling and re-open his business. In late 2004, a young man, also from Uupindi, was shot dead while working in a local grocery store during a robbery by a local *botstsotso* (*The Namibian*, 12 November 2002). "There is not one day without a serious crime being committed in these shantytowns" a policeman living in Evululuku told me.

There is, in fact, a silent power struggle between the community and people it considers particularly "harmful" (*aayekelwaki*). In Oshoopala, the poorest and most volatile of the shantytowns, many people knew who the *botsotsos* were but did not report them to the police or local 'community court' for fear of repercussions from what they knew was a close-knit *botsotso* network. In Uupindi, less poor and with a history as a village before it became part of Oshakati (see Chapter 2), a strong community leader had managed to make extended families accountable for crime and had engineered several cases of public flogging of *botsotsos* – giving them less leeway. One day in November 2001, I saw close to one hundred people run after a young man in Uupindi who was caught stealing from an old, respected lady, hitting and shouting at him in anger and distress.

Such efforts notwithstanding, crime had a hold on all the Oshakati shantytowns in the sense that it made people careful about whom they entered relationships with and thus narrowed their potential social networks. And for poor families with members known to have been involved in robberies, theft or sexual violations, it was particularly difficult since they were commonly marginalised or excluded as a consequence of their association with crimi-

---

[6] According to the Oshakati police in 2001, "less than five percent" of the crimes in Oshakati are committed by women.
[7] The crime rate in Namibia is one of the highest in Southern Africa (UNDP 2000), and it is particularly high in urban slum areas.

nals. In the case of a father and son from Uupindi who were known to be *botsotsos* and had their shack destroyed by fire, the community leaders and neighbours inhibited them setting up a new one by refusing to reallocate the land and help out and eventually forced them to move out of the shanty together with their family.

Localised Women

While most poor unemployed men who have retreated to the shanties are caught up in social relations and networks of poverty which tend to further marginalise them, most poor women combine their involvement in the informal economy with being involved in localised shanty relations of the *amushiinda shiinda* (literally "neck-to-neck") type with better options for reciprocal relationships involving material as well as non-material exchanges. The gendered differences in types of social relations of urban poverty in the shantytowns follows a line from the status and role of women in matrilineal Owambo society; via their relatively independent position during times of male labour migration; to their economic independence following urbanisation and the informalisation of the economy. It is also, as we shall see in the next chapter, related to what I call the crisis of manhood in the poor urban shantytowns.

The community water-posts (with one for approximately every 75 households) are the most common social arenas for women who stay in the shanty-town during the day, where they feel relaxed and can talk freely – knowing well that the men who have to fetch water themselves are "harmless" as they do "women's things" as some women expressed it. Discussions centre around the hardships of shanty life, jokes and stories, crime, the blessings of children – and men. Indeed it is remarkable the extent to which the content of their discussions tends to separate male and female spheres, as if men (most of whom we have seen are unemployed and poor) are redundant in women's lives. Talking with seven or eight women at a water-point one day, they openly discussed a man who was approaching with a bucket saying that they all considered him to be no good as he had a reputation for being lazy and drinking. Their comments were such that he soon left, with his bucket still empty. During such water-post discussions, moreover, women who have put themselves in dependency relations with men who turn out to be no good are often rebuked, and some are taken aside and given advice by older and wiser women.

Felicidade Nakala lived in Oneshila, sold *okapana* in the shanty-town and was well-liked by everybody. Her husband had a good job as a labourer with the municipality, but was notorious among the women in the neighbourhood for having many girlfriends and treating Felicidade badly. He did not give her the money she needed to take proper care of their children, and frequently beat her. When I first met Felicidade she said she had tried to get out of the marriage for a long time, but that she needed the little money he gave her and didn't know how to leave him. A few months later neighbours found Felicidade badly beaten. Then her *amushiinda shiinda* neighbours took action: They took her to the hospital, and took care of her children while she was there. When Felicidade came out of the hospital they took her and the children into another house, guarded them there until the story had calmed down, and supported her economically to get restarted with her *okapana* business. Her husband eventually realised that it was difficult to live in a neighbourhood with so many being against him, and left the shack to Felicidade who moved back.

Women's *amushiinda shiinda* relationships are not only filled with money and material resources through *cuca*-shops, *okapana* and other shanty-based enterprises; they also involve children and reciprocal childcare, social support networks and physical protection. Being less commoditised than male relationships, they are also easier to enter and maintain for poor women without own income who can contribute by taking care of children while economically active women are away at work; "watching the gate" (*okutonatela*) of neighbours who are away for short or longer periods of time; and helping out with cooking, preparing *okapana* or performing other practical tasks when friends and neighbours need help. Social networks are usually more restricted for women than for men, rarely extending outside their sub-area where they know most people and feel safe. And most *amushiinda shiinda* relationships tend to involve only three to five particularly close women who have known and trusted each other over time.

In 1995 Emilie Katana from Omusati moved into an area in central Evululuku with her three children. She settled in the backyard of an older widow, originally from her village who was living alone in a brick house. When I met her she had only lived there for a week. Emilie had hired some young boys to put up her shack, and had already found a woman to look after her children, another woman who she cooperated with making food, and a third who helped her establish her *okapana* along the main road in town. She told me she was surprised at how easy it had been to make friends in town, but that she still did not feel really safe with all the people and noise around. When I came back after about two months, she told me that she had struggled in the beginning because she did not get enough customers for her *okapana*. People, including her widow landlord, had helped her out with small loans. Her plan was to extend her shack to include a small *cuca*-shop that the widow could look after when she was herself working in town. I asked her if things might not be easier if she met a man who could help her out and protect her. Emilie said she would not "risk it", and explained that she trusted the women she had come to know and that men could easily be an additional burden and cause problems. Last time I saw her in 2001, she still lived under the same arrangement.

While the combination of involvement in the informal economy and *amushiinda shiinda* relationships are vital for poor women in the Oshakati shantytowns, the very poorest women falling outside such networks find themselves in a particularly difficult situation. These are usually women who have become destitute by not being able to care for themselves and their children, with the violation of motherhood being seen as particularly serious. Monika Homateni told me she was only 16 years old when she came to Oshakati in 1985, and already had a child with a man who she claimed had raped her. She was pregnant again with a South African soldier before independence, but he left and she had never heard from him again. The first three years after independence Monika Homateni had managed by staying with different ex-soldiers, but when I met her in the end of 1993 she stayed alone in a small shack. Her attempts to earn money ("I have tried everything" she told me) did not work out, and it was obvious from their looks that the children suffered. Others in the neighbourhood seemed to shun her: According to one lady in the neighbourhood she was "loose and lazy", probably referring to her many relationships with men and that she sometimes spent late hours in *cuca*-shops. One day in 1995 I was told that several women in the neighbourhood had come to pick up her two children, while leaving Monika Homateni in the shack. They eventually located the women's sister in another shantytown, who agreed to look after both children.

Such poor women are not only marginalised in relation to what may be vital flows of material resources, social prestations and security, but these relations also form the main basis for friendship – a type of social relationship often overlooked in the anthropology of urban poverty (Bell and Coleman 1999). For destitute women in the Oshakati shanties, their inability to engage in such relationships tends to make them even more isolated than destitute men. While poor unemployed men seek some comfort with other men in a similar situation in *cuca*-shops or other public arenas, the very poorest women are scorned by other women for not making an effort to make money and take care of their children and have few if any shanty arenas to turn to.

Social Isolation

The very poorest men and women in the shantytowns who are marginalised because other shanty-dwellers *know* they will not be able to pay back or return favours develop subtle ways of securing basic needs, primarily by trying to play on the moral responsibilities of individuals and the community at large. Often this is done by sending children with cups and plates to people in the neighbourhood who are eating; by adults who simply sit down in begging positions (some older people hold out empty baskets as a sign of their hunger) outside *cuca-shops* and *okapana* stalls where many people pass; and by households displaying their sick outside their shacks, to show others they are suffering. Some signs also give themselves: "A house without smoke is a poor house" a common saying goes, alluding to the link between fire and food. With the fragile sense of community that has arisen from the general poverty in most neighbourhoods, however, the material outcome of such calls for sympathy is usually meagre.

Moreover, subtle avoidance takes place when the poorest people walk around in the shanty's dirt roads. Such activity is usually a social affair, with people greeting, giving comments, asking questions or pulling out a chair. Yet when the poorest approach neighbours or friends to borrow food or money, the latter might pretend not to be home or will talk about something else. They may ask people to stay away from their house or immediate neighbourhood (a very rude behaviour among Owambos). And they may gossip and pass around rumours, making life in the shantytown even more difficult for the poor. As one young man said of his life in Oneshila: "A snake does not have legs, but because of hunger it moves on its belly to find food somewhere" (*ondjala oye li pwedifa eyoka*) – alluding to the snake as a detested and feared reptile and his own search for food as if he were himself a snake who had to slither around stealthily in search of something to eat.

The dramatic consequences of such social isolation were highlighted in Oshoopala, the poorest of the shantytowns, in January 2002. Water for washing, cleaning and drinking has always been freely available to the shanty population through communal taps. But, as noted in an earlier chapter, the municipality had made neighbourhoods accountable for paying water charges in 1999. People who did not pay their share had thus to be covered by others in the group to avoid a whole neighbourhood's water supply being cut off, and in some neighbourhoods that led to the poorest and most marginalised eventually being refused access even to water. The only alternative for such people in Oshoopala is the Owambo Canal that passes the shanty with its green-coloured water contaminated by manure, garbage and other disposals. And, as *The Namibian* (10 January 2002) reported, several people from Oshoopala died from drinking the water in early 2002.

Concluding this chapter, images of hybrid socio-cultural formations between urbanism and modernity, on one hand, and rurality and tradition on the other have become a central theme in the urban anthropology of Southern Africa. Ferguson (1999:95) writes about differences of style between "cosmopolitans" and "localists" in urban areas as "accomplished strategies of survival in deteriorating economic space". Hansen (1997:18) argues that "reinvented traditions" mediate deeply felt tensions between local and global influences in the context of one of Africa's most dreadful economic downturns as it impacts on Zambian city dwellers. And Bank (2002:270) argues that people relate to their economic context of oppression and poverty by establishing "hybrid social forms that constitute a peculiarly African process of cultural creativity and innovation". In all cases, choice and innovation seem to be central aspects of people's coping strategies.

People in the Oshakati shantytowns perceive and relate to their poor and violent communities as a distinct socio-cultural formation, with very limited options for the poorest to make strategic and alternative choices. As we have seen is the case with their rural relationships, the nature of the shanty-dwellers' relations with the formal urban town is significantly affected by economic position and gender. Better-off men and women with permanent employment and income segregate their lives in the formal town from their lives in the Oshakati slum areas as best they can. Poor unemployed men try to integrate their lives in the shanties with piecemeal or intermittent employment and income in town, but often with limited success due to the scarcity of such work and the competition that exists between those seeking it. Poor unemployed women try to integrate their shanty-lives with informal employment in town, usually with more success than for men due to the importance of matrifocal and mutual support networks in both settings. And the very poorest men and women, who are unable to exploit any options for employment and income, are increasingly marginalised and encapsulated in the shantytowns where they depend on closed networks with friends, neighbours and other acquaintances who themselves are poor and vulnerable.

For all shanty dwellers, their position of well-being, poverty or destitution ultimately depends on the social relationships and distribution of material resources within the household as the basic unit of social reproduction. This is the topic of the next chapter.

8 Intra-Household Relationships

In the preceding two chapters, we have seen how economic positions and gender affect the types of social relationships that shanty-dwellers establish with others in rural areas and in the urban setting. The employed and better-off, I have shown, are in positions to use such relationships as part of a long-term strategy for well-being, while the unemployed and poorest are marginalised or excluded from them. Encapsulated in the shanties, poor men usually have few if any options for employment and income while most poor women enter close reciprocal relationships centred around the informal economy and child-care. This chapter will explore relations of impoverishment, marginalisation and exclusion within households as basic units of social reproduction. The household is a central (and for some of the poorest the last) resort for access to food, clothing, shelter and other basic necessities as well as for a sense of belonging; and being marginalised within or excluded from their household effectively leaves people in destitution and isolation.

Recent years have seen major changes in the anthropological analysis of the household (Moore 1994:87; O'Laughlin 2007). One is a shift away from the perception of the household as a bounded unit towards a view which stresses its permeability in form and structure. And a second is a move away from understanding the household as a social unit mobilising around common interests to an understanding of the household as a locus of competing interests and obligations, particularly around gender and age. As a consequence of the first shift, intra-household relations are now seen as significantly affected by political, economic and social processes outside the household; and as a consequence of the second those processes are understood to affect individual members of a household in diverse ways.

In Chapter 2 I showed how households in Owambo had changed from being centred around a polygamous unit to an increasingly nuclear unit resulting from the dual pressure of Christianity and labour migration. With the pauperisation and urbanisation that took place from the mid 1960s, reproduction of the household changed character again. Most men who moved to Oshakati did so alone, to work for the colonial regime and armed forces; and they lived in barracks or shacks. And, as poor women or single mothers, most women who moved to Oshakati ended up in the shantytowns, alone or cohabiting with soldiers or unemployed men. With independence and the opening up of Oshakati and its shantytowns, a more diverse set of people and household formations emerged with the result that there was variation in households' headship, size and composition albeit still in a context of oppression and generalised poverty (see Chapter 4).

Arriving in Oshakati's shantytowns in the early 1990s, the internal stress of poverty and the permeability of household boundaries soon became evident to me. Returning to dwellings where I thought I knew every resident from previous visits, I repeatedly experienced that household compositions had shifted radically – even over brief periods of time: The man in the house had left; children seemed to have disappeared; youngsters had arrived; relatives and friends had moved in; new men had appeared; and some had suddenly found themselves all alone after having lived in a dwelling full of people.[1] With the boundaries between private and public spaces separated by just thin corrugated iron sheets, moreover, I also soon sensed that household disputes and quarrels were common (as were acts of love and affection, for sure, but they tend to be quieter in their expression). And, as I got to know the members of individual households better, I came to recognise that domestic conflicts around resources and responsibilities were clearly widespread, particularly along lines of gender and age.

In the following, I argue that most households in Oshakati's shantytowns are under considerable pressure. Wedged in their own history and structural oppression, the instability of the household as a social unit is closely related to the stresses induced by poverty. The instability of poor household units is also related to changing conditions of womanhood and manhood. Poor households have become increasingly matrifocal, and poor unemployed men have become increasingly marginalised as members of domestic units, resulting in a sharp increase in the proportion of female-headed households (see Chapter 4). Following from my discussion of poverty and changing domestic roles along lines of gender and age, I finally argue that poor households are becoming scenes of increasing violence and abuse as men try to assert themselves – which in itself undermine household stability and instigate processes of marginalisation and exclusion.

Forms of Domesticity

The historical and structural processes of impoverishment and marginalisation of people in Oshakati's shantytowns, as outlined in the first part of this study, find their expression in household organisation. 35 percent of the household heads are formally married in church, traditionally, or by a magistrate; 33 percent of the households are based on extra-marital cohabitation of a man and a woman; and 31 percent have single household heads (the large majority being single mothers). Each category is closely linked to economic position, with a high frequency of formal marriages and stability in better-off households, and a high frequency of cohabitation and instability in poorer households. Among the best-off households (with an income of more than NAD 1000 per month), 62 percent are centred around a for-

---

[1] A similar finding in Cape Town led Reynolds (1997) to argue that an earlier focus on the household development cycle in anthropology should be substituted by a focus on co-residency, in order to understand processes of maintenance and change of households in this type of society.

mally married couple; among the poorest (with an income of NAD 250 per month or less), 73 percent are single or are based on unmarried cohabiting partners.

Cohabitation

Cohabitation or *okwaotekathana* (literally to "thicken the milk by putting in resin from the *omunkuzi* tree") has become increasingly common in the shantytowns, normally based on a combination of love, sex and immediate practical considerations – or what Ferguson (1999:97) describes in the case of Zambia as "less exalted reciprocities of money, economic cooperation and sex". They are entered without any formalities or celebrations and without extended families being involved – and hence as relatively *ad hoc* decisions in order to relate to specific personal and material circumstances (or "situational immediacy" to use Ross' [1995:95] terminology) of poverty and vulnerability. The relationship between Tuhafeni Grasiano and Kornelia Kalamba is a case in point.

Tuhafeni moved into Kornelia's shack in Evululuku in early 1994 just weeks after he arrived from Ohangwena to search for a job. Kornelia had recently been left by another man with their common child, and had problems making ends meet even though she had kept the shack. "Tuhafeni", she told me, "seemed like a nice person. He even brought me presents the first day we were together". They had been staying together a little over a year the last time I met them, and Kornelia was pregnant with Tuhafeni's child. She planned to send her first child to her rural village-based mother because, as she put it, "when the new one comes Tuhafeni will not like to have both here even though I run the household [i.e. own the shack and make most of the money]." Her main worry was that Tuhafeni often became rude and violent, particularly when he had been drinking with his friends. She would, she conceded to me, ask him to leave – at least if it turned out that he didn't support his own child properly.

Relationships of cohabitation of this type are usually of short duration, and riddled with intense struggles over resources when the first excitement of meeting one another has calmed down. A major source of instability in such units is that the men do not bring home money in support of the other household members, either because they cannot hold down a job or because they spend their income on themselves. The latter is, according to Loide Namwandi – a widow and single mother living in Evululuku whose insights and acute observations I will draw on throughout this chapter – the most problematic: "If unemployment is the real problem, we can live with it. The problem is when our men earn money, go to the *cuca*-shop to get drunk, and then come home and beat up their women because there is no food on the table". The topics of these struggles vary from daily expenses for food, clothes, water and school fees to rights and obligations over children. The internal allocation of household income is at the centre of concern, but with no legal or culturally based specifications of rights or obligations, struggles also take place over the control of property like dwellings, furniture and other household utensils.

Women often break up such relationships when their male cohabitants turn out not to support the rest of the household with money or other means, or become violent. Men often move out when the woman gets pregnant, because it leads to additional pressure on them to contribute economically to the household. Many men also move out when they realise that their girlfriends have other partners, precisely because they know their days are running out. Over a period of six months during 1994, Priscilla Iiyambo lived in her shack with three different men and her three children who came from two fathers. The father of the youngest child, who was resident early in 1994, had been asked to leave when he stopped bringing home money, even though Priscilla knew he was working. Another man moved in after a few weeks. He left when he found that Priscilla had another boyfriend in town. Getting pregnant by the latter, she eventually moved to his house in a neighbouring shantytown while renting out her own. When I met her again two years later, she was back in her shack living with just her four children.

The most stable type of cohabitation seems to be where there is a large difference in income between the partners, yielding skewed relations of power between them. These are particularly cases where older employed men, many with a wife in the rural area who knows about their husband's "town wife" [*omukulukadhi gwoponto*], enter relationships with younger women. Some young women in Oshakati's shantytowns have also entered relationships with men usually living in the southern part of Namibia and employed by government or the private sector, who stay in Oshakati for short periods of time when on business. Balancing her relationships on a tight rope, Elise Tobias – who normally cohabited with a local shantytown boyfriend – made sure that he stayed away for two-three days at the end of each month which was when her short-term Windhoek-based partner came to town. She thus ensured receipt of support from two men in this local shanty version of polyandry. Like a number of women, she received a fixed monthly "allowance" from her man from the South in order to be on standby, and she maintained that this was a good arrangement for her.

Receiving "gifts" (*omagano*, lit. "soap") of this type is not considered prostitution by most men and women. The term *ohonda*, which is how such women are described, can best be translated by "girlfriend", as opposed to the term *oshikumbu* which is used to refer to a "prostitute". Many women readily acknowledge that getting "gifts" in cash or kind is an important aspect of such relationships. But, they argue, it is not prostitution as long as nothing explicit is agreed in advance.[2] The types and sizes of transfers are the subject of negotiations, with

---

[2] In fact, prostitution has only very recently become an issue in Oshakati and is usually associated with young school-leavers. They stop cars on the main road and look up places where men are gathered (including Oshakati's only *de facto* all-white club) to offer sexual services against up-

women having the option of breaking up the relationship as their main sanction.³ For the very poorest who lack their own dwelling and income, however, staying in difficult relationships that are based on sexual services in exchange for material benefits may be the only possibility they can find. Indeed, one finds many women in the shantytowns who hardly get any support from their boyfriends and are constantly violated and beaten, but who keep coming back to the same man knowing that the situation will only get worse.

Particularly for the poorest, having experienced one broken cohabitantship often leads quickly to another in a type of informal serial monogamy. I know of women who have lived with six different men over a period of three years, usually with dramatic and tearful terminations of each relationship. They argue that they cannot stop hoping that one day they will find a man who will take care of them or even marry them, even though they know that the chances of establishing a permanent relationship get smaller and smaller the more children they have and the older they become. The common perception is that with one child by another man there is still a chance; with two children the possibility is slight; and with three or more children it is impossible.⁴ As argued earlier, children in matrilineal Owambo society are traditionally secured a place in the matrilineal group, irrespective of the identity of the biological father. But poor women from poor families know that the burden of taking care of themselves and of their children is likely to fall on them alone (see below).

Poor and unemployed men who enter *okwaotekathana* relationships often have an immediate short-term economic motive, as the women with whom they cohabit are usually involved in the informal economy. A young man in Uupindi told me how he maintained relationships with his girlfriend in Uupindi and with another in Evululuku. And he bragged that "one is making *okapana* and the other is selling clothes", apparently to tell me that he was both fed and dressed through his relationships. However, living with women and having many sexual partners is also a way of proving oneself in a situation of poverty and marginalisation. Men in this situation talk and boast about the number of relationships and children they have – to assert, I will argue later, what is left of their own masculinity as unemployed and poor men. When I inquired about this in a social setting where men of all ages were present, one argued as follows, with reference to history and "needs" (*ompumbwe*): "You see", he said, "it is our culture. Owambos used to have many wives. Then Christianity came and said that we couldn't. Now we do it this way instead". "And, my

---

front payment.
3   Helle-Valle and Talle (2000) describe a similar situation from Tanzania and Botswana: Sex and money may be combined without becoming prostitutes, they argue, because the sexual mores imply that sex may be an element in economic exchange. What is central is to present their choice as part of longer term (social) reproduction rather than short-term (private) transactions.
4   In Oshakati we have seen that 39 percent of all women have their first child before they are 20 years old; and women in Owambo give birth to an average of six children (MHSS 2001; see also MHSS 2008).

friend", a young man about half my age said, offering a variation of a theme many men bring up, "We are men. We have to eat" (*Tse aalumentu otwa pumbwa okulya*).

Okwaotekathana relationships raise questions about structures of authority and household headship. Clearly defined in formal marriages as vested in the husband, and in single parent households as vested in the single parent, headship in living-together relationships is a matter of constant contention between traditional male dominance and patriarchy on the one hand, and women's economic power, particularly related to dwelling ownership and provisioning, on the other. Loide Namwandi expressed the issue of gender authority in living-together relationships in the following way, referring as she did to the importance of women for household income: "Petrus will say it is his house; people in the neighbourhood will say it is Petrus' house; but everybody, including Petrus, knows that it is not really Petrus' house" (*Kehe gumwe ota ti egumbo olya Petrus shaasi oye omulumentu, ihe ayehe oye shi shi nawa kutya egumbo kali shi lye*).

Cohabitation, then, is a basis for a type of household unit that shows the clearest signs of instability. It is usually established on an *ad hoc* basis as a result of a combination of sexual courtship and difficult economic circumstances; and it easily yields to pressure when relationships cool down and turn out not to resolve the economic problems people face. Not being embedded in extended family structures, there is also little external pressure or support for those in them to maintain such units. Rather than being flexible social units "responding to circumstances in a way that the nuclear family has never been able to" as Ferguson (1999:191) argues in the case of Zambia, *okwaotekathana* relationships in Oshakati's shantytowns are closely related to the stress of poverty. Establishing a household based simply on cohabitation, the chances of the unit disintegrating are high, often leaving its weakest and most vulnerable members in very difficult situations without shelter and economic support.

Single-Headed Households

Turning to single headed households, my data from 1994 show that 27 percent of households in Oshakati's shantytowns are headed by women. With the household permeability under the stress of structural oppression, poverty and the crisis of manhood (to which I will return below), however, this figure has increased substantially: The proportion of *de facto* female headed households is now believed to be as high as 54 percent in Owambo (GON 2003; see also NPC 2006 and 2008), and there is little reason to believe that it is lower in the Oshakati shantytowns. The increase is accompanied by an enhanced proportion of marginalised single men in the shanties.

As shown in Chapter 4, female-headed households tend to be smaller, to have a larger proportion of non-family members, and to have a lower household income than male-headed households. In this sense, they reflect the common perception about the "feminisation of poverty" as seen to mean that women have a higher incidence of poverty than men, that their poverty is more severe than that of men, and that there is a trend towards greater poverty among women that is particularly associated with rising rates of female-headed households (Chant 2007). In Oshakati's shantytowns, however, female-headed households show large variations in their access to economic resources, composition, stability and inter-household relations, which suggests that the notion of a feminisation of poverty is more complex than often assumed.

Women heading better-off households often have their own income, obtained through the formal or informal economy, have children from one or several fathers, and have control of their own dwelling. Many have made a deliberate choice of staying alone. Independence, through own income and children, often through "polyandrous motherhood", are central to their perception of themselves as women and to their social status. Or, as Loide Namwamdi, herself a single mother, said: "Men are nice to have sometimes [making a gesture implying that she is thinking about our reproductive capacity], but that doesn't mean you have to live with them". In Oshakati's shantytowns women who can make it on their own criticise certain kinds of men, such as those who drink, those who have extramarital affairs and those that don't bring home their wages. But they nonetheless establish relationships with men when they consider it advantageous, as the following case shows.

One of the most popular places to meet in Uupindi was a *cuca*-shop run by an Angolan woman of Kwanyama origin called Amalie, located along the main road to Uukwangula. It was actually more than a *cuca*-shop (but "not a real restaurant" Amalie insisted), as it not only sold drinks and food but also had tables and chairs. As were most Angolan women, Amalie was more open and vocal than the local Namibian women, and her *cuca*-shop-cum-restaurant was always full. Abandoned by her husband many years previously, and never really having adjusted to life in Oshakati (as indicated by her inadequate English), she was quite open about her relationships with different men. "I let men who I like stay with me in my house to make me forget Angola", she told me; "but I always make sure that they understand that I am the boss (*que sou eu que manda*). If they get too homely (*domesticados*) I tell them to leave".

A second category of female-headed households comprises single mothers staying alone because they have no other alternative. They are either seeking men, or are single because their social or economic situation makes them unattractive as cohabitation partners for shantytown men who are looking for a woman to support them. These women are often among the very poorest (such as Emilia Uushona whose case I presented in Chapter 5). They lack both the authority of women with their own income and dwelling, and they lack a male supporter. Their situation is particularly difficult when it implies neglect of their children, which is perceived to be the responsibility of women and at the core of womanhood. There are, in fact, few ways out for single women who cannot take proper care of themselves and their children.

For several months during the early parts of my stay in Oshakati, Martha Kandenge, a young single mother in Oshoopala, desperately tried to feed her children by sending them around the shantytown begging for food. While they were given food, and ultimately took up residence with an older couple, Martha Kandenge personally became increasingly marginalised. Even children in the area seemed to sense that she was an "outcast", teasing her and calling her names they would never have used with other adults. I saw her become increasingly isolated, not being able to maintain her appearance and with her body "sinking together" when she walked around, as if trying to hide herself. She ultimately moved out of the shantytown to another similar area where she was less well known – according to an old neighbour because "she could not take the shame of not being able to take care of her children".

Single women with children and some economic means often share their dwelling with close female matrilineal relatives or friends. My survey data show that close extended family members are more common in female-headed households than in male-headed households, whereas "other relatives" and "non-relatives" are more common in male-headed households. Living with any male relatives other than uterine brothers is considered difficult,[5] but female relatives (mothers, daughters, sisters and cross-cousins) not only usually constitute people with whom an amiable relationship is regarded as very likely, but are also practical co-residents for a woman in terms of sharing child-care, cooking and in supporting each other in informal economic activities. There is, in other words, a feminisation of such households around a cell of mother and children, which is also reported from urban townships and shantytowns in South Africa (Barabarin and Richter 2001, Bank 2002).

Female members of many female-headed households have created strong social and economic units between themselves. In one case from Oneshila three sisters (all single mothers) shared a dwelling, owned by their mother who had moved back to her natal village in Ohangwena. One sister was formally employed in a new supermarket in Oshakati; one was very active in the informal economy with a base at the Omatala market; and the third stayed in Oneshila running the extended household with child-care, cleaning and cooking duties and a small *cuca*-shop too. At one stage two of the sisters had babies, both breast-fed by the sister staying at home. Income and other resources were shared for running expenses, but they all also had separate savings accounts. All three sisters seemed happy with the situa-

---

[5]   The Owambo have a kinship classification system in which the term brother (*omwameme mati*) denotes brothers from the same mother (uterine brothers) as well as mother's brothers' sons (Estermann 1957).

tion, and none expressed any urge to live with the fathers of their children – or with other men for that matter.

Female-headed households are an increasingly common feature in the Oshakati shantytowns, and tend to be stable over time. Women centre their attention on the upbringing of their children through cooperation with matrikin (see Chapter 6), and through neighbourhood relations with other women (see Chapter 7). Women with resources make deliberate choices to limit their relations with men in their everyday lives. They may have several partnerships, and produce children by a number of different men (a standard phrase when talking to people about children or siblings is to specify whether they are by the same father or not [*uunona woohe yi ili*]); but they do not anticipate economic support from the fathers of their children. In other words, many female-headed households in the Oshakati shantytowns are not a residual category of women who for some reason have not managed to find a husband, as implied by e.g. Ferguson (1999) and Hansen (1997) in the case of urban Zambia, but are shaped by images and ideals about what is best for women and their children within the structural confines of poverty. Only the very poorest women, who are unable to take care of their children, end up being marginalised and excluded from such matrifocal networks; and as indicated earlier that is both because they lack any resources to bring into such networks and because they lose others' respect through their not caring for their children.

Single men who do not manage to support their women or children and thereby to fulfil the normative expectations of fatherhood are, for their part, often transformed into "domestic nomads", as Bank (1996:73) expresses it for East London in South Africa. "Dumped" by women before they can claim to be part of the household (i.e. before they claim the status of household heads or even cohabitants rather than just lovers), some have to manage alone by trying to relate to other households and individuals on an *ad hoc* basis to secure food and other basic necessities. Others live with parents, brothers or married sisters, where they tend to have an accessory position due to their inability to be economically and socially independent.

John Shinyala was one of the young soldiers in the Oshakati shantytowns whom we met in the beginning of Chapter 2, dressed in fashionable clothes and being a small "king" with easy access to women. His downfall after independence was hard and brutal. From earning more than 3000 Rand[6] per month, he could not find a job any longer and became dependent on badly paid casual work. According to a neighbouring girl his charm was still intact, though he soon received a reputation for being fond of women but not contributing anything to their households. After having had three children with three different women

---

[6] After independence the Rand was substituted by the Namibian Dollar, albeit retaining the same value.

and given no support to any of them, people in the shantytown talked about him as a "womaniser" ("*okhole iipala*"). As noted above many single men of age 30-40 years have a strong influence over poor young women who hope to be supported. But in John Shinyala's case, his reputation went before him and such women legitimately refused and avoided him. When I last met John Shinyala in 1999, he was living with his sister who was married to a manual worker in local government and lived in a shack in Oneshila; but, he told me, he did not get along with his brother-in-law and really did not know what to do.

There are examples of single and independent male-headed households, but they are typically part of a support network making them reminiscent of 'extended households', as the following case shows: David Fillipus was born in Namibia in 1931, and as a child he suddenly became blind. He stayed with his uncle in Angola for several years before he came to Oshakati in 1982 and settled with his sister and her adolescent son in Evululuku. The latter later died while fighting in Angola against Swapo, and his sister died in the middle of the 1990s. Tate Fillipus inherited the erf and iron shack, and stayed all alone for nearly three years, surviving on his small disability pension. He then decided to let people he knew make houses on the plot. As he explained:

> There are now six houses, and all are working like one unit. We eat together, we drink *tombo* together from one glass, and I have access to their children and can send them to do things for me. I can borrow money from people on the plot, and they can borrow from me. I do not have big goals in life. I am blind, and as long as I can eat, drink and play with the children I am happy... The children are my biggest friends. They call me *tatekulu* [grandfather].

Summing up this section, female headed households are an increasingly common form of domestic unit in Oshakati's shantytowns – currently representing more than 50 percent of the total number of households. While the responsibility for household management, provisioning and childcare represents a hard toll on many women, for those with sufficient means, being single-headed is often a deliberate choice to avoid what many perceive as the burden of men. Only the poorest women, who are without sufficient income or other resources and hence unattractive to men as partners, seem compelled to make it on their own, often leading to problems in taking care of children and to those women's ultimate marginalisation and seclusion. Poor single men attach themselves to households of relatives or girlfriends on an *ad hoc* and short term basis, but will also stay alone. Being forced to do domestic chores themselves, such as cooking and cleaning, their marginal position is evident not only for themselves but also for the rest of the immediate community.

Conjugal Unions

The permeability, competing interests and increasing matrifocality in many households do not mean that marriage is considered irrelevant. On the contrary, to be married is the goal of most young men and women (at least, as Loide puts it in her regular sarcastic tone, until the latter have seen how much trouble men cause). The continued attraction of marriage as an institution is the outcome of what it may entail for provisioning and security, and a combination of a romantic view of the traditional past (framed in images of the authoritative man or woman surrounded by children and grandchildren in the traditional setting of the *egumbo*), and images of modern romantic love and marriage mediated through locally performed marriage ceremonies among better-off couples in the formal parts of town.[7]

For many young women the dream is to marry someone who is securely employed, brings home money, takes care of the children and can take them out of the shanty-town. For young men, secure employment, a proper house, marriage and children is the fulfilment of deeply felt cultural expectations of tradition as well as modernity. In the shanties, "complete" households with a husband, a wife, children and other dependants are, as we shall see, respected by others. In Ferguson's (1999:177) words, the experienced failure of the myth of the nuclear family in many urban African contexts signifies a rupture not only with the ideologically conceived "normal family", but also with images of modernity.

Why, then, is marriage currently the basis for only one-third of the households (see Chapter 4) and on the decline with an increasing number of cohabitating and single headed households? One immediate and apparently paradoxical reason is the exorbitant costs related to becoming married – paradoxical also because dowry (*iigonda*) has no tradition in matrilineal Owambo society (Williams 1991). The costs for gifts to in-laws, expensive dress and suit for the spouses, bridesmaids to be dressed up, transportation, church and traditional ceremonies, and not least extravagant parties in town, in the village or both have become extremely high: The reason often given for this apparent paradox by unmarried and married alike is that "Owambos like to celebrate" (*aawambo oye hole iituthi*); but the pressure for a large and expensive celebration should equally be seen as a "test" that the people involved are serious about the relationship and capable of supporting the spouse economically in a context of poverty and insecurity. One young man from Uupindi, working as a low-paid gas-station attendant, told me that he still needed to save 1500 Namibian Dollar to get the 5000 he needed before the parents' of his girl-friend would let him marry their daughter, adding that most of it would be used to give them presents and organise a proper wedding.

The importance of money in a commoditised urban context means that men with secure formal employment and income are coveted marriage partners. And their marital re-

---

[7] Ceremonies of national and international celebrities also play a role for those with access to the right media. The much-publicised marriage in 2001 of the then Minister of Fisheries carried by the national press, and the marriage of Nelson Mandela and Grace Machel carried by glossy magazines, are cases in point.

lationships tend to be stable over time – or for as long as the male partner is employed and brings home money. Being closer to cultural expectations for conjugal unions than are simple living-together relationships, household authority is, in such cases, also more clearly vested in men. As the case of Ndemuweda Nambadja below shows, there are households in the shanties where the partners live up to ideal expectations of pooling resources, investing in appropriate housing, and supporting children and their education, even though some of these households leave the shanties to settle elsewhere when they reach this stage.

Ndemuweda Nambadja was in his mid-forties when I met him in 1995, and was one of the few people in the shantytown who had married traditionally. He and his wife had six children aged from 20 to five years, four of whom still stayed at home. Ndemuweda Nambadja was employed as a foreman at Oshakati's Coca-Cola bottling factory, and his wife stayed at home. They lived in a large brick house in Uupindi, built immediately after independence and which also housed an additional five residents. Three were of Ndemuweda Nambadja's matrilineal kin, and two were youngsters from his rural village: they were studying in Oshakati and had been sent to him by his father's neighbour and friend. Often at least two or three other people would stay for short periods of time. With the exception of rural goods like *mahangu* and *etaka* sent by the father of the two youngsters, Ndemuweda Nambadja and his wife were responsible for supporting the entire household of nine persons. Representing a hard toll on his own and his wife's income, he evaluated this against the status it gave him to head and provide for such a large household and the outstanding claims this represented in relation to his extended family and village (see Chapter 6).

All this does not mean that such households are not susceptible to the kinds of external and internal pressures and processes of marginalisation and exclusion that affect poorer household units in the shantytowns. However, with a more binding conjugal relationship involving extended families and a better economic situation, the pressure is smaller and the tolerance larger than in other households, as both husband and wife may have much to lose by breaking up. For the female partner the ability to provide for herself and her children may be at stake, and for the male partner his status and power as a man may be jeopardised. The ambiguities surrounding the distribution of resources in cases of divorce, with traditional and Roman law underlining the rights of the matrilineage and the spouse and children respectively being juxtaposed (Hinz 2002), also mean that divorce is a risky business.[8] Many married women know that their husband is sleeping with other women; they may realise that they have "private children" as the saying goes; they may suspect that the husband does not bring home everything he earns; and they may experience problems

---

[8] The role of traditional law is enshrined in the Constitution, and there are traditional courts at the level of the shantytowns (presided over by the headman), the town (presided over by the senior headman), and for each of the seven Owambo groups (presided over by the chief and his council).

with domestic violence – but they will still stay. The status of men in such households gives them considerable leeway regarding their own life and conduct, even to the point of openly having relationships with and supporting other women.

Yet conjugal households tend to disintegrate if the man as the main provider becomes unemployed, loses his income or somehow becomes economically dependent on his wife. Not being able to provide for the household over time is seen as a legitimate reason for a wife to leave the house and even to enter relationships with other men. For a husband in such a situation, the choice is between making it on his own or staying in the household as a powerless figure where his lost status as main provider further contributes to his marginalisation and loss of a sense of manhood (see below). These are the men Loide thinks about when she emphatically states that "Our fathers were real men [*omakondombolo*]. The men here are not real but fake [*iikopi ndooha*]". These are men like José António, whose story I told in Chapter 6, who had experienced a downfall from being a powerful and respected soldier to becoming completely dependent on his wife for survival. Every time I met him this dependence was the focus of his sense of disgrace, rather than the fact that his household had become exceedingly poor. Sakeus Nepando from Oshoopala, on his part, was literally squeezed out of his dwelling when his girlfriend simply took another cohabitant after Sakeus lost his job. "In 1992 my wife left me for someone else, after I became unemployed. She also took my son, who is now 18. They never visit me. I still love her, but I cannot afford her as I am unemployed".

Let me finally exemplify relations of impoverishment and marginalisation in households as domestic units by paying a visit to three families living next door to each other in Evululuku. The cases show that level of poverty not only has implications for internal household organisation and processes of integration and disintegration, but also for how households relate to opportunities for employment and income and hence options for social mobility.

When I first met them in 1998, Lukas Mateus and his wife of Angolan origin lived with three children and had visitors from Angola constantly coming and going in their home. Lukas was a pastor in the local Tocoist church, and his wife stayed home and helped out with church-related chores such as preparing the near-daily services. Their income from the church – in the form of contributions from the mother-church in Angola as well as collections – was good and stable. Their neighbouring household consisted of a single mother (Tiodesia Kalamba) with three children, staying with her sister and often being visited by their mother from the village. The sister took care of the children during the day, and made a little money by also looking after the child of a friend. Tiodesia ran a successful *okapana* business, with dried cat-fish bought via middlemen from the Caprivi region. And the third neighbouring household comprised an unmarried couple (Tomasina Negonga and Emanuel Ashikoto) living together with a total of four children only one of whom was their joint biological child. Both were unemployed, though Tomasina sometimes helped out with small chores for neighbours doing *okapana* or having *cuca*-shops.

About a year later an older man moved into the shantytown neighbourhood who would come to represent an opportunity and upward social mobility for all the three households. Erastus Haifiku was one of the few "real entrepreneurs" based in the shantytown itself. With a background as a cook in hotels and restaurants in the southern part of the Namibia, he established an informal school for cooks in an extended shack in Evululuku. After a while his cooking school grew in popularity, particularly among unemployed secondary-school graduates, who came from all over northern Namibia with the objective of qualifying for work in hotels, restaurants and other similar establishments. *Tate* Haifiku sought a collaborator in the neighbourhood where the three families lived to help invest in a larger shack and help out with practicalities.

Lukas Mateus stated to me that he was not interested. He had a good income already, and argued forcefully that his wife had no business working for a would-be school in the shantytown (even though, he insisted equally forcefully, Angolans were the ones who really knew how to make food...). His intention was also to move out of the shanty and back to Angola with his family as soon as the war ended – which he ultimately did in 2001. Tomasina and Emanuel did not have the money that Erastus wanted, and Tomasina herself also turned down an offer to help out. She did not have anyone to look after her children when she was gone, and she feared that Emanuel would take off with the money she would earn. Tomasina eventually forced Emanuel to leave her (leaving him with no income whatsoever), and she was left with her meagre income from helping neighbours. Tiodesia Kalamba, by contrast, seized the opportunity with both hands. She left her existing *okapana* business to her sister, brought her mother permanently into the shanty to look after the children, and ended up as co-owner of a business that thrived on fees of 100 Namibian Dollars for a week-long course and an increasing number of students. Last time I met Tomasina in November 2001, she was in the process of building a brick house for herself and her children, her mother and her sister.

Summing up this sub-section on the relation between well-being, poverty and household organisation, I have shown that the poorest households are particularly fluid and unstable, often established on the basis of *ad hoc* and short-term moves to relate to love, sex and economic difficulties. The most vulnerable men or women in such units of cohabitation are easily marginalised or excluded, leaving them in precarious situations of deep poverty and vulnerability. In households with a more solid economic base, household members are not only in a position to stabilise their relationships through marriage and the involvement of their respective extended families, but also to plan and act on the basis of images and ideals of what constitutes a proper, urban and modern household in terms of organisation, relations of authority and consumption. Having said this, the frequent failure of the ideal nuclear or extended household in the face of structural oppression and poverty has led to a competing cultural discourse about women, children and matri-relations being the optimal household unit – a type of unit that currently represents more than 50 percent of the households in the Oshakati shantytowns and in which men have little more than a very marginal place.

Manhood and Womanhood

The permeability of the household as a unit of social reproduction should also be understood with reference to profound changes in local perceptions of manhood and womanhood (Walker 1995, Morell 2001, Cornwall et al. 2007). In Chapter 2 I showed how the basis for the changing discourses and perceptions of manhood and womanhood in Owambo and Oshakati was the disconnection between public and domestic power following urbanisation and modernisation, exacerbated by war and violence. In poor urban areas like Oshakati's shantytowns, men were excluded from participation in the broader political system (changing as we have seen from traditional authority structures to the apartheid state, and later to "elite democracy"). And, with the transition from agro-pastoralism and male labour migration to a labour market largely outside their reach, they were no longer essential for access to economic resources. This meant, as Bank (1996:66) has argued for East London in South Africa, that men who did not earn became *dispensable* within the functioning of poor urban households, where cash income was vital. Today the notion of manhood as protector and provider of the household is in the process of becoming impossible for poor men in Oshakati's shanties to relate to, and manhood has increasingly come to be about simply producing children whilst escaping any responsibility for those children's upkeep.

The frustration and feeling of inferiority this instils in poor men is palpably noticeable, particularly in their frequently finding outlets for it in their withdrawing from immediate family relationships, their use of violence and their excessive use of alcohol (see next section). Many men stay away from their own dwelling for large parts of the day, spending time with other men talking not only about problems of employment and income but also about how they have been "sidelined by women in their households" (*aakiintu ya peife oyi-ili*) as one put it. People in the shanties also argue that one can see when men are poor and excluded, not only by the amount of time they spend in the shantytowns and the way they dress, but also in their body language. "A poor man", the headman in Oshoopala told me, "will not look you in the eye but to the side and he will mumble instead of speaking out like a real man". Jacob Nelenge is one of them:

> I did not attend school, as schools in the 1960s were not regarded as important. I was a cattle herd-boy, taking care of my grandmother's cattle. She used to mistreat me, and [when I was]

seven years old I moved to Oshakati to live with my cousin who was employed as a police soldier [Koevoet]. At the time, Amunkambya [now Oshoopala] was a rough place. There was no respect for human lives, or other people's property. There was a lot of killing, knifing and shooting. As a child I was always scared, but I got used to it as I grew up. In 1986 I joined the police force myself, and did horrible things. ... Now I am not employed, and I don't have money. My neighbours sometimes give me food, and share their *tombo* with me. I do small piecework for them, such as fetching the water for the *tombo*. Not all my neighbours are good people. There are good neighbours, and there are just neighbours. People get tired of someone [like me] who does not have money.

For women, the 'crisis of manhood' has implied additional burdens but also possibilities for them to develop new roles and to challenge male authority. In town, many women have come to occupy a position not only to accumulate their own income mainly through the informal economy, but also to accumulate and control property. Thus the shantytown notion of womanhood has changed from being one of bringing up children (on behalf, so to speak, of the biological father and the woman's male matrikin) to one of social reproduction in a broad sense, including provisioning, socialisation and, in many cases, household and family headship.[9]

In the private sphere, the enhanced position of women in many households in Oshakati's shantytowns is reflected in their discourses as well as their behaviour. In the course of the more than 10 years during which I have worked in Oshakati, I have noticed salient changes in the way women receive me and talk to me in an ever more open and direct way, as compared with previously when they would have referred me to husbands, male cohabitants or male relatives. In matters concerning money and loans, women have told me that, whereas previously they would leave decisions to the man in the household, they now simply inform him when decisions have been made by themselves. Women also more openly share domestic issues with friends and neighbours, and do so now in a language that those who catch the finer tunes of Oshiwambo describe as "sexist". Indeed, men who come home late and intoxicated may well find themselves publicly ridiculed by their women in a blurring of the private-public space boundary that older people regard as unheard of.

Poverty is embodied also by poor women in the way they dress, speak and comport themselves. They may wear worn-out clothes, they may only know the Oshiwambo vernacular and they may withdraw particularly from public arenas. But at the same time most

---

[9] While this finds resonance in much of the urban anthropology and related disciplines in South Africa (van der Vliet 1991, Bank 1996, Morrell 2001), both Tranberg Hansen (1997) and Ferguson (1999) seem to argue for a much more dependent position of women in Zambia, implying more limited economic independence and a stronger hold of tradition. Hansen (1997) argues that a woman's access to productive resources is still mediated through men as fathers, uncles, brothers and husbands. And Ferguson maintains that the connection with wage-earning men is of extraordinary importance for women (1999).

women seem to maintain what people call *okwiituma* (best translated as "grace"), and they reveal it in the ways they move and behave with an upright posture and looking people straight in the eyes. People explain this "bodily grace" with reference to women's habit of carrying things on their head, but this is not common in an urban environment. Rather, the bodily movement expresses deeper sentiments of increasing independence and self-esteem, reinforced by the system of matrilineality in Owambo. Only the very poorest women – who are not economically secured through marriage, unable to attain an independent economic position and violate notions of motherhood by not being able to take care of their children – are marginalised and ashamed of their situation.

Intergenerational Relations

In the context of the oppressed and poor Oshakati shantytowns, the permeability and instability of households also involve intergenerational relations. As we saw in Chapter 4, very few older people live with their children and grandchildren as Owambo custom prescribes, this being related to the difficulty of supporting economically inactive people in a poor urban context as well as the problem of "crowded living" in urban slums (Hansen 1997:151). And older shantytown residents who have been able to maintain rural relationships, or have a long employment career and savings, have moved either back to their rural villages or (less commonly) into the formal parts of Oshakati. In fact, older people remaining in the shantytowns are often without viable rural relationships and tend to be socially marginalised and among the poorest people there.

Emilia Uushuno, whom I presented at the beginning of Chapter 5, is a case in point. She has not been able to maintain her contacts with her rural area of origin; her children who still live in Oshakati have no room to accommodate her and in any case cannot support her; and she has no income of her own. "Myself", she told me, "I am supposed to get a pension. But they [i.e. the government] are telling me that my age is not correct. Apparently I appear young. But my baptism certificate shows that I am 60, meaning that I have reached the age to get a pension". Ambrosius Sippora was 62 years old and lived in Uupindi with his wife when I met him in 2001. He told me he had moved to Oshakati already in 1970, to seek employment. With his age and a partly paralysed leg he never made it to the military, and ended up helping a shoe-maker who had established himself in Uupindi. Ambrosius Sippora's economic situation remained difficult: When I met him he was in the process of giving up his own little shoe-repair business ("People cannot afford to pay me, and those who can buy new shoes" as he put it), and his wife made a meagre income from looking after a neighbour's children. Ambrosius Sippora and his wife had lost contact with their rural families many years ago ("We know they are all struggling hard"), and in the shantytown they mainly stayed by themselves, saying that most people they knew had left or died. "Uupindi is no place for old people like us", Ambrosius Sippora's wife complained. "People are too busy to talk [to old people], and we don't have anything [to offer]".

Relations between parents and their children are often particularly strained among poor households, with limited possibilities for mutual support. When older parents are people who have grown up in rural areas where relationships (at least in their own recollection) were based on respect and obedience, they tend bitterly to complain that young people nowadays "show no consideration" (*ka yena esimaneko*) in their behaviour, as reflected in their not contributing economically to the household. According to one 51-year-old widow living in Uupindi,

> [O]ne reason why traditional values are ignored is that the children have turned into parents and the parents have turned into the children. We the parents are now respecting the children. Today's life is built on money. This is the means of survival. A child today has access to different sources of money, which we did not have.

Young people are also bewildered by the changing nature of domestic unions, womanhood and manhood and intergenerational relations. They may have been exposed to or heard about large extended family units in rural areas, or the urban ideal of a nuclear family, but find themselves in a shanty- and family context of poverty where the household frequently is a scene of internal struggles and disintegration. Maria Kalwenia grew up in exile in Zambia, where her father was the family head, a freedom fighter and a farmer. Coming back to Namibia after independence they had nothing, and settled in Evululuku. Her father now suffers from depression and "slowly disappears from us" as Maria puts it. The family totally depends on income generated by Maria and her mother in the informal economy where the two of them run a small *okapana* business. They cope, said Maria, only "because my mother is very strong and she has made us to be strong". Thinking loudly about the situation of poor families in the shantytown and her own future, she stated:

> But for myself, marriage is not on my mind now. I have better things to do. I am also discouraged from getting married, because people do not value marriage any more the way they used to in the past. In the past, marriage was viewed as a guarantee of life and prosperity. Young boys were taught by their parents that it is their responsibility to take care of the family once they were married, and any failure of taking care of the family was regarded as a cowardly act. But nowadays marriage is seen as a burden, it ties you down. On top of that, you cannot go into a marriage empty-handed: You will be treated `as nothing´ by your partner and his extended family. In the past marriage was viewed as a guarantee. A married couple was expected to take care of each other, but nowadays people do not care anymore. Everybody in marriages is misbehaving, both male and female. They go out with other partners even though they are married. They do not ask themselves how the partner will feel. This is true. For example, where a partner commits adultery (*oluhondelo*), this act is done without any guilt and it is repeated without any guilt. If asked about the action, the answer is always: `If this was allowed during

the polygamy time, why not now?' Their actions have something to do with declining moral values. Loose contact [*okwaasimaneka ondjokana osha talika shili mondjila*] is viewed as normal. If you are not behaving according to these loose values [then people say that] something is wrong.

Concluding this part of my analysis of intra-household processes of impoverishment, marginalisation and exclusion, manhood and womanhood in Owambo have undergone dramatic changes with urbanisation and the commodification of social relationships. Anthropological studies of masculinity from the southern African region (Morell 2001; Barker and Ricardo 2005) tend to emphasise expressions in the form of cosmopolitan styles and "comradism", which are often contrasted with traditional rurally-based perceptions of fathers as breadwinners and household heads. While the better-off shanty-dwellers in Oshakati are in a position to embody at least one of these expressions, the poorest shanty-dwellers are not able to fill any of them. They cannot support a family, and they do not have the money or the cultural competence to play out their masculinity in accordance with hegemonic perceptions of modernity. For these men, the fall from manhood leaves them vulnerable to household-based processes of marginalisation and impoverishment.

The core of womanhood in the Oshakati shantytowns continues to be household management and child rearing, but for many women urbanisation and modernity have added responsibilities for employment, income and household headship. Werbner (quoted in Bank 2002:194) argues that the conditions for the feminisation of citizenship in patriarchal postcolonial societies usually begins with "the reconstruction of citizenship in terms of encompassing qualities associated with women's roles as nurturers, carers and protectors of the family and its individual members". In Oshakati, as I have shown, such a role is becoming increasingly widespread with the changing nature of manhood, but it also presupposes an independent economic position for women that, as I have demonstrated, not all women have.

Violence and Abuse

Poverty and the changing positions of manhood and womanhood have not only contributed to permeability of social relations of the household and processes of marginalisation and exclusion, but have also found their expression in a dramatic increase in domestic violence. According to a 2000 UNDP report (see also KAS 2008):

> There is a fairly high level of aggression in Namibian society ... due to the large number of changes. These changes are ... redefining previously held norms and values and causing expectations that are virtually impossible to fulfil. This causes frustration and aggression that results in social problems, such as general violence and violence against women (UNDP 2000:xvii).

Also in the Oshakati shantytowns I have seen how violence further increases marginalisation and social exclusion in households – of men who usually are the violators as well as of women who usually are the victims. The case below reveals the extent to which those involved in domestic violence – both as perpetrators and as victims – all too often find that it also leads to their becoming socially marginalised; and that that in turn leads those among them who are already very poor to being unable to maintain any of the social connections, even within the household itself, to sustain themselves.

A poor family in a neighbourhood in Uupindi had a particular history of violence and instability. The father in the household was a returnee from exile in Angola, who, when I met him in the early 1990s, always complained about having ended up in a slum after having "spent years fighting for my country". He could only hold small, part-time jobs, usually in construction. People shunned him because he had a reputation for beating up his wife and girlfriends ("Once he even beat up the foreman at a road where he worked" one told me). The wife's brothers ultimately forced him to leave the household, and she was left to support the family with a meagre income from *okapana*. In the late 1990s, a son of around 17 years of age was caught raping a girl about the same age in the neighbourhood. It was done at night, but neighbours were alarmed, caught the boy, beat him up and took him to the police-station the next morning – only to see him released after a couple of days. After this neighbours refused to help out in the *okapana* business and support the family with money and food as they had done in times when the mother had pleaded for help. She was ultimately forced to denounce her son, and he eventually moved to his father in Rundu (in the Kavango region) leaving the mother with only two daughters. Not considered outcasts anymore with the violent son gone, she was re-integrated into the neighbourhood and managed to make ends meet through her *okapana* business.

In the anthropological literature domestic violence is often seen as the outcome of men's loss of intra-household authority and an (imagined or real) inability to control the sexual behaviour of their partner (Moore 1994; see also Whitehead et al. 2006). In the case of the Oshakati shantytowns, additional reasons for the frequent violence in households may to be found in the combination of poverty and subjective histories. We have seen that many men and women in the shanties have had direct personal experiences of violence in war and during the processes of early urbanisation, and that many children are brought up in contexts where violence is commonplace. For many, then, violence seems to be the only way out when cornered in a difficult situation or relationship. Having said this, however, there is no *necessary* relationship between poverty and violence. In fact Loide, whom I have quoted earlier as regards her search for alternative explanations, said that people with *some* employment and *some* income are the most violent "because they can afford to buy the alcohol that brings violence about. The poorest don't have enough [money to buy alcohol], and the rich don't have problems that can't be solved".

Recognising that many people in the shantytowns use alcohol excessively is necessary if one is to fully understand the processes that lead to the disintegration of household relationships in the Oshakati shantytowns.[10] As a visitor one is likely immediately to be struck by the large number of drinking places (our survey showed that every third dwelling includes a *cuca*-shop), and one will always see people drinking or drunk. In Oshakati's shantytowns, people often refer to drinking as one of the most destructive forces to influence the domestic economy, leading all too often to domestic violence and hence the instability of households as social units. This concern is epitomised in the local expression *okutombolola*, meaning "*tombo* takes out your wisdom". Or, as Evelina Hangula, who lived in Oneshila when I met her in 1999 and has close contact with the problem as a nurse assistant, expressed it:

> People who are living here are poor and unemployed, and there are signs of malnutrition, particularly among those who are drinking without eating. ... I see, every day, frustrated people, filled with anger and a feeling of [being] betrayed. And so they drink, become alcoholics, and some become thieves. Those who are drinking start in the morning and finish very late in the night. The following morning is the same thing, because there is nothing to do. When they are sober they think that something is wrong with them – and [so they] start to drink again.

For the Oshakati shanty-dwellers finding themselves marginalised in situations of deep poverty, violence and despair, the spread of HIV-AIDS represents an additional serious threat to the reproduction of their household (Sorrell and Rafaelli 2005, Mufune 2005; see also Bähr 2007). The disease affects an estimated 30 percent of all adults between 15 and 49 years (SIAPAC 2002, based on data from Ministry of Health and Social Services). As indicated by the shifts in the term used for AIDS in the years since I first came to Oshakati in the early 1990s, people are increasingly aware of the danger involved. While AIDS was previously known as *omukithi gwomashenge* (meaning a disease affecting only homosexuals), people now refer to it as *omukithi gwekomba* (meaning a disease that wipes away people). With such a large part of the population affected, shanty-dwellers are also confronted with the implications of AIDS on a daily basis, through the presence of sick people and death.[11] Despite this, AIDS is still associated with taboos and sanctions, and very few are open about their suffering from the disease.

---

[10] According to the 1999 UNDP Namibia report, there is "an alarming prevalence of alcohol use and abuse among Namibians" (UNDP 2000: Foreword).

[11] With many people being malnourished, it is often difficult to see if people are sick because of AIDS infection or "only poor". Local 'diagnosticians' also say that with people being malnourished and their immune systems being weak, people die so quickly that you hardly realise that they are sick.

The fact that so many people in Oshakati's shantytowns are affected has a number of implications for household organisation and processes of marginalisation and exclusion. Steadily increasing numbers of deaths (SIAPAC 2002) mean that the proportion of single-parent households is on the rise. Moreover particularly women have become more sceptical to marriage or permanent relationships because they perceive the risk of being infected as too high. And with an estimated one out of every eight child being an AIDS orphan (SIAPAC 2002) a new marginalised group of street-children is becoming part of the shantytown scene. While people in the shantytowns argue that the better-off are just as likely to get AIDS as the poorest (because "the better off men are more popular with the ladies" as Loide puts it), they also acknowledge that the poorest tend to be less informed about the risk, less likely to go to hospital for tests and medication, and less likely to get support from family or others once affected – because they often find themselves in a situation where their relations with their kin has been weakened or discontinued (see Chapter 6).

Many households with HIV-positive members thus become ever poorer as those members' ability to work is reduced. With reduced or no income, and with the stigma still being attached to the disease, the burden they represent for their respective households leads to their being particularly easily marginalised and excluded. An Angolan lady with the name of Lídia Fumo, who had lived in Oshoopala since 1989 with a husband, five children and a young sister, told me that one of the hardest choices she had ever made in her life related to her husband being inflicted with AIDS: As he had become weaker and weaker, it had become increasingly difficult for her to continue trading goods from Oshakati over the border into Angola which had come to be the household's main source of income, and expenses particularly for medicines meant that she had less and less money for their children. She eventually had to stop buying the medicines, and her husband was put on a bus to his village in Angola (which many do to save the much higher expenses for transporting a coffin) where he later died. For poor households, having members with AIDS epitomises their own powerlessness and vulnerability. When poor AIDS-victims are sent away or not given medicines that will relieve their suffering and sustain their life, this is not because their family do not care but because the poorest have to make brutal choices on how to spend meagre resources.

Concluding this chapter, the nature of intra-household relations in Oshakati's shantytowns is closely related to the stress of poverty and gender. Rather than representing one type of shanty household – in the form of Hansen's (1997:97) households embedded in traditional norms about kinship and marriage, Ferguson's (1999:192) flexible households responding to circumstances "in a way that the nuclear family has never been able to do", or Ross's (1995:95) notion of households being so permeable that they appear to have no boundaries save those imposed with situational immediacy – all three types are present in the Oshakati shantytowns. The better-off households are formalised and stable, with their members in positions to pool resources and pursue strategies to attain hegemonic perceptions of the good life both for themselves and their children. An increasing number of women establish their own households and alleviate their material poverty by entering flexible matrifocal networks around the informal economy, child-care and domestic tasks. And the poorest men and women are constantly on the move through permeable "living together relationships" and other temporary *ad hoc* relations, which together with the often ensuing violence and abuse (for men) and inability to take proper care of children (for women) contributes to their marginalisation and impoverishment as shanty-dwellers.

In the final chapter, I will address the issue of the extent to which the very poorest – who we now have seen are marginalised from vital relationships with rural areas and the extended family, from urban areas and relations of employment and provisioning, and in relation to the immediate context of the shanty neighbourhood and their own household – are *trapped* in their poverty in the sense of being chronically poor and without expectations of improving their lives (see Chapter 1). This makes it necessary to go beyond the confines of the structuration of poverty and social relationships treated thus far, and look at the shanty-dwellers' own perceptions of their situation and options for social mobility.

9 Overwhelmed by Poverty

I end my analysis of people's experiences of processes of impoverishment, marginalisation and social exclusion in the Oshakati shantytowns by relating to the aspect of the life of the poorest part of the population living there that has puzzled me the most: I have shown that the better-off shanty dwellers strove to improve their situation by establishing and maintaining social relationships with rural and urban socio-cultural formations outside the shantytowns, with the goal of ultimately getting out of shantytowns. And most of the poor struggled to go on with their lives as urban slum dwellers, maintaining relationships with people in the shantytowns as well as with people in rural and urban areas as best they could. But some of the very poorest apparently succumbed to their fate as destitute shantydwellers by spending practically all their time in shantytowns and seeming literally to give up on improving their lives.

So far I have explored the overall shantytown history and structural oppression, and how the ensuing differences in economic positions and gender have channelled social relationships in different directions. While this has gone a long way in explaining the strategies of well-being and social mobility for the better-off, and the strategies for coping with poverty by most of the poor, it has not fully explained the extent to which the very poorest and most destitute are *trapped* in poverty. "Too many people in this place give up their lives" a community worker told me during a discussion we had at the end of my last stay in Oshakati – capturing his impressions by using the Oshiwambo word *uuthigona* ('to be overwhelmed by poverty') to describe the lives of many of the poorest people in the shantytowns.

In the preceding pages I have shown how, as a whole, each of the Oshakati shantytowns was at odds with and lacked effective integration into the larger political and economic social order, and how the shantytown population, if viewed as community, was characterised by poverty and a minimal level of organisation. At the same time, I have emphasised that such conditions were created by historical and structural forces beyond the control of the individual shanty dwellers, that there were differences in the way shanty dwellers have related to those forces, and that these differences are closely related to those people's particular economic position and gender. Actively relating to the world outside the shantytown had material implications, and broadened their social and cultural repertoire. By contrast, effectively being so overwhelmed by poverty as to become trapped in the shantytowns, without employment and income-generating opportunities and in confined social relations and networks, narrowed people's social and cultural repertoire and contributed to their ongoing impoverishment and sense of exclusion. The dominated thus contribute to their own domination, and as Bourdieu contends (quoted in Wacquant 1992:24, see also Hannerz 1992) "the dispositions which incline them to this complicity are also the effect, embodied, of domination".

Seen this way, the shantytowns can be understood to be constituted by, and to contribute to the reproduction of, enduring structures of inequality in the larger society of which they are part (Ortner 1991). They also represent a joint point of reference for the people living there. On the one hand, a sense of community is enforced on them from the outside, as an ascribed identity. The Namibian state demands legality, the market demands money, the media demands literacy and the presence of organisations representing global social movements demand involvement – all conditions that most shanty-dwellers do not and cannot fulfil and that make them part of a community understood to be detached from the mainstream. Even those who do fulfil all or some of the expectations of the larger society, by their being part of other communities (rural or urban, imagined or not), are constantly reminded of their otherness in encounters with the world outside. When shantytown residents reveal to others that they come from Uupindi, Oneshila, Evululuku or Oshoopala, they are continuously confronted with specific reactions and responses that have social and material implications in their own right as I demonstrated in Chapter 3.

As I have stressed throughout the chapters above, however, if seen from inside the shantytowns, any sense that their residents form a coherent community is more contradictory. While anthropology traditionally has used a notion of community as being "a social environment to which people would expect, advocate or wish to belong" (Rapport 1996:116), contemporary shantytowns in Oshakati are too full of contradictions to create such a notion, with their violent pasts, their disconnection from mainstream society, their poverty and the HIV/AIDS that afflicts their residents. Nor do there seem to be any particular institutions or incidents that have created a positive sense of belonging.

Politically, Oshakati's shanty areas were (and still are) fragmented by their apartheid history and the inability of the Swapo government to deliver social services and security. That, and the persisting poverty and inequality, continued to discourage the establishment of joint institutions or associations for community management, for the provision of social services or of finance and credit, or for religious and social affairs – associations that are common in many other slum areas (Tostensen et al. 2001). Moreover, there were no joint heroic experiences of resistance and triumph over the previously oppressive political power in Oshakati's shantytowns, such as there are, for example, in many poor South African urban areas. The most encompassing joint experience is probably the inundation of large parts of the shantytowns by the *efundja* in years of high floods, sweeping away shacks and other property and – as Bank (1996:54) argues in the case of devastating fires in Duncan Village in East London – leading to a situation where "people believe in their own powerlessness and fear, [encouraging] them to be fatalistic and despondent and to view the urban environment as insecure, unstable and violent".

Looking at the level of social relationships, the better-off men and women in the shantytowns had a shared experience of being at least partly within mainstream rural and urban society. For them, oppression and generalised poverty spurred their perceptions and practices aimed at getting themselves as far away as possible from slum life and as close as possible to an urban life-style and rural rootedness. This was the case for Vitus Nangola (Chapter 6), Filemon Shiimi (Chapter 5), Johannes Martin (Chapter 5), Frieda Shigweda (Chapter 6), Ndemuweda Nambadja (chapter 8) and others whom we met in the preceding pages. It was also the case for Puys Nepando, a teacher I have known since I first came to Oshakati and whom I accompanied to his village, to his workplace, to bars he patronised and to family gatherings. Wherever he was he always seemed to have an air of supremacy and control in the way he dressed and spoke, and he had his attention and relationships directed beyond the shantytown area in which he lived – resulting even in his taking an occasional trip to Windhoek.

Contrasting with those people, many poor men shared experiences of impoverishment and of marginalisation from rural and from urban social formations, and found themselves without employment and options for taking care of their families in accordance with their understanding of tradition and of contemporary expectations of manhood and fatherhood. They related to forces of oppression and poverty primarily by seeking individuated solutions through intermittent, piecemeal work in town or by establishing relationships with better-off households in the shantytowns. They were all men who at times had found themselves unable to take proper care of their families, and some of them had become "domestic nomads" during periods of the time I knew them. This was the case for example for Mateus Shonga (Chapter 6), Shilongo Nampila (Chapter 6), João Dungo (Chapter 7) and Silas Litta (Chapter 7). Another example is Mateus Hangula, a 40 year old ex-soldier who lived in a shack in Uupindi when I met him in 1999. He had struggled to make ends meet after his military days had ended in 1990. He told me he was usually not able to hold jobs more than a few days, either because the task ended or because he was fired. He blamed "bad luck"; but people in his neighbourhood said that his trouble was his aggressive behaviour which frequently got him into trouble with employers as well as with the women he stayed with. But he did not give up, and constantly sought ways out in his troubled life – including smuggling and theft.

Many poor women too shared experiences of having been marginalised from rural and urban relationships and having had to take on heavy responsibilities for their own lives. For them, their experience of oppression and poverty had instigated them to find coping strategies that required them to establish their own spheres and niches of survival, most notably in the form of feminised networks and informal employment and income-generating activities. The female and mother centred households they created are expressions of innovative practices in the face of poverty and new socio-cultural space. Lucia Mbunde (Chapter 6), the three sisters living together in Oneshila (Chapter 8), Ndeulita Henock (Chapter 7), Ndeulita Henock (Chapter 7) and others were all in positions to cope largely through such networks. Loide Namwandi, who we met several times in Chapter 8, was poor but confident, particularly in her relationships with other women. Her way of dressing, speaking and moving bore clear evidence of material poverty; but she was self-assured, and she seemed to have had her position as a strong and independent woman confirmed in her relationships with other women, both in the shantytowns and outside.

It was the very poorest and socially marginalised men and women – those who seemed overwhelmed by poverty – who eventually became socially encapsulated in the shantytowns. The poorest and most destitute were those who shared the long-term experience of being marginalised in, and excluded from their relations with the rural areas and their extended families, with the formal urban setting of employment and provisioning, and also, all too often, with their own households or domestic units in the shantytowns themselves. This in turn not only led to their further impoverishment, but also instilled in them a sense of powerlessness and vulnerability, leading them to focus, if they could, on immediate shanty-based relationships or to become socially isolated. On the preceding pages, we have met Emilia Ushoona (Chapter 5), Sofia Kallo (see Chapter 6), Jacob Nelenge (see Chapter 8), John Shitenya (see Chapter 7), Paulus Abiata (see Chapter 6) and others who all demonstrated awareness of their marginal position in relation to the larger society. And it was they who seemed to have become increasingly encapsulated in their shantytown-based poverty and relationships. One of my most vivid and sad memories of such extreme poverty and isolation is two brothers in Uupindi who slept and spent most of their days sitting in the ruins of a brick building, only leaving it to search for food in a garbage-pile used by people in the neighbourhood. People told me they had originally come from a village in Omusati to join the South African army or to work, but had accomplished neither, that they had lived alone for as long as people could remember, and that, as one person put it: "poverty has ruined them".

The salient features of such a type of poverty and social encapsulation are, I would argue, twofold: One is the disjuncture between the hegemonic cultural flows of urbanisation and modernity and of rurality and tradition, on one hand, and the real life situations of the very poorest in the shantytowns on the other – effectively making the dominated give up and contribute to their own exclusion through their acts of compliance (Bourdieu 1990, Wacquant 1992). The second is a sense of emergency in the acts in which they engage and the events in which they participate to secure food and other basic necessities – all spurred on by their abject poverty (Douglas 1982). Both contribute to a perception among the very poorest of being trapped in their poverty; they give up making much of their lives; and they act in ways that tend to further undermine their situation. The situation is thus one that, were one to phrase it in terms of Hannerz's (1992) characterisation of a micro-culture of destitution, might be seen as reflecting an interplay between concrete personal experiences of impoverishment, marginalisation and social exclusion, on one hand, and generalised understandings and dispositions of being trapped in poverty on the other – all then maintained in encapsulated networks between the poorest and most destitute in the Oshakati shantytowns.

The shantytowns' poorest men and women have all, of course, been exposed to the larger rural and urban socio-cultural formation. But they have been so marginalised from both over a long period of time that they appear to have given up establishing relations outside the shantytown in which they reside. As we have seen, most of the destitute men staying there either wandered around between the shanties searching for money, food or other basic necessities, or met in one of the many *cuca*-shops, some to drink local brew, others just to sit there talking or remaining silent for hours. Most of the destitute women seemed to seek more individualised personal relations or solitude to escape the stigma of not being able to earn a living and take care of children, but they also primarily related to other people in the shantytown who were in a similar situation to their own.

A striking feature of conversations I have been part of or listened in to with such people is the extent to which they talk as if the shantytown represent their whole world. They do of course refer to personal experiences in their rural areas of origin, to incidents during the war and to encounters and setbacks in the formal urban areas. But they do not do so in ways that make these references part of their contemporary coping strategies and relationships. Rather, most conversations centre around acts and events in the shantytowns themselves. They concern ways to acquire money, food, shelter and other basic necessities from neighbours and acquaintances, and problems they face in the shantytowns relating to poverty, crime and abuse that often involve the very poorest themselves.

Fernando Morales was born in a village in Angola just across the border in 1960. He told me he had grown up on a Portuguese-owned *fazenda* (farm), with his parents and six siblings. They were poor and treated badly by the owner, and three of his siblings died when they were young. He said they often starved, and were left with nothing when the owner fled in 1972 as a result of the war. His father had disappeared at independence in 1975 (Mr. Morales thought he had left for the Angolan capital Luanda), and his mother barely managed to feed herself and her three remaining children from their small homestead. Mr. Morales himself left in 1983 to join UNITA and subsequently the South African 32nd Battalion (see chapter 3). For seven years he was involved in war and acts of atrocity, for the most time living and moving around in the border areas between Namibia and Angola. In 1990 when the war ended, he was in Oshakati but with nowhere to go. His family in Angola was dead or had disappeared, and he could not find employment or other sources of income in town. The combination of being an ex-soldier and of Angolan origin, he told me, had made it impossible. When I first met Mr. Morales in 1993, he lived in a small tent in Oshoopala. He had had two children with two different Namibian women (one in the rural areas and one in Oshakati), but no contact with any of them. He managed by helping neighbours with small tasks and some help from the Tocoist church, but most of the day he spent in or around his tent sleeping, or talking to others (mainly men) who found themselves in similar situations. Every time I came to Oshakati, I always found him near to his tent or close by in the neighbourhood. What struck me was that, despite being only around 40 years old, he seemed to have accepted (or succumbed to) his fate. He told me he had stopped trying to find work (saying that it had become impossible with the poor state he was in), and lamented that it was difficult for him to get to know people who could help him (women in the neighbourhood called him a *maluco*, a term which signifies a mixture of poverty and lunacy). His main source of food seemed to be occasional left-overs and *tombo* (beer) given to him by neighbours. When I last met him in 2001, he was malnourished and sick and I could see that he was afraid and had lost hope.

In parallel with their exclusion or withdrawal from social relationships outside the shantytowns and the concomitant sense of social isolation among the poorest and most destitute shanty-dwellers, I have shown that their abject poverty and vulnerability is characterised by its situational immediacy. Poverty *demands* a constant search for food, shelter, clothing and other basic necessities, making *ad hoc* and short-term moves an integral part of the lives of the poorest and most destitute in the shanty population. Poverty itself, embodied in hunger and illness thus has its own logic in the form of instant experiences of hunger or fatal disease that bring what Douglas (1982) calls immediacy or emergency into life. Psychologists like Barbarin and Richter (2001) tell us that chronic poverty with what they call its stress of daily living is especially devastating. Studying children growing up in Soweto, they conclude that, for children especially, extreme poverty is among the most consistent predictions of behavioural and social problems.

The very poorest in the Oshakati shantytowns often have a long personal history of relations of poverty and marginalisation. In their relationships with rural areas and rural kin, as we have seen, the poorest based themselves on rare and *ad hoc* visits to solve an urgent problem rather than longer-term investments in rural rootedness, often with negative consequences for their ability to cope at decisive moments in life, and sometimes resulting in the termination of rural relationships altogether. We have also seen that in the urban context their inability to obtain employment and relate to an urban life-style has ultimately led to their withdrawal to shanty life, to focussing on establishing *ad hoc* relationships and, often, to becoming involved in closed networks with people in similar situations (in the case of men) and relative isolation (in the case of women). And as parts of households as social units, we have seen that they entered cohabitation relationships, in defiance of both traditional and modernist expectations – relationships that led all too often to further poverty and vulnerability when they disintegrated. We have also seen how the children in many of the poorest households, and the increasing numbers of street-children, remain in the shantytowns during the day, looking for food or other basic necessities and becoming encapsulated in the shantytown and its relationships.

Anna Iipinge was born in a rural village in Ohangwena in 1974, in a family with "many children and little food" as she said. She described her childhood as "hard": Her father was known as the village drunk, and her mother did her best to feed her four children (Anna thought that "at least four" had died when they were babies). When Anna became pregnant by an older village man at age 15 years, she left the village: the child's father did not want her there and her mother could not care for an extra household member. With this decision, she effectively also left her rural relationships behind. Coming to Oshakati in 1989, she settled in Kanjengedi (a small shantytown neighbouring Oneshila), living with a cousin who worked for SWATF. But he "was not nice to me and my child" as Anna put it, and after a few months she moved in with another soldier in Uupindi. He too mistreated her and, when she got pregnant with twins, he left her. When I met Anna Ipinge in 1994, she was living alone with no man to support her in a small shack with her three children. She could barely make ends meet by selling small things like bottles and empty tin-cans collected in the shanties and fish and frogs caught in dams during the flooding season. In desperation, she co-habited with five different men during the subsequent years, all relations lasting for a short time, without improving her situation and with further suffering. When I last saw her in 2001, she was living alone again. She had by then lost one child and her other children were malnourished and sick, and her neighbours said she simply could not take care of herself and her children and had effectively cut her off from her social network by then. As I have described in chapter 8, when women were unwilling or unable to care for their children, they were soon socially ostracised.

Common to many of the *ad hoc* and short-term moves of the poorest is that they further undermine their own situations and their ability to get by. Getting out of their abject poverty necessitates social relationships and investments in ways that the poorest find to be out of reach. The differences between the longer term strategies of the better-off and the situational immediacy of those living in utter poverty or destitution are evidenced in people's behaviour and discourses. I have shown how the better-off as well as many of the poor have their days set up with working or seeking employment, domestic tasks, school for the children, and visits to family, friends and bars or *cuca*-shops in the evenings. In contrast, the poorest tend to peddle rather sporadically between frantic activities to secure basic necessities and an apparent withdrawal from life. As Shifiona (2001) has pointed out, depression is a common problem in Oshakati's shantytowns, a state reflected in one woman's comment that "I felt sad most of the time. When looking at the situation I found myself in, and all the unfulfilled promises, I felt abandoned" (Shifiona 2001:9).

A telling example of the effect of abject poverty on acts and events is the issue of safe sex practices in a context where AIDS is prevalent. Using condoms reflects a long-term strategy and a concern with the reproduction of oneself and one's immediate social relationships; not using them during sexual encounters implies a concern with the present only, where one's longer term vision is curtailed (even though the decision about condom usage is still largely vested in men). Also, other self-destructive acts I have witnessed or heard of during my years in the Oshakati shanties have been performed by shanty-dwellers in the most desperate situations as either a call for help or in defiance of life itself. These are acts such as those of poor men who spend their last money on drinks for friends and hold nothing back for critical food provision even though they know they will only get drinks in return; of poor men who are totally dependent on their women beating those same women and treating them so badly that they *know* they will be chased out; of people committing serious crimes of child molestation around the belief that having sex with a virgin will cure AIDS,[1] *knowing* that they will likely be jailed and even more marginalised when they come out; and (as an ultimate act of defiance of life) people committing suicide in a public space rather than in a private place.[2] The case of a young mother from Uupindi who left her baby in a plastic bag in bushes in central Oshakati in March 2000 (*The Namibian*, 9 March 2000) may reflect that kind of desperation and defiance of life by a shantytown resident who could not handle being a woman in a chaotic shanty setting and could not take care of her child.

People's different relationships to the material and cultural manifestations of poverty is also reflected in their understanding of poverty itself – or of why some people are poor and others are better off. Throughout my time in Oshakati I have asked hundreds of shanty-dwellers why they think some people are poor and others better off. There are of course overlapping perspectives, but three types of perceptions stand out.

First there is the notion that people in the shanties are victims of political and economic forces outside their own control. Such ideas as usually expressed by people in better-off or *mbwiti* households. In the words of a teacher in Uupindi:

---

[1] A community worker in Oshakati recently urged people to "refrain from cultural myths of sexuality, and abuse of alcohol and drugs, which can lead them to practising immoral habits, such as rape and murder of infants" *(The Namibian*, 07.04.2005).

[2] Shifiona (2001:2) reports that there is an exceptionally high suicide rate in the Oshakati shantytowns among men as well as women.

> I think some people are poor and some are rich because there is mismanagement and misuse in the economy of this country. Money is improperly distributed among different groups and as a result some people suffer and become poorer and poorer. The poor need to be employed for them to afford basic needs, and the rich must play a role by employing them.

The second notion of poverty and differentiation centres around the responsibility of each individual shanty-dweller for their own situation, often expressed by women, and often with reference to men. As a poor woman in Oneshila put it:

> Rich people are hard working and always strive for even better things. A poor household is not well constructed, and cannot afford what it needs. Some people have to be poor and others rich, because some are lazy and some are not. Poor people are afraid to explore things, while rich people socialise easily because they are free.

And the third notion of poverty and economic differentiation, which sees those conditions as God-given and unavoidable, is the one that is most often expressed by the very poorest themselves such as a destitute man in his mid-40s in Oshoopala:

> I think it is God's will to have poor and rich, because the poor have to work for the rich. It is just like the fingers on our hands: some are long, and some are short. People are created differently by God; some rich and some poor. If a person is born poor, it doesn't help if he works hard. Most poor people don't have the courage to improve their lives, because they don't believe they can do it.

The last sentence of this third quote sums up the essence of the sense among the poorest and most marginalised in the Oshakati's shantytown of being trapped in their poverty – closely related to the socio-economic context in which they find themselves.

What I have shown in this chapter is how specific epistemic and organisational structures predominant in, and in the context of, the shanties contribute to the perpetuation of poverty both at the community and at the individual level. Confined and encapsulated social relations tend to reproduce a social formation that is conducive to producing an outcome of marginality. For the very poorest who are also the most marginalised, their own long-term experiences of discrepancy between their own lives and the hegemonic perceptions of modernity and tradition, along with the sense of emergency created by their very poverty, together create a sense of inferiority and hopelessness, indeed of being overwhelmed by poverty. For some, as reflected in the title of this work, the final confirmation of being that poor and so utterly marginalised is to be hastily buried in an urban graveyard that is filled with litter, instead of in their rural village attended by family, relatives and friends and surrounded by the remains of deceased kin, in accordance with culturally acceptable ideas about how the end of life should be.

10 Conclusions

My point of departure for this book has been a search for an understanding of the processes that enable some people living in the oppressed and poor Oshakati shantytowns to strive to go on with their lives or improve their situation, while others, living in the same setting and apparently under the same conditions, seem to be trapped in their poverty and to give up making more of their lives.

My analysis has been carried out with reference to the long tradition in the anthropology of Southern Africa of looking at issues of urbanisation, modernity and social change (Hannerz 1980:119-162) – starting with Hellman's (1948) *Rooiyard*, going on to the Manchester School (see e.g. Epstein 1958; Gluckman 1961; Mitchell 1966) and the Xhosa in Town trilogy (the East London studies: Reader 1961; Mayer 1963; Pauw 1963), and ending with recent studies by James Ferguson (1999), Karen Tranberg Hansen (1997) and Leslie Bank (1996, 2002) – as well as a number of other urban studies more limited in scope (see e.g. Andersson 2001; Englund 2002; Frayne 2004; Bähr 2007). The focus has been a remarkably consistent approach in regional ethnography, and contributed not only with insights into urban lives but also with innovative perspectives in methods and approaches. While drawing on these, my main concern has been the inadequate attention they pay to the implications of structural oppression and level of material poverty for people's coping strategies and cultural identities – captured in Spiegel's (1997) call for a "new materially grounded culturalism" as a paradigm for the anthropology of Southern Africa.

My central thesis has been that levels of well-being and poverty among shanty-dwellers depend on the ways and extent to which people come to terms with and possibly internalise structural oppression, and their ability to establish and maintain social relations with rural and urban areas outside poor shantytowns. I have related to this through a focus on the dominant effect of social structures and processes on people's lives, where history (Comaroff and Comaroff 1997) and material and cultural flows (Hannerz 1992) have been seen to define Oshakati and its shantytowns as oppressed and poor urban space and place. Social relations of impoverishment and marginalisation have been analysed through a focus on social practise (Bourdieu 1977 and 1990; Ortner 1984 and 2006), with economic positions and gender largely determining the nature of the shanty-dwellers' relationships with rural areas and kin, the formal town and provisioning, people in the shantytowns themselves and intra-household relationships – following Bourdieu (1990) and Hannerz (1992) in their notion that cumulative exposure to extreme oppression and poverty instils in the very poorest and most marginalised shanty-dwellers a sense of being trapped in and overwhelmed by chronic poverty.

In support of my thesis, the first part of the book (Chapters 2-4) looked at how historical processes and structural conditions have shaped the Oshakati shantytowns with their particular distribution of population and material realities. I started by tracing the history of the shanty population. The pressure on traditional Owambo society from the colonial authorities, the church and system of labour migration led to changing social relationships between authorities and their subjects, young and old and men and women – all exacerbated by an increasing commodification of relationships following the capitalisation of labour and land. Those Owambos who lost out in the process, found themselves with limited access to both employment opportunities and rural resources. In turn that resulted in their being pauperised and marginalised from rural society and relationships. The outbreak of war that led to acts of violence and atrocities exacerbated these processes of socio-economic disintegration and differentiation. From the mid-1960s, primarily the poorest and rurally most marginalised men and women in Owambo started moving to the recently established town of Oshakati, to join the South African colonial forces or work in the informal economy. Most soon found themselves marginalised in apartheid-structured urban space, living in dense and tense urban shantytowns. With Namibian independence and the withdrawal of the colonial power, the economic conditions of the existing shanty population deteriorated while new people with a more varied socio-economic background moved in and increased socio-economic differentiation.

Moving on to the contemporary structural position of Oshakati and its shantytowns in the Namibian political economy, I then showed how the flows of the modern state, the market, the media and social movements were at odds with shanty-life – making the shantytowns increasingly susceptible to forces of oppression and marginalisation. For the state, the shantytowns were at odds with its project of modernisation and governmentality, as evidenced by the illegality of tenure and limited state investments in physical and social infrastructure – conditions that maintained the shantytowns as poor and illegitimate social spaces. For the market, the shanty population remained important, as evidenced by its signs and symbols of modernity and consumption that penetrated into the shantytowns – but whose commodities were out of reach for the poorest parts of the population who could afford only its informal and second-hand expressions. The cultural flows of the media largely carried the meanings of the state and the market, relevant for those in a position to relate to them but deepening the gap between hegemonic flows and the real lives of the shantytown's poorest. And social movements, carrying western ideologies of democracy, participation and gender equality, met shanty realities where only parts of the population were in positions to become involved in their ideas.

The demographic and material expressions of the historical processes and structures treated revealed a situation of general material poverty in the Oshakati shantytowns, but also exposed internal inequalities implying differences primarily along lines of economic positions and gender – in a situation where even small differences in income and social organisation affect whether individuals and households find themselves in positions of well-being, poverty or destitution. Albeit necessary to understand the making of the Oshakati shantytowns as poor urban spaces, and of the materiality of poverty, descriptions of structurally driven processes through quantitative data cannot, however, explain the processes of impoverishment, marginalisation and exclusion among the shanty population that isolated some people in abject shanty poverty while others were able to maintain constructive urban and rural relationships or to move out of the shantytowns altogether.

That is better achieved by the data and analyses I have introduced and developed in the second part of the book (Chapter 5-9). There I focused on social relations of poverty as practice and argued that, even though structures do have a powerful effect upon human action and events, they do not preclude social change. With reference to the importance of social relationships for understanding relative well-being and poverty in the Oshakati shantytowns, I used four basic conceptual tools. The first was the notion of the rural, the urban and the slum as separate socio-cultural configurations in which people's options for relating constructively to them varied between the better-off and the poor. The second was the notion of a commodification of social relationships across rural, urban and shanty space, with money and material means being increasingly important for their maintenance. The third was the notion that the social reproduction of both households and individuals rests on socially established patterns of power and poverty, with the social space for women and men resting on changes in their status and roles. And the fourth was the notion that the very poorest develop particular dispositions and actions for dealing with their circumstances that tend to contribute to their impoverishment and destitution.

The shanty-dwellers' social relationships with rural areas and kindred were important both for access to rural resources such as land and cattle and for support at decisive moments of childbirth, marriage, divorce and death. The situation of generalised poverty in which many people found themselves made it necessary for them to fill rural relationships with material content if those relationships were to be sustained, and particular expectations were vested in men as traditional family heads and providers. Shantytown women had closer rural relationships through matrilineal family and children, but in their case too their relationships had to be maintained through material exchanges if they were to be sustainable over time. The poorest shantytown men and women could not maintain rural relationships, and they thereby jeopardised their access to rural resources and support from the extended family – leading them to be and to feel particularly vulnerable. Thus while rural relationships represented important material as well as emotional parts of the coping strategies for the better-off – with options for fulfilling ultimate goals of moving back to their respective villages during old age – for the poorest shanty-dwellers their inability to maintain such relationships not only affected their material well-being and security, but also deepened their sense of being overwhelmed, marginalised and encapsulated within the shantytowns.

Social relationships with the formal urban area were crucial for access to employment and income, necessary to alleviate poverty and for upward social mobility. Yet connecting to the formal urban town itself required a set of resources, including education and command of urban cultural codes, which only the better-off part of the shanty population possessed. Unemployed and poor men came to depend on erratic, piecemeal and individuated work in a highly competitive formal labour market, with fluctuating returns. For such men, finding themselves marginalised and excluded from all urban relations of provisioning, the only alternative became a search for food and other basic necessities through shanty-based social relationships. Poor shanty-town women were in a position to relate to the formal urban space through the informal economy, transgressing the boundary between the two types of urban settings and giving them a small but regular income and a sense of belonging. The irrelevance of men in these women's employment strategies led to the development of close matrifocal relationships – for all but the very poorest women who were unable to contribute with money or labour.

People's most immediately important social relationships for access to food and other basic necessities, indeed to social reproduction as a whole, were those found in households. Yet through colonial encounters, commodification and urbanisation the household had itself come under pressure – pressure that, for people in Oshakati's shantytowns, was exacerbated by the stress of living in oppressed urban slums and in poverty. While better-off shanty-dwellers did manage to marry and integrate their relationships with their extended families, poorer shanty-dwellers entered less stable relations of cohabitation that frequently disintegrated and left people marginalised and in precarious situations where they felt quite overwhelmed by poverty. With many women being the main providers through the informal economy, men were also increasingly seen as redundant as household members, leading to a sharp increase in the proportion of *de facto* female headed households. The marginal position of poor men in the domestic sphere often led to violence and abuse, further undermining their position, while the poorest women who were unable to take care of themselves and their children violated local perceptions of woman- and motherhood and were among the most destitute shanty-dwellers.

Shanty dwellers with a long-term experience of oppression, impoverishment and marginalisation from rural, urban as well as shanty relationships withdrew and entered into confined or encapsulated relations primarily with people in their own situation. The discrepancy between the larger urban and rural socio-cultural order, and their own abject poverty in confined slum areas, led them into a situation in which they gave up trying to make much of their lives and acted with reference to short-term goals for survival. For destitute men this primarily took the form of small closed networks around *cuca*-shops and other shanty arenas, often combined with destructive acts of violence which further undermined their situation. Destitute women usually led more isolated lives with their children, instilling in them a desperate sense of being overwhelmed by their poverty and being encapsulated. The very poorest part of the shanty population, who have been my main concern in this study, thus found themselves chronically poor as the combined outcome of structural oppression, a long-term experience of impoverishment and social marginalisation, and a sense of being trapped in the shantytowns with no options for improving their lives.

Abbreviations

AIDS	Acquired Immune Deficiency Syndrome
BBC	British Broadcasting Corporation
CNN	Cable News Network
CBDO	Community Based Development Organisation
CDC	Community Development Committee
CoD	Congress of Democrats
DAPP	Development Aid from People to People
DSTV	Digital Satellite Television
ESPN	Entertainment and Sports Programming Network
GDP	Gross Domestic Product
HDI	Human Development Index
HIV	Human Immunodeficiency Virus
MHSS	Ministry of Health and Social Services
NBC	Namibian Broadcasting Corporation
NDC	Natioanl Development Corporation
NGO	Non-Governmental Organisation
OHSIP	Oshakati Human Settlement Development Project
OTC	Oshakati Town Council
PLAN	People's Liberation Army of Namibia
SADF	South African Defence Force
Swapo	South West Africa People's Organisation of Namibia
SWATF	South West African Defence Force
UNICEF	The United Nations Children's Fund
UNITA	União Nacional Para a Independência Total de Angola
UNAM	University of Namibia

List of Figures

Figure 1: Population Pyramid 1994 (Age Cohorts). Source: Tvedten and Pomuti   8

Figure 2: Household Income Distribution by Sex of Household Head 1994. Source: Tvedten and Pomuti   8

Figure 3: World apart. Photographer: Jacob Holdt. (http://www.american-pictures.com/english/jacob/index.html)   60

Figure 4: Monthly Household Income Distribution 2002. Source: Oshakati Town Council (OTC)   78

Figure 5: The Shopkeeper Maria Nangolo. Photographer: Albertina Abiatar   84

Figure 6: Lahia Endjala from the Oneshila location. Photographer: Albertina Abiatar   84

Figure 7: Parents constructing kindergarten classes in their community to give their children the opportunity to learn. Photographer: Lydia Uudhingu   85

Figure 8: Family having dinner, the traditional Owambo porridge. Photographer: Paulina Iindongo   85

Figure 9: Joung women meeting at a Cucashop. Photographer: Albertina Abiatar   86

Figure 10: Girl sent out by her mother to go and get some tombo, the traditional Owambo beer. Photographer: Aline Naule   86

Figure 11: Man taking a bath. Photographer: Anton Silveira   87

Figure 12: Kids playing a game called Ndilimani. Photographer: Lydia Uudhingu   87

Figure 13: John Nandjembo Ndaunda-Onya practising the art of singing and playing the guitar. Photographer: Albertina Abiatar   88

Figure 14: A kindergarten teacher teaching her young pupils. Photographer: Lydia Uudhingu   88

Figure 15: Kuku Johanna selling apples at the Okamukuku Open Market at the Oshakati main road. Photographer: Albertina Abiatar   89

Figure 16: One of the houses built through loans from the Build Together Programme in the informal settlements. Photographer: Magdalena Samuel   89

Figure 17: Daniel Indongo after breaking the wall of silence about his HIV-status. Photographer: Karen Shiimi   90

Figure 18: Elisabeth Vilho from the Oshoopala Location making a living from doing baskets made of dried palm-leaves. Photographer: Rosalia Uushona   90

Figure 19: Mamy using Revlon to stretch her hair. Photographer: Magdalena Samuel   91

Figure 20: Child gathering food in the dustbin. Photographer: Karen Shiimi   91

List of Maps

Map 1: Namibia and its regions. Adapted from G. Hopwood: 'Guide to Namibian Politics', 2008 edition, Windhoek, p. 4   6

Map 2: Oshakati and its Shantytowns. Designed by Robert Sjursen, Chr. Michelsen Insitute   7

List of Tables

Table 1: Population in the Oshakati Shantytowns, 1994 & 2002. Sources: OHSIP 1994; OTC 2002   68

Table 2: Age Structure of Oshakati Shantytown Population (Percent). Source: Tvedten and Pomuti 1994   68

Table 3: Sex Structure of Oshakati Shantytown Population (Percent). Source: Tvedten and Pomuti 1994   69

Table 4: Levels of Education of Oshakati Shantytown Population (Percent). Source: Tvedten and Pomuti 1994   69

Table 5: Health Conditions of Oshakati Shantytown Population. Source: UNICEF 1995; MHSS 2001   70

Table 6: Monthly Household Income by Shantytown (Percent). Source: Tvedten and Pomuti 1994   73

Table 7: Employment Status by Shantytown Population (Percent). Source: Tvedten and Pomuti 1994   74

Table 8: Employment Status of Adult by Sex in Shantytown Population (Percent). Source: Tvedten and Pomuti 1994   74

Table 9: Employment Status and Sex of Household Head by Income (Percent). Source: Tvedten and Pomuti 1994   75

Bibliography

Adongo, Jonathan and Mariama Deen-Swarray (2006). *Poverty Alleviation in Rural Namibia through Improved Access to Financial Services. NEPRU Working Paper No. 109.* Windhoek: The Namibian Economic Policy Unit.

Africa Research (2003). *Annual Economic Profile: Namibia January 2003.* Web-site: www.sarpn.org.za/ d0000206.

Amukugo, Elisabeth Magano (1995). *Education and Politics in Namibia: Past Trends and Future Prospects.* Windhoek: Gamsberg Macmillan.

Andersson, Jens A. (2001). "Reinterpreting the Rural-Urban Connection: Migration Practises and Socio-Cultural Dispositions of Buhera Workers in Harare." In: *Africa* Vol. 71(1) pp.82-112.

Appadurai, Arjun (1995). "The Production of Locality". In: R. Fardon (ed.) *Counterworks. The Uses of Knowledge. Global and Local Relations.* London and New York: Routledge.

Appadurai, A. (1996). *Modernity at Large. Cultural Dimensions of Globalization.* Delhi: Oxford University Press.

Arce, Alberto and Norman Long (2000). "Reconfiguring Modernity and Development from an Anthropological Perspective". In: A. Arce and N. Long (eds.) *Anthropology, Development and Modernities. Exploring Discourses, Countertendencies and Violence.* London: Routledge, pp.1-31.

Askew, Kelly (2002). "Introduction". In: K. Askew and R. R. Wilk (eds.) *The Anthropology of Media. A Reader.* Oxford: Blackwell Publishers, pp.1-13.

Banghart, Peter D. (1969). *Migrant Labour in South West Africa and its Effects on Owambo Tribal Life.* Stellenbosch: University of Stellenbosch.

Bank, Leslie (1996). *Poverty in Duncan Village, East London: A Qualitative Assessment.* East London, South Africa: Institute of Social and Economic Research (ISER).

Bank, Leslie (2001). "Living Together, Moving Apart: Home-Made Agendas, Identity Politics and Urban-Rural Linkages in the Eastern Cape, South Africa." In: *Journal of Contemporary African Studies* Vol. 19(1) pp.129-147.

Bank, Leslie (2002). *Xhosa in Town Revisited: from Urban Anthropology to an Anthropology of Urbanism. Department of Social Anthropology.* Cape Town: University of Cape Town.

Barbarin, Oscar A. and Linda M. Richter (2001). *Mandela's Children. Growing Up in Post-Apartheid South Africa.* New York and London: Routledge.

Barker, Gary and C. Ricardo (2005). "Young Men and the Construction of Masculinity on Sub-Saharan Africa: Implications for HIV-AIDS, Conflict and Violence". *Social Development Paper No. 26 / June 2005*. Washington: World Bank

Barth, Fredrik (1992). "Towards Greater Naturalism in Conceptualising Societies". In: A. Kuper (ed.) *Conceptualising Society*. London: Routledge, pp.17-33.

Barth, Fredrik (1994). "A Personal View of Present Tasks and Priorities in Cultural and Social Anthropology". In: R. Borofsky (ed.) *Assessing Cultural Anthropology*. New York: McGraw-Hill, pp.349-361.

Becker, Heike (2000). "A Concise History of Gender, `Tradition´ and the State in Namibia". In: C. Keulder (ed.) *State, Society and Democracy. A Reader in Namibian Politics*. Windhoek: Gamsberg Macmillan.

Becker, Heike (2001). "Living the Post-Colonial Empirical. New Perspectives on Doing Anthropology in South Africa". Paper Presented for the American Anthropological Association Conference in Washington DC 28.11-02.12 2001.

Becker, Heike and Manfred Heinz (1995). "Marriage and Customary Law in Namibia". *CASS Working Document No. 30*. Windhoek: Centre for Applied Social Sciences.

Bell, Sandra and S. Coleman (eds) (1999). *The Anthropology of Friendship*. Oxford: Berg.

Bloch, Maurice and Jonathan Parry (1989). "Introduction: Money and the Morality of Exchange". In: J. Parry and M. Bloch (eds.) *Money and the Morality of Exchange*. Cambridge: Cambridge University Press, pp.1-32.

BtP (1992). *'Build Together' National Housing Programme. Implementation Guidelines*. Windhoek: Ministry of Local Government and Housing.

Bourdieu, Pierre (1977). *Outline of a Theory of Practice*. Cambridge: Cambridge University Press.

Bourdieu, Pierre (1990). *The Logic of Practice*. Stanford: Stanford University Press.

Bourdieu, Pierre and L. J. D. Wacquant (eds.) *An Invitation to Reflexive Sociology*. London: Polity Press

Bourgois, Philippe (1995). *In Search of Respect. Selling Crack in El Barrio*. Cambridge: Cambridge University Press.

Brown, Susan (1995). "Diplomacy by Other Means – SWAPO's Liberation War". In: C. Leys and J. S. Saul (eds.) *The Two-Edged Sword: Namibia's Liberation Struggle*. London: James Curry.

Bryceson, D.F. and D. Potts (eds.) (2006). *African Urban Economies. Viability, Vitality or Vitiation?* Basingstok: Palgrave Macmillan.

Buraway, Michael (2000). *Global Ethnography. Forces, Connections and Imaginations in a Postmodern World*. Los Angeles: University of California Press.

Bähr, Erik (2007). "Reluctant Solidarity. Death, Urban Poverty and Neighbourly Assistance in South Africa". In: *Ethnography* Vol. 8 (1) pp.33-59.

Caldeira, Teresa P.R. (2000). *City of Walls. Crime, Segregation and Citizenship in São Paulo*. Berkeley: University of California Press.

Carrier, James (1996). "Consumption". In: Barnard, Alan and Jonathan Spencer (eds.). *Encyclopaedia of Social and Cultural Anthropology*. London: Routledge, pp 128-129.

Carrier, James D. and Miller. D (1999). "From Private Virtue to Public Vice". In: H. Moore (ed.) *Anthropological Theory of Today*. Cambridge/Oxford: Polity Press, pp.24-43.

Castells, M (1999). *The Rise of the Network Society*. London: Blackwell Publishers.

Chambers, Robert (1989). *Vulnerability. How the Poor Cope*. IDS Bulletin. Sussex: Institute of Development Studies.

Chant, Sylvia (2007). *Gender, Generation and Poverty. Exploring the 'Feminisation of Poverty' in Africa, Asia and Latin-America*. London: Edward Elgar.

CLGF (2004). *The Local Government System in Namibia*. London: Commonwealth Local Government Forum.

Comaroff, John L. and Jean Comaroff (1999). "Occult Economies and the Violence of Abstraction: Notes from the South African Postcolony." In: *American Ethnologist* Vol. 26(2) pp.279-303.

Comaroff, John L. and Jean Comaroff (1997). *Of Revelation and Revolution. The Dialectics of Modernity in a South African Frontier*. Chicago: The University of Chicago Press.

Cornwall, Andrea (2007). "Myths To Live By? Female Solidarity and Female Autonomy Reconsidered " In: *Development and Change* Vol. 38(1) pp.149-168.

Cornwall, Andrea, Elisabeth Harrison and Ann Whitehead (2007). "Gender Myths and Feminisation Fables: The Struggle for Interpretive Power in Gender and Development." In: *Development and Change* Vol. 38(1) pp.1-20.

CPRC (2005). *The Chronic Poverty Report 2004-05*. Manchester: Institute for Development Policy and Management, The Chronic Poverty Research Centre.

DaMatta, Roberto (1995). *On the Brazilian Urban Poor. An Anthropological Report*. Notre Dame: University of Notre Dame Press.

D'Andrade, Roy (1995). "Moral Models in Anthropology." In: *Current Anthropology* Vol. 36 pp.399-408.

Devereux, Stephen and John Hoddinott (1992). *Fieldwork in Developing Countries*. New York: Harvester Wheatsheaf.

Devisch, René (1995). "Frenzy, Violence and Ethical Renewal in Kinshasa." In: *Public Culture* Vol. 7 pp.593-629.

Dobell, Lauren (1998). *Swapo's Struggle for Namibia, 1960-1991. War by Other Means*. Basel: P. Schlettwein Publishing Switzerland.

Douglas, Mary (1982). *In the Active Voice*. London: Routledge and Kegan Paul.

Eames, Edwin and J.G. Goode (1977). *Anthropology of the City*. Englewood Cliffs: Prentice Hall.

Eames, Edwin and J.G. Goode (1996). "An Anthropological Critique of the Culture of Poverty", in: Gmelch, George and N.P Zenner (eds): *Urban Life. Readings in Urban Anthropology*. Prospect Heights, Illinois: Waveland Press.

Edelman, Marc and Angelique Haugerud (2005). *The Anthropology of Development and Globalization. From Classical Political Economy to Contemporary Neoliberalism*. Oxford: Blackwell Publishing Ltd.

EIU (2008). *Country Profile 2008. Namibia*. London: The Economist Intelligence Unit.

Englund, Harri (2002). "The Village in the City, the City in the Village: Migrants in Lilongwe." In: *Journal of Southern African Studies* Vol. 28(1).

Epstein, A.L. (1958). *Politics in an Urban African Community*. Manchester: Manchester University Press.

Erasmus, Paul (1995). *Inside the Dark Heart of Koefot. Mail and Guardian*. Johannesburg.

Erichsen, Casper W. (2000). *"Shoot to Kill. Photographic Images in the Namibian Independence/Bush War"*. Paper delivered at the conference "Public History: Forgotten History", University of Namibia, Northern Campus 22-25 August 2000.

Eriksen, Thomas Hylland (2003). "Introduction", in: Eriksen, Thomas Hylland (ed): *Globalisation. Studies in Anthropology*. London: Pluto Press.

Eriksen, Thomas Hylland and Finn Sivert Nielsen (2001). *A History of Anthropology*. London: Pluto Press.

Escobar, Arturo (1991). "Anthropology and the Development Encounter: The Making and Marketing of Development Anthropology." In: *American Anthropologist* Vol. 18(4) pp.658-682.

Estermann, Carlos (1957). *The Ethnography of Southwestern Angola. The Non-Bantu Peoples, the Ambo Ethnic Group*. New York: Africana Publishing Company.

Fairweather, Ian (2003). "`Showing Off´: Nostalgia and Heritage in North-Central Namibia." In: *Journal of Southern African Studies* Vol. 29(1) pp.279-296.

Fardon, Richard (1990). "Localising Strategies: The Regionalization of Ethnographic Accounts". In: R. Fardon (ed.) *Localising Strategies: Regional Traditions of Ethnographic Writing*. Edinburgh: Scottish Academic Press, pp.1-31.

Ferguson, James (1994). *The Anti-Politics Machine. "Development", Depolitization and Bureaucratic Power in Lesotho*. Minneapolis: University of Minnesota Press.

Ferguson, James (1997). "The Country and the City on the Copperbelt". In: A. Gupta and J. Ferguson (eds.) *Culture, Power, Place. Explorations in Critical Anthropology*. Durham and London: Duke University Press.

Ferguson, James (1999). *Expectations of Modernity: Myths and Meanings of Urban Life on the Zambian Copperbelt*. Berkeley: University of California Press.

Ferguson, James and A. Gupta (2005). "Spatializing States. Towards and Ethnography of Neo-Liberal Governmentality". In: Inda, Jonathan Xavier (ed). *Anthropology of Modernity. Foucault, Governmentality and Life politics*. Oxford: Blackwell Publishing.

Frayne, Bruce (2004). "Migration and urban survival strategies in Windhoek, Namibia." In: *Geoforum* Vol. 35 pp.489-505.

Frayne, Bruce (2005). "Rural Productivity and Urban Survival in Namibia: Eating Away from Home." In: *Journal of Contemporary African Studies* Vol. 23(1) pp.51-75.

Frayne, Bruce, W. Pendleton and A. Pomuti (2001). "Urban Community Participation in Oshakati, Northern Namibia". In: Tostensen, A., I. Tvedten and M. Vaa (eds). *Associational Life in African Cities: Popular Responses to the Urban Crisis*. Uppsala: Nordiska Afrikainstitutet.

Frayne, Bruce and Wade Pendleton (2003). "Mobile Namibia: Migration Trends and Attitudes". The Southern African Migration Project, Migration Policy Series No. 27. Ontario: Queens University

Fuller, Ben and Isolde Prommer (2000). *Population – Development – Environment in Namibia. Background Readings*. Windhoek: MRCC, University of Namibia.

Gardner, Katy and David Lewis (1996). *Anthropology, Development and the Post-Modern Challenge*. London: Pluto Press.

Gledhill, John (2000). *Power and its Disguises. Anthropological Perspectives on Politics*. London: Pluto Press.

Gluckman, Max (1961). "Anthropological Problems Arising from the African Industrial Revolution". In: *A. Southall (ed.) Social Change in Modern Africa*. London: Oxford University Press.

Gmelch, George and Walter P. Zenner (1996). *Urban Life. Readings in Urban Anthropology*. Prospects Heights, Ill.: Waveland Press.

GON (2003). 2001 *Population and Housing Census. National Report. Basic Analysis with Highlights*. Windhoek: Government of Namibia, National Planning Commission.

Gordimer, Nadime (2000 [1979]). *Burger's Daughter*. London: Bloomsburg Publishing.

Gordon, Robert J. and Andrew D. Spiegel (1993). "Southern Africa Revisited." In: *Annual. Review of Anthropology* Vol. 22 pp.83-105.

Graefe, Olivier, Daniel Oherien and Pascal Renaud (1994). *Informal Settlement and Institutional Survey in Rundu Town.* Windhoek: Department of Geography, University of Namibia and CRIAAA.

Graefe, Oliver and Elisabeth Pyroux (2001). "Decentralisation Put to the Test: The Case of Oshakati, Economic Capital of Ovamboland". In: I. Diener and O. Graefe (eds.) *Contemporary Namibia. The First Landmarks of a Post-Apartheid Society.* Windhoek: Gamsberg Macmillan Publishers.

Gregory, C.A. (1997). *Savage Money. The Anthropology and Politics of Commodity Exchange.* Amsterdam: Harwood Academic Publishers.

Greiner, Clemens (2009). "Beyond the Rural-Urban Divide: Migration in Post-Colonial Namibia". *BAB Working Paper No.1 2009.* Basel: Basler Afrika Bibilographien.

Grillo, R.D. (1997). "Discourse of Development: The View from Anthropology". In: R. D. Grillo and R. L. Stirrat (eds.) *Discourses of Development. Anthropological Perspectives.* Oxford: Berg, pp.1-35.

Groth, Siegfried (1995). *Namibia. The Wall of Silence.* Wuppertal, Germany: Peter Hammer Verlag.

GSA (1963). «Report of the Commission of Inquiry into South African Affairs 1962-63». Johannesburg: Government of South Africa.

Guilinotti, Richard and Roland Robertson (2009). *Globalization and Football.* London: Sage

Hahn, C.H., Heinrich Vedder and Louis Fourie (1928). *The Native Tribes of South West Africa.* London: Frank Cass.

Hakulinen, Maija (1992). *Means of Livelihood in Northern Namibia.* Helsinki: University of Helsinki, Institute of Development Studies.

Hangula, Lazarus (1993a). *The International Boundary of Namibia.* Windhoek: Gamsberg Macmillan.

Hangula, Lazarus (1993b). *The Town of Oshakati: A Historical Background.* Discussion Paper 9. Windhoek: Social Sciences Division, University of Namibia.

Hangula, Nehason (2000). *The Impact of War on the Ohangwena Region.* Paper presented at the conference Public History: Forgotten History, August 2000. Oshakati, Namibia.

Hannerz, Ulf (1980). *Exploring the City. Inquires Towards an Urban Anthropology.* New York: Columbia University Press.

Hannerz, Ulf (1992). *Cultural Complexity. Studies in the Social Organisation of Meaning.* New York: Columbia University Press.

Hannerz, Ulf (1996). *Transnational Connections. Culture, People, Places.* London: Routledge.

Hansen, Karen Tranberg (1995). "Transnational Biographies and Local Meaning: Used Clothing Practices in Lusaka." In: *Journal of Southern African Studies* Vol. 21(1) pp.131-145.

Hansen, Karen Tranberg (1997). *Keeping House in Lusaka*. New York: Colombia University Press.

Hansen, Karen Tranberg and Mariken Vaa (2004). «Introduction». In: K. T. Hansen and M. Vaa (eds.) *Reconsidering Informality. Perspectives from Urban Africa*. Uppsala, Sweden: Nordic Africa Institute, pp.7-25.

Hartmann, Wolfram (1998). ""Ondillimani!" Iipumbu ya Tshilongo and the Ambiguities of Resistance in Owambo". In: P. Hayes, J. Silvester, M. Wallace and W. Hartmann (eds.) *Namibia under South African Rule. Mobility and Containment 1915-46*. Oxford: James Currey, pp.263-289.

Hartmann, Wolfram, Jeremy Silvester and Patricia Hayes (1998). *The Colonising Camera. Photographs in the Making of Namibian History*. Windhoek: Out of Africa Publishers.

Hayes, Patricia (1998). "Northern Exposures: The Photography of C.H.L. Hahn, Native Commissioner of Owamboland 1915-1946". In: W. Hartmann, J. Silvester and P. Hayes (eds.) *The Colonising Camera. Photographs in the Making of Namibian History*. Windhoek: Out of Africa, pp.171-187.

Hayes, Patricia, Jeremy Silvester and Marion Wallace (eds.) (1998). *Namibia under South African Rule. Mobility and Containment 1915-46*. Oxford: James Currey.

Helle-Valle, Jo and Aud Talle (2000). "Moral, marked og penger: Komparative refleksjoner over kvinner og sex i to afrikanske lokaliteter." In: *Norsk Antropologisk Tidsskrift* Vol. 11 pp.182-196.

Hellmann, Ellen (1948). *A Sociological Survey of an Urban Native Slum Yard*. Manchester: Manchester University Press.

Herbstein, Denis and John Evenson (1989). *The Devils are Among Us. The War for Namibia*. London: Zed Books

Hiltunen, Maija (1986). *Witchcraft and Sorcery in Owambo*. Helsinki: Finish Anthropological Society.

Hiltunen, Maija (1993). *Good Magic in Owambo*. Helsinki, Finland: The Finnish Anthropological Society.

Hinz, Manfred O. (2002). "Two Societies in One: Institutions and Social Reality of Traditional and General Law and Order". In: V. Winterfeldt, T. Fox and P. Mufune (eds.) *Namibia. Society. Sociology*. Windhoek: University of Namibia Press.

Hishongwa, Ndeutala (1983). *Women of Namibia. The Changing Role of Namibian Women from Traditional Precolonial Times to the Present*. Vimmerby, Sweden: Förlaget By och Bygd.

Hishongwa, Ndeutala (1992). *The Contract Labour System and its Effects on Family and Social Life in Namibia. A Historical Perspective*. Windhoek: Gamsberg Macmillan.

Hiyalwa, Kaleni (2000). *Meekulu's Children*. Windhoek: New Namibia Books.

Hooper, Jim (1988). *Koevoet!* Johannesburg: Southern Book Publishers.

Hulme, D. and A. Sheperd (2003). "Conceptualising Urban Poverty". In: *World Development* 31 (3) pp. 403-423.

Iken, A. (1999). *Women-Headed Households in Namibia. Causes, Patterns and Consequences*. Frankfurt am Main: Verlag für Interkulturelle Kommunikation.

Johannsen, Agneta M. (1992). "Applied Anthropology and Post-Modern Ethnography". In: *Human Organisation*, Vol. 51, No. 1, pp. 71-81.

Johnson-Hanks, Jennifer (2002). "On the Limits of Life Stages in Ethnography: Toward a Theory of Vital Conjunctures." In: *American Anthropologist* Vol. 104(3)

Kamete, Y., A. Tostensen and I. Tvedten (2001). *From Global Village to Urban Globe. Urbanisation and Poverty in Africa: Implications for Norwegian Development Aid*. Report R 2001: 2. Bergen: Chr. Michelsen Institute.

Kanbur, Ravi and P. Schaffer (2007). "Epistemology, Normative Theory and Poverty Analysis: Implications for Q-Squared in Practise." In: *World Development* Vol. 35(2) pp.183-196.

KAS (2008). *Understanding the Perpetrators of Violent Crimes against Women and Girls in Namibia*. Windhoek: Konrad Adenauer Stiftung

Kedir, A.M. (2005). "Understanding Urban Chronic Poverty: Crossing the Qualitative and Quantitative Divide." In: *Environment and urbanization* Vol. 17(2) pp.43-54.

Kessides, Christine (2006). *The Urban Transition in Sub-Saharan Africa. Implications for Economic Growth and Poverty Reduction*. Washington D.C.: Cities Alliance.

Kiernan, Jim (1997). "David in the Path of Goliat. Anthropology in the Shadow of Apartheid". In: P. McAllistar (ed.) *Culture and the Commonplace. Anthropological Essays in the Honour of David Hammond-Tooke*. Johannesburg: Witwatersrand University Press, pp.53-69.

Knauft, Bruce (1997). "Theoretical Currents in Late Modern Cultural Anthropology." In: *Cultural Dynamics* Vol. 9(3) pp.277-300.

Knauft, Bruce (2002). "Critically Modern: An Introduction", in: Bruce Knauft (ed.) *Critically Modern: Alternatives, Alterities, Anthropologies*. Bloomington and Indianapolis: Indiana University Press.

Konings, Piet and D. Foeken (eds) (2006). *Crisis and Creativity – Exploring the Wealth of the African Neighbourhood*. Leiden: Brill

Krüger, Gesine and Dag Henrichsen (1998). «We have been Captives Long Enough. We Want to be Free.» In: P. Hayes, J. Silvester, M. Wallace and W. Hartman (eds.) *Namibia under South African Rule. Mobility and Containment 1915-1946*. Oxford: James Curry, pp.149-174.

Kuper, Adam (1992). "Introduction". In: A. Kuper (ed.) *Conceptualising Society*. London: Routledge, pp.1-14.

Lamont, Michèle and Mario Luis Small (2008). "How Culture Matters for the Understanding of Poverty: Enriching Our Understanding". In: Lin, Ann and David Harris (eds): *The Colors of Poverty: Why Racial and Ethnic Disparities Persist*. New York: Russel Sage Foundation.

Lebeau, Debbie (1992). *Namibia: Ethnic Stereotyping in a Post-Apartheid State*. NISER Research Report No. 5. Windhoek: Namibian Institute of Social and Economic Research.

Leeds, Anthony (1994). "Towns and Villages in Society: Hierarchies of Order and Cause". In: R. Sanjek (ed.) *Cities, Classes and the Social Order*. Ithica, N.Y.: Cornell University Press, pp.71-97.

Lewis, Oscar (1966). *La Vida*. New York: Rarndom House.

Lewis, Oscar (1996 [1966]). "The Culture of Poverty". In: G. Gmelch and W. P. Zenner (eds.) *Urban Life*. Prospect Heights, Illinois: Waveland Press, pp.393-417.

Leys, Colin and John S. Saul (1995). "Introduction". In: C. Leys and J. S. Saul (eds.) *Namibia's Liberation Struggle. The Two-Edged Sword*. London: James Currey, pp.1-19.

Little, Daniel (1991). *Varieties of Social Explanation. An Introduction to the Philosophy of Social Science*. Boulder, Colorado: Westview Press.

Low, Setha M. (1999). "Introduction: Theorizing the City". In: S. M. Low (ed.) *Theorizing the City*. Brunswick, New Jersey: Rutgers University Press, pp.1-33.

Low, Setha M. and Gary W. McDonough (2001). "Introduction to Remapping the City: Place, Order and Ideology." In: *American Anthropologist* Vol. 103(1) pp.5-6.

Low, Setha M. and Denise Lawrence-Zúñiga (eds.) (2003). *The Anthropology of Space and Place. Locating Culture*. Oxford: Blackwell Publishing.

Lush, David (1993). *Last Steps to Uhuru. An Eye-Witness Account of Namibia's Transition to Independence*. Windhoek: New Namibia Books.

Lynch, Kenneth (2005). *Rural-Urban Interaction in the Developing World*. London: Routledge.

Magnani, José Guilherme Cantor (2003). A Antropologia Urbana e os Desafios da Metrópole. In: *Tempo Social*. Vol. 15. No. 1 April 2003.

Malkki, Liisa H. (1997). "News and Culture: Transitory Phenomena and the Fieldwork Tradition". In: A. Gupta and J. Ferguson (eds.) *Anthropological Locations: Boundaries and Grounds of a Field Science.* Berkeley: University of California Press.

Marcus, George E. and M. Fischer (1986). *Anthropology as Cultural Critique. An Experimental Moment in the Human Sciences.* Chicago: University of Chicago Press.

Mayer, Philip (1963). *Townsmen and Tribesmen.* Cape Town: Oxford University Press.

Mbuende, Kaire (1986). *The Broken Shield.* Malmö, Sweden: Liber Förlag.

McKittrick, Meredith (1998). "Generational Struggles and Social Mobility in Western Owambo Communities 1915-1954". In: P. Hayes, J. Silvester, M. Wallace and W. Hartmann (eds.) *Namibia under South African Rule. Mobility and Containment 1915-1946.* Oxford: James Curry.

Meena, Ruth (ed.) (1992). *Gender in Southern Africa. Conceptual and Theoretical Issues.* Harare: SAPES Books

Melber, Henning (1996). *Urbanisation and Internal Migration: Regional Dimensions in Post-Colonial Namibia.* NWP No. 48. Windhoek: The Namibian Economic Policy Research Unit (NEPRU).

Merry, Sally E. (2001). "Spatial Governmentality and the New Urban Social Order. Controlling Gender Violence Through Law". In: *American Anthropologist* 103(1) (pp 16-29).

MHSS (2001) "Health Survey. Peri-Urban Areas of Oshakati" (mimeo). Windhoek: Ministry of Health and Social Services.

MHSS (2008). *Namibia. Demographic and Health Survey 2006-2007.* Windhoek: Ministry of Health and Social Services.

Miller, Daniel (1994). *Modernity. An Ethnographic Approach. Dualism and Mass Consumption in Trinidad.* Oxford: Berg.

Miller, Daniel (1995). "Introduction: Anthropology, Modernity and Consumption". In: D. Miller (ed.) *Worlds Apart. Modernity through the Prism of the Local.* London: Routledge, pp.1-23.

Mitchell, J.C. (1966). "Theoretical Orientations in African Urban Studies". In: M. Banton (ed.) *The Social Anthropology of Complex Societies.* London: Tavistock.

Mitchell, J.C. (1969). *Social Networks in Urban Situations. Analysis of Personal Relationships in Central African Towns.* Manchester: Manchester University Press.

Moore, Henrietta (1994). *A Passion for Difference. Essays in Anthropology and Gender.* Cambridge: Polity Press.

Moore, Henrietta (1999). "Anthropological Theory at the Turn of the Century". In: H. Moore (ed.) *Anthropological Theory Today.* Cambridge: Polity Press, pp.1-23.

Moore, Henrietta and Todd Sanders (2001). "Magical Interpretations and Material Realities. An Introduction". In: H. L. Moore and T. Sanders (eds.) *Magical Interpretations, Material Realities, Modernity, Witchcraft and the Occult in Postcolonial Africa.* London: Routledge, pp.1-27.

Moorsom, Richard (1995). *Underdevelopment and Labour Migration: The Contract Labour System in Namibia.* Windhoek: Dept. of History, University of Namibia.

Morrell, Robert (2001). "The Times of Change. Men and Masculinity in South Africa". In: R. Morrell (ed.) *Changing Men in Southern Africa.* Pietermaritzburg, South Africa: University of Natal Press, pp.3-37.

Moser, Caroline (1996). "Confronting Crisis: A Comparative Study of Household Responses to Poverty and Vulnerability in Four Poor Urban Communities". *Communities Environmentally Sustainable Development Studies and Monographs Series* No. 8. Washington D.C. The World Bank.

Mosse, David (2005). *Cultivating Development. An Ethnography of Aid and Aid Practise.* London: Pluto Press.

Mufune, Pempelani (2005). "Myths About Condoms and HIV/AIDS in Rural Northern Namibia". In: International Social Science Journal Vol. 57 (4) pp. 675-686.

Narotzky, Susana (1997). *New Directions in Economic Anthropology.* London: Pluto Press.

Norman, Siv Jorun (1996). *Kvinner og jordbruk i Owamboland. En sosiologisk analyse av bondekvinners arbeids- og livssituasjon i post-apartheid Namibia.* Institutt for sosiologi og samfunnsgeografi. Oslo: Universitetet i Oslo.

NPC (1999). *Levels of Living Survey. Main Report.* Windhoek: National Planning Commission.

NPC (2004). *Vision 2030: Prosperity, Harmony, Peace and Political Stability.* Windoek: National Planning Commission.

NPC (2006). *Namibia Household Income and Expenditure Survey 2003/2004.* Windhoek: National Planning Commission.

NPC (2008). *A Review of Poverty and Inequality in Namibia.* Windhoek: National Planning Commission

NPC (2008). *2nd Millennium Development Goals. Report Namibia 2008.* Windhoek: National Planning Commission.

O'Callaghan, Marion (1977). *Namibia: The Effects of Apartheid on Culture and Education.* Paris: United Nations Educational, Scientific and Cultural Organisation.

OHSIP (1992). "Programme Document. The Oshakati Human Settlement Improvement Project (OHSIP)". Windhoek: Ibis (WUS-Denmark).

OHSIP (1994) "The Population in Informal Settlements Being Parts of the Oshakati Human Settlement Improvement Project (OHSIP)". Unpublished mimeo.

O'Laughlin, Bridget (2007). "A Bigger Piece of a Very Small Pie: Intrahousehold Resource Allocation and Poverty Reduction in Africa." In: *Development and Change* Vol. 38(1) pp.21-44.

Ortner, Sherry (1984). "Theory in Anthropology since the Sixties." In: *Studies in Society and History* Vol. 26 pp.126-166.

Ortner, Sherry (1991). "Reading America. Preliminary Notes on Class and Culture". In: R. G. Fox (ed.) *Recapturing Anthropology. Working in the Present.* Santa Fe, New Mexico: School of American Research Press, pp.163-189.

Ortner, Sherry (1995). "Resistance and the Problem of Ethnographic Refusal." In: *Comparative Studies in Society and History* Vol. 37(1) pp.173-193.

Ortner, Sherry (2006). *Anthropology and Social Theory. Culture, Power and the Acting Subject.* Los Angeles: UCLA University Press.

OTC (2002). *Oshakati Statistics.* (Mimeo) Oshakati: Oshakati Town Council.

Pauw, B.A. (1963). *The Second Generation.* Cape Town: Oxford University Press.

Pels, Peter (1997). "The Anthropology of Colonialism: Culture, History and the Emergence of Western Governmentality." In: *Annual Review of Anthropology* Vol. 26 pp.163-183.

Pendleton, Wade (1974). *Katutura: A Place Where We Do Not Stay.* San Diego: San Diego State University Press.

Pendleton, Wade (1996). *Katutura. A Place We Stay. Life in a Post-Apartheid Township in Namibia.* Athens, USA: Ohio University Center for International Studies.

Pendleton, Wade and Bruce Frayne (1998). *The Namibian Migration Project.* SSD Research Report 35. Windhoek: Social Sciences Division, University of Namibia.

Peyroux, Elisabeth, Olivier Graefe and Pascal Renaud (1995). *Precarious Settlements at Windhoek's Periphery. Investigation into the Emergence of a New Urban Phenomenon.* Windhoek: CRIAA.

Rakodi, Carole and Tony Lloyd-Jones (eds.) (2002). *Urban Livelihoods. A People-Centered Approach to Reducing Poverty.* London: Earthscan.

Rapport, Nigel (1996) "Community". In: A. Barnard and J. Spencer (eds.) *Encyclopaedia of Social and Cultural Anthropology.* London: Routledge,

Reader, D.H. (1961). *The Black Man's Portion, History, Demography and Living Conditions in the Native Locations of East London, Cape Province.* Cape Town: Oxford University Press.

Reynolds, Pamela (1997). "The Ground of All Making: State Violence, the Family, and Political Activists". In: V. Das, A. Kleinman, M. Ramphele and P. Reynolds (eds.) *Violence and Subjectivity*. Berkeley: University of California Press

Rohde, Rick (1998). "How We See Each Other: Subjectivity, Photography and Ethnographic Re-Vision". In: W. Hartmann, J. Silvester and P. Hayes (eds.) *The Colonialising Camera. Photographs in the Making of Namibian History*. Windhoek: Out of Africa, pp.188-204.

Rothenbuhler, Eric W and Mihai Coman (2005). *Media Anthropology*. London: Sage

Ross, Fiona (1995). *Houses Without Doors: Diffusing Domesticity in Die Bos*. Pretoria: Human Sciences Research Council, Cooperative Research Programme on Marriage and Family Life (HG/MF-25).

Ross, Fiona (2010). *Raw Life, New Hope. Decency, Housing and Everyday Life in a Post-Apartheid Community*. Cape Town: UCT Press.

Sanjek, R. (1990). "Urban Anthropology in the 1980s: A World View." In: *Annual Review of Anthropology* Vol. 19 pp.151-186.

Scheper-Hughes, Nancy (1992). *Death Without Weeping. The Violence of Everyday Life in Brazil*. Berkeley: University of California Press.

Scheper-Hughes, Nancy (1995). "The Primacy of the Ethical. Propositions for a Militant Anthropology." In: *Current Anthropology* Vol. 36(3) pp.409-420.

Schmidt, Matthias (2009). *The Estimation of Poverty Trends in Post-Independence Namibia*. IPPR Briefing Paper No. 45, March 2009. Windhoek: Institute for Public Policy Research.

Schmidt-Kallert, Einhard (2009). 'A New paradigm of Urban Transition: Tracing the Livelihood Strategies of Multi-Locational Households' in: *Die Erde*, No. 140, Vol. 3 (319-336)

Scott, James (1985). *Weapons of the Weak. Everyday Forms of Peasant Resistance*. (Yale): Yale University Press.

Seckelman, Astrid (2001). *Development of Urban Settlements in Namibia*. NEPRU Occasional Papers No. 20. Windhoek: The Namibian Economic Policy Research Unit.

Shifiona, Napeua (2001). *Life Histories of Adult Depressed Women in Peri-Urban Namibia*. Paper Presented at the Research Forum Conference – UNAM Northern Campus June 2001.

SIAPAC (2002). *Impact Assessment of HIV/AIDS on the Municipalities of Ongwediva, Oshakati, Swakopmund, Walvis Bay and Windhoek. Volume 3: Oshakati*. Windhoek: Social Impact Assessment and Policy Analysis Corporation (SIAPAC).

Siiskonen, Harri (1990). *Trade and Socio-Economic Change in Ovamboland*, 1850-1906. Helsinki: Finska Historiska Samfundet.

Siiskonen, Harri (1998). "Migration in Ovamboland. The Oshigambo and Elim Perishes". In: P. Hayes, J. Silvester, M. Wallace and W. Hartmann (eds.) *Namibia under South African Rule. Mobility and Containment 1915-46*. Oxford: James Currey, pp.219-241

Silvester, J., M. Wallace and W. Hartmann (1998). "Trees never meet. Mobility and Containment: An Overview 1915-1946". In: P. Hayes, J. Silvester, M. Wallace and W. Hartmann (eds.) *Namibia under South African Rule. Mobility and Containment 1915-46*. Oxford: James Curry, pp.3-51.

Sorrell, Jill Brown James and Marcela Raffaelli (2005). "An exploratory study of constructions of masculinity, sexuality and HIV/AIDS in Namibia, Southern Africa." In: *Culture, Health and Sexuality* Vol. 7(6) pp.585-598.

Southall, Adrian (1961). "Introductory Summary". In: Aiden Southall (ed). *Social Change in Modern Africa*. London: Oxford University Press

Sparks, D. and D. Green (1992). *Namibia. The Nation after Independence*. Boulder: Westview Press.

Spiegel, Andrew D. (1997). "Continuities, Culture and the Commonplace. Searching for a New Ethnographic Approach in South Africa". In: P. McAllistar (ed.) *Culture and the Commonplace. Anthropological Essays in Honour of David Hammond-Tooke*. Johannesburg: Witwatersrand University Press, pp.9-31.

Stoler, A.L. (1995). *Race and the Education of Desire: Foucalt's History of Sexuality and the Colonial Order of Things*. Durham/London: Duke University Press.

Talle, Aud (2002). "Kvinner og utvikling. Tjue år senere." In: *Norsk Antropologisk Tidsskrift* Vol. 5(1-2) pp.34-47.

Tapscott, Chris (1990). *The Social Economy of Livestock Production in the Owambo Region*. NISER Discussion Paper No. 4. Windhoek: Namibian Institute of Social and Economic Research.

Tostensen, Arne, I. Tvedten and M. Vaa (2001). "The Urban Crisis, Governance and Associational Life". In: A. Tostensen, I. Tvedten and M. Vaa (eds.) *Associational Life in African Cities: Popular Responses to the Urban Crisis*. Uppsala: Nordiska Afrikainstitutet, pp.5-27.

Tvedten, Inge (1997). *Angola. Struggle for Peace and Reconstruction*. Boulder, Colorado: Westview Press.

Tvedten, Inge (2004). "Moving to Town or Staying Behind: Social Relations of Migration in Namibia." In: *Canadian Journal of African Studies* Volume 38 Number 2. pp 393-423.

Tvedten, Inge and Akiser Pomuti (1994). *The Oshakati Human Settlement Improvement Project: A Socio-Economic Baseline Study*. SSD Report 9. Windhoek: Social Sciences Division, University of Namibia.

Tvedten, Inge and Moono Mupotola (1995). *Urbanization and Urban Policies in Namibia. A Discussion Paper Prepared for the Annual Meeting of the Association of Local Authorities in Namibia July 1995*. SSD Report 10. Windhoek: Social Sciences Division, University of Namibia.

Tvedten, Inge and Selma Nangulah (1999). *Social Relations of Poverty: A Case Study from Owambo, Namibia*. CMI Report R 1995: 5. Bergen: Chr. Michelsen Institute.

Tönjes, Herman (1911). *Ovamboland. Country, People, Mission*. Windhoek: Namibia Scientific Society.

UNDP (1999). *Namibia. Human Development Report 1999. Alcohol and Human Development in Namibia*. New York: United Nations Development Programme.

UNDP (2000). *Namibia. Human Development Report 2000/2001. Gender and Violence in Namibia*. Windhoek: United Nations Development Programme.

UNDP (2007). *Human Development Report 2007. Fighting Climate Change: Human Solidarity in a Divided World*. New York: United Nations Development Programme.

UN-Habitat (2003). *The Challenge of Slums. Global Report on Human Settlements*. Nairobi, Kenya: United Nations Human Settlement Programme (UN-Habitat).

UN-Habitat (2009 [2008]). *State of the World's Cities Report 2010/11. Bridging the Urban Divide*. Nairobi: UN-Habitat.

UNICEF (1990). *Household Health and Nutrition in Namibia*. Windhoek: UNICEF.

UNICEF (1995). *Children in Namibia: Reaching Towards the Rights of Every Child*. Windhoek: UNICEF and Government of Namibia.

United Nations (2008). *World Urbanisation Prospects: The 2007 Revision*. New York: United Nations

Urban Dynamics (2001). *Oshakati. Structure Plan. August 2001*. Windhoek: Urban Dynamics. Town and Regional Planners.

Uukwambi, Traditional Authority (n.d). *Coveta dhUukwambi [Uukwambi Traditional Law]*. Oshakati: Uukwambi Traditional Affairs Office.

Vliet, Virginia van der (1991). "Traditional Husbands, Modern Wives? Constructing Marriages in a South African Township". In: P. McAllistar (ed.) *Culture and the Commonplace. Anthropological Essays in the Honour of David Hammond-Tooke*. Johannesburg: Witwatersrand University Press.

Wacquant, Loic J.D. (1992). "Towards a Social Praxeology: The Structure and Logic of Bourdieu's Sociology". In: P. Bourdieu and L. J. D. Wacquant (eds.) *An Invitation to Reflexive Sociology*. London: Polity Press.

Walker, Cherryl (1995). "Conceptualising Motherhood in Twentieth Century South Africa." In: *Journal of Southern African Studies* Vol. 21(3) pp.417-439.

Wallace, M. (1998). "Looking at the Locations: The Ambiguity of Urban Photography". In: W. Hartmann, J. Silvester and P. Hayes (eds.) *The Colonising Camera: Photographs in the Making of Namibian History.* Windhoek: Out of Africa Publishers, pp.132-137.

Whitehead, A., A. Cornwall and E.A. Harrison (2006). *Feminisms and Development: Contradictions, Contestations and Challenges.* London: Zed Press.

Williams, Frieda-Nela (1991). *Precolonial Communities of Southwestern Africa.* Windhoek: National Archives of Namibia.

Willis, Paul (1977). *Learning to Labour. How Working Class Kids Get Working Class Jobs.* Farnborough: Saxon House.

Wilson, Godfrey and Monica Wilson (1945). *The Analysis of Social Change.* Cambridge: Cambridge University Press.

World Bank (2007). *World Development Report 2007. Development and the Next Generation.* Washington DC: World Bank

World Bank (2008). GenderStats. Database on Gender Statistics (www.devdata.worldbank.org/genderstats)

Index

A

Acquired Immune Deficiency Syndrome (AIDS) 10, 58, 70, 71, 72, 83, 108, 109, 110, 127, 156, 157, 160, 166
Amunkambya (see also Oshoopala) 31, 32, 38, 56, 57, 125, 151
Angola IX, 1, 7, 21, 22, 27, 32, 36, 39, 45, 52, 53, 54, 57, 58, 101, 103, 108, 110, 112, 118, 124, 142, 145, 148, 149, 155, 157, 163

B

Bantustan 24
Battalion 32 163
Benguela 22
Berlin 45
bin Laden 43
Bom Jesus de Mata 13
Botha, P.W. 23
Bourdieu, Pierre 15, 16, 20, 25, 43, 52, 64, 65, 81, 160, 162, 168
British Broadcasting Corporation (BBC) 57
Build Together Programme 94, 119

C

Cable News Network (CNN) 57
Cairo 44
Cape Town IX, XIII, 44, 102, 137
Caprivi 27, 45, 109, 148
Caspir 30
Castle 43
Catholic Church 117
Cazenga 2
China 52, 58
Club Fantasy 44
Coca-Cola 52, 54, 147
Commonwealth 58
Community Based Development Organisation (CBDO) 63
Community Development Committee (CDC) 62, 63
Congress of Democrats (CoD) 60
Copperbelt 14, 32, 35, 38, 39, 112
Cuca-shop 26, 31, 39, 43, 52, 55, 92, 95, 96, 99, 112, 115, 119, 127, 129, 132, 133, 138, 142, 143, 149, 156, 163, 166, 172
Cunene 101

D

Denmark 61
Deutsche Rundfunk 58
Development Aid from People to People (DAPP) 50, 51, 125
Die Republikein 59
Digital Satellite Television (DSTV) 55
Doornfontein 14
Duncan Village 160

E

East London 14, 32, 35, 39, 107, 112, 144, 150, 160, 168
Eemwandi 7, 67
Engen 44
Entertainment and Sports Programming Network (ESPN) 57
Erundu 31, 34
Europe 46, 50, 57
Evululuku XIII, 3, 7, 9, 32, 37, 44, 50, 67, 68, 69, 72, 73, 74, 97, 101, 105, 124, 127, 129, 130, 132, 138, 140, 145, 148, 149, 153, 160

F

Ferguson, James 11, 14, 16, 39, 48, 61, 94, 107, 111, 112, 120, 134, 138, 141, 144, 146, 151, 157, 168
Finnish Missionary Society 22
Fourie, Louis 23
France 46

G

Game Shopping Centre 53
Gamsberg MacMillan 58
Germany 17, 22, 27, 45
Goldberg, Whoppi 55
Gordimer, Nadine 1

H

Hahn, C.H.L. 23
Human Immunodeficiency Virus (HIV) 10, 70, 72, 156, 157, 160

I

Ibis 61, 63, 83

J

Johannesburg 14

K

Kanjengedi 7, 67, 99, 165
Kaoko 45
Katutura (see also Windhoek) 14, 27
Kavango 155
Kentucky Fried Chicken 43, 44
Koevoet 27, 28, 29, 30, 35, 36, 37, 38, 41, 151
Kwanza Sul 2

L

Lanterna 59
Lewis, Oscar XI, 11, 33, 40, 41
Liverpool 57
Luanda 1, 2, 163
Lusaka 14, 53, 113

M

Manchester School 168
Manchester United 57
Mandume 25, 27
Meatco 54, 126
Ministry of Finance 46
Ministry of Health and Social Services (MHSS) 10, 70, 71, 140
Ministry of Local Government and Housing 46
Ministry of Trade and Industry 51
Moçámedes 22
Moore, Henrietta 11, 16, 39, 81, 111, 136, 155
Mtendere 113

N

Namibian Broadcasting Corporation (NBC) 58, 59, 60
Nandos 45
National Development Corporation (NDC) 51
New Era 58, 59
Non-Governmental Organisation (NGO) 50, 51, 83
Nujoma, Sam 43, 60

O

Odendaal Commission 24, 31
Ohangwena 25, 50, 80, 98, 102, 103, 117, 138, 143, 165
Okatana River 31
Okavango 27
Okuriangawa 2

Olupale 108
Omashaka 32, 37, 38, 50, 51
Omatala 40, 45, 47, 50, 55, 111, 112, 125, 126, 127, 143
Ompumbu 7, 67
Ompundja 99, 103, 104, 106, 107
Omugulumbashe 27
Omusati 26, 60, 124, 132, 162
Ondangwa 59
Oneshila XIII, 3, 7, 9, 10, 25, 32, 37, 38, 39, 44, 63, 67, 68, 69, 72, 73, 74, 94, 96, 99, 109, 110, 117, 123, 125, 129, 131, 134, 143, 145, 156, 160, 162, 165, 167
Onheleiwa 110
Oniihende 99, 103, 104, 105, 106, 107
Ortner, Sherry 13, 15, 16, 81, 83, 160, 168
Oshakati Country Lodge 45
Oshakati East 32, 37, 38, 44
Oshakati Human Settlement Development Project (OHSIP) 61, 62, 63, 65, 67, 68
Oshakati Town Council (OTC) 3, 7, 9, 51, 63, 67
Oshakati West 32, 36, 37, 45
Oshana 69, 72, 80, 103
Oshikoto 80, 96, 98, 101
Oshimbangu 7, 67
Oshoopala 7, 9
Oshoopala (see also Amunkambya) XIII, 3, 10, 31, 32, 38, 47, 48, 56, 67, 68, 69, 72, 73, 74, 103, 109, 121, 124, 128, 130, 134, 143, 148, 150, 151, 157, 160, 164, 167
Otshipuku 31
Out of Africa 58
Owambo Region 20, 21, 22, 23, 24, 25, 26, 27, 28, 29, 31, 33, 34, 35, 36, 37, 38, 42, 43, 45, 51, 60, 67, 69, 92, 93, 103, 106, 108, 111, 116, 117, 119, 131, 134, 136, 140, 141, 143, 146, 147, 150, 152, 154, 169

P

People's Liberation Army of Namibia (PLAN) 27, 30, 31
Portugal 21, 54, 108, 110, 118, 163
Pretoria 27
Private Sector Foundation 51
Put More Fire 44

R

Radio Swapo 58
Rhenish Missionary Society 22, 23
Ruacana 80, 126
Rundu 155

S

Sharpeville 27
Shoprite 123
Sky 1 67
Sky 2 67
South Africa IX, 5, 14, 17, 20, 21, 23, 24, 25, 27, 29, 30, 31, 32, 33, 35, 36, 37, 39, 41, 43, 45, 50, 52, 54, 57, 58, 61, 62, 66, 104, 107, 110, 117, 133, 143, 144, 150, 151, 160, 162, 163, 169
South African Defence Force (SADF) 27, 28, 35
Southern Africa 3, 14, 17, 21, 35, 39, 71, 112, 113, 130, 134, 168
South West African Defence Force (SWATF) 25, 27, 28, 29, 30, 32, 38, 41, 165
South West Africa People's Organisation (Swapo of Namibia) 17, 28, 46, 104, 145, 160
Soweto 164
Spain 46
Standard Bank 45, 127
Stefanus, Jacobus 33, 36, 37, 38
Supersport 57

T

The Namibian 30, 47, 49, 55, 58, 59, 130, 134, 160, 166
The Observer 58
The United Nations Children's Fund (UNICEF) 70, 72
Third World 11
Tocoist church 148, 164
Travis 43

U

União Nacional para a Independência Total de Angola (UNITA) 36
United Nations Transition Assistance Group (UNTAG) 31
United States 50
Universal Church 45
University of Namibia (UNAM) XIII
Urban Dynamics 32, 47, 48, 49, 67
Uukwaludhi 22, 96
Uukwambi 22, 31, 108
Uukwangula 108, 142
Uukwanyama 22, 24
Uupindi XIII, 3, 7, 9, 25, 26, 30, 32, 34, 37, 38, 43, 53, 62, 67, 68, 69, 72, 73, 74, 96, 97, 101, 102, 108, 109, 110, 112, 115, 120, 121, 126, 127, 130, 131, 140, 142, 146, 147, 152, 153, 155, 160, 161, 162, 165, 166

V

Vedder, Heinrich 23
Verwoerd, H. 24
Voice of America 58

W

Walvis Bay 6, 45, 117
Windhoek 4, 1, 2, 6, 27
Windhoek (see also Katutura and Okuriangawa) 27, 33, 57, 58, 59, 82, 109, 118, 139, 161

Z

Zambia 14, 32, 45, 53, 58, 94, 107, 138, 141, 144, 151, 153

Forthcoming Titles

Julie Taylor
Naming the Land: San Identity and Community
Conservation in Namibia's West Caprivi.
Introduction by William Beinart
Basel Namibia Studies Series 12
Basel 2011. ISBN 978-3-905758-25-2

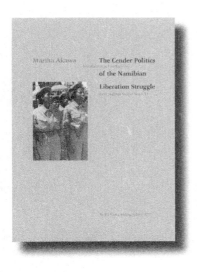

Martha Akawa
The Gender Politics of the Namibian
Liberation Struggle
Basel Namibia Studies Series 13
Basel 2012. ISBN 978-3-905758-26-9

Forthcoming Titles

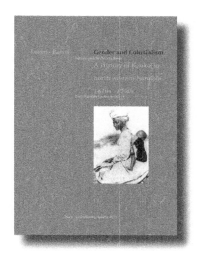

Lorena Rizzo
Gender and Colonialism.
A History of Kaoko in north-western Namibia,
1870s –1950s.
Introduction by Patricia Hayes.
Basel Namibia Studies Series 14
Basel 2012. ISBN 978-3-905758-27-6

www.baslerafrika.ch

CPSIA information can be obtained at www.ICGtesting.com
Printed in the USA
BVOW09s1856130715

408582BV00008B/29/P